BEYOND FICTION

A Critical Evaluation of The Non Fictional Writings

BEYOND FICTION

A Critical Evaluation of The Non Fictional Writings

Editor

Dr. Rajshree Roselean Kapoor

AUTHORSPRESS

Worldwide Circulation through Authorspress Global Network
First Published in 2023
by
Authorspress
Q-2A Hauz Khas Enclave, New Delhi-110 016 (India)
Phone: (0) 9818049852
E-mail: authorspressgroup@gmail.com
Website: www.authorspressbooks.com

Beyond Fiction: A Critical Evaluation of the Non Fictional Writings
ISBN 978-93-5529-486-9

Printed in India at Thomson Press (India) Limited

Preface

It gives me immense pleasure, to respectfully place this book in the hands of the readers (students and teachers) whose role cannot be overlooked. This book is compiled in an easy and comprehensive form assuming that they would pursue this subject with a view that this perspective can opt in a stand-alone form for research. The purpose of selecting this topic: "Beyond Fiction: A Critical Evaluation Of The Non-Fictional Writings" is to catch the attention of scholars to connect these themes in the areas of research. Students pursuing English literature will find it very interesting and useful. The chapters contributed by authors provide a better understanding of this function of non-fiction writing. I assume that this book will be an excellent text for readers to develop their ability to explore these topics and will furnish them with essential areas of acquiring specialization. The merit of this is that it contains excellent contributions of chapters by academicians from different Colleges, Universities, and Institutions nationwide. Features like Travelogues, Diaries, Letters, Advertisements, Narrative nonfiction, Newspaper Articles, Information Leaflets, Magazine Articles Expository Non-fiction, Persuasive Non-fiction, Descriptive Non-fiction The Non-Fictional Writings Of Writers, and any other related themes, show the connection of concepts in different areas of literature, in general, to break the monotony and enliven the book. With the turn of every page of this book, the readers will get the author's approach, ideas, and insight and their just evaluation. After thanking The Almighty and my family and friends for their never-ceasing support. I would fail in my duty if I do not thank a few people here. I am indebted to Dr. Rajesh Trivedi Sir for his enlighting support, as I long wanted to respected Sir, about exploring this area of nonfiction writings in English literature and Sir very enthusiastically appreciated my approach. Working on this subject was a steep learning curve for me as Sir did not only polish my topic but also gave me an insight into the dimensions of the subject. I took his perspectives, maxims, and thoughts seriously and started my work. I acknowledge all the efforts of the intellectuals for their contribution as they paved the way for me to bring my diligent work on paper. It has been a pleasure to work on this book with a dedicated team who were committed to the task of developing, reviewing, designing, refining, approving, and correcting the drafts. I extend my gratitude towards the experts who drafted the Forwards after their extensive reading of the chapters of the various authors minutely observing the topics and then jotting down their expert appreciation for each respectively. I'm ever grateful to the Patron of my Institution for always being ready to render his support and help for such academic pursuits. I also thank the seniors and colleagues in my department for their appreciation and good wishes for my academic endeavors. I also thank Authors Press, New Delhi, India for the publication. They provide the very best paper quality and excellent printing. I welcome suggestions and comments from valued readers. I wish the readers a happy journey into the exciting realm of English literature compile this book, and I shared my thoughts with the

Dr. Rajshree Roselean Kapoor

Foreword

I am delighted to express my admiration and have to appreciate the endeavour to bring a wonderful book. It's not hyperbole to say that this is an era of nonfiction because if there is something that is useful or solid to be used in writing is nonfiction. One must admit that no scholar or reader minds the importance of the genre which is a tool through which sensational information or some revolutionary thoughts that are so helpful are revealed through real-time experiences of writers. Nonfiction is a wonderful genre to share our knowledge to motivate, inspire, educate or make things better known to the world around. The present publication can be considered a treatise on the prominent role of nonfiction in the literary world.

The Editor of this book Dr. Rajshree Roselean Kapoor, meticulously chosen the theme of the book to elevate the value of nonfiction literature and to intact the idea with learned scholars who fulfilled the objective of the editor in meeting the ends with great expectations on the theme of the book. The Editor's inclination to the theme reveals her commitment to the work and proves her to be a strong adherent of nonfiction genre. The authors of the chapters wholeheartedly immersed in quality of thoughts and presentation by embracing new ways with unique topics to create interest on the genre. The editor's role to make it intact is immense and praiseworthy. The book covers most of the aspects, dimensions, issues beyond fiction.

I'm sure this book will enhance the dignity and respect for nonfiction in the minds of writers and scholars – especially readers with its subtle and insightful knowledge. It guides the readers and scholars to inspire, rethink about and re-explore on nonfiction writing!

Raja Kumar Tenali

Freelance Writer, Former Head, Department of Visual Communication (PG), Andhra Loyola College, Vijayawada, Andhra Pradesh. Email: rktenali@yahoo.com

Foreword

It gives me immense pleasure to write the Foreword for this book titled Beyond Fiction – A Criitical Evaluation of the Nonfictional writings.

English language reminds an effective tool for communication beyond boundaries of the world. It is the language which can be called as the window of the world. It also still continues to be an official language tool, at all levels of communication, administration and medium of instruction. The rapid development in Science and Technology, Travel, Newspaper, Media, Communication Cinema, Literature and all Fine Arts has carried the value of English language across boundaries. The use and application of English in the Education sector to obtain proficiency for better opportunities in Government and Private for employment is increasing day by day.

The acquisition of communicative skills in English is a boon to the aspirants who are trying to secure a job. In the international global trade competition, competency and credibility are the main ingredients to seek job in corporates.

I feel very happy and proud to present this book before the readers. It covers much of the areas related to ELT which is the essential part of student's proficiency. I do hope that the pages in the book runs through the topic like, Travelogues, Diaries, Advertisements, Reviews, Letters, Neswspapers, Article's, Magazines, Nonfictional writings of writers Narratives,, Nonfiction, Expository nonfiction, Persuasive, Nonfiction etc. will be of very effective for students in acquiring language skills. This Book is of great use for the student community, and who are the best beneficiaries. It is a great boon to the readers of all walks – of life. Congratulations to the contributors, editors and the entire team for making the book a great success. My heartfelt thanks to the editor for this opportunity. May God bless you all. Once again I thank one and all for this beautiful creation.

N. Karpagavalli

Assistant Professor of English,
Rani Anna Government College Tirunelveli.

Foreword

Non-fictional writings with its divers forms and manifestations have always offered a claim for the identity which is parallel to the fictional writings or any other form of literature such as drama, poetry etc. However the fact cannot be denied that the non-fictional writings, instead of offering a challenge to the fictional writings, such as short story (or novella) and novel have always played a supporting role for a just and honest appreciation for the critical endeavors for the fictional works. The non-fictional works being free from all confines of technical parameters loom out with more unbiased point of view of the writer thus enable the criitic to approach the work of fiction with more authenticity providing a landmarked route to the just and honest criticism to the text produced by the author.

It is however a difficult task to put non fictional writings into a well-defined category as they may cover any topic under the sun with same gravity and technical exuberance. If Francis Bacon directs his preferences to the grave philosophical concepts of the Truth and Friendship and interprets them with utilitarian acumen, then Rober Lynd picks up the trivial objects like the kitten and the noises and renders them profound metaphorical value through subtle application of the wit and wisdom. If Milton's *Areopagitica* a seemingly political treatise on freedom of expression and Thomas *Brown's Urn Burial* depicts the complex issues related to life and death then Lamb's personal essays are the deep and profound but playful revelation of the personal whims and eccentricities; pains and pangs of an individual in an engrossing manner. It is an interesting phenomenon that the question marks have been raised to the subjective writings of various genres by great critics like T S Eliot but the non-fictional prose writings have always been free from allegations of subjectivity and inclusion of personal elements thus wider range of non-fictional writings is ratified and authenticated. In fact the biographies and autobiographies where subjective and personal elements have been enshrined and adored, have been amongst the most popular forms of non-fictional writings. Essays and travelogues are unquestionably the most popular forms of non-fictional writing that share the space and claim for super-numeracy with the autobiographies and biograophies.

It is noticeable that in either case the personal elements are welcome and seldom questioned for inclusion and proportion.

Essays – personal or otherwise – aptly been defined as "loose sally of mind" by Samuel Jonson – account for a vivid description of the form and function of the genre in the literary firmament. In either case the essay gives us the point of view of the author and in case of the non-fictional writings of a fiction writer the reader comes across the point of view of his narrators in a clear and lucid manner with lambent reflections on mist of the technical complexities of their narratives. R K Narayan's *My Dateless Diary*, Kamla Das's *My story* and Salman Rushdie's *Imaginary Homelands* are few scintillating examples of the undeniable correlation between non-fictional and fictional writings and these books provide the critics with sufficient pabulum for criticism on creativity writings.

There has been a parallel stream of non-fictional works however they are originally not in scripted form but in form of lectures and that are later put into scripted form and made available to the readers. In British English literature, the series of lectures by Carlyle titled Hero and Hero Worship is a fine instance of the same. In American English Literature, the lectures of Emerson enjoy respectable status comparable with that of the poetic works of Robert Frost and novels of Natheniel Hawthorne. In criticism also, the lectures of E M Forster complied and published as *Aspects of Novel* enjoy a respectable place in the modern criticism. It can however not be denied that the criticism of Forster server much to make the points of view of his narrator clear and perceptible. In India, the speeches of M K Gandhi, J L Nehru and S Radhakrishnan have earned great fame in the field of literature and are treated respectfully in literary arena.

The present book serves to explore different aspects of non-fictional writing of the masters of letters from different fields and literature. It is a humble effort of the author to unify the views of young critics on this genre of literature with immeasurable span and unfathomable depth. I express my sincere thanks to all the contributors who responded the author's call with promptitude and devotion. The books enshrines certain objectives, whether those objectives have been fulfilled or not, will be ascertained by the honest appreciation by the reader.

Dr RajeshTrivedi

Professor-Department of English,
Shriram Institute of Technology Jabalpur

Contents

CHAPTER 1

Feminist Sensibility and Identity in the Short Stories of Sashi Deshpande

Dr. Susheela. B

Abstract

Sashi Deshpande's short stories sensitively portray a woman's frustrations, despair, pain and anguish in a society governed by the rigid codes laid down by the patriarchal social order. Sashi Deshpande's short stories featuring female protagonists, reconstruct aspects of women's experience and attempt to give voice to 'muted ideologies. Sashi Deshpande's short stories prove the authenticity of her claim that," a world without frightened, dependent, trapped, frustrated women are a better world for all of us to live in.'

Keywords: Feminist, Woman, Sensibility, Muted Ideologies, Society

The fruition of Indian writing in English is beyond now. English became an 'Indian' Language in the post-colonial context. It originated as a necessary outcome of the introduction of English education in India under the colonial rule. In recent years, it 'has attracted widespread interest, both in India and abroad'. Indian women writing in English is being recognised as major contemporary current in English language – Literature. Traditionally, the work of Indian Women Writers has been undervalued to patriarchal assumptions about the superior worth of male experience factors contributing to this prejudice is the fact that most of these women writers have observed no domestic space. The Indian women's perceptions of their aspirations and expectations are within the framework of Indian social and moral commitments. Indian women writers in English are victims of a second prejudice vis-à-vis their regional counterpart's. Proficiency in English is available only to writers of the intellect, affluent and educated classes. Writer's works are often therefore, belong to high school strata and cut off from the reality of Indian life. The majority of novels written by Indian women writers depict the psychological sufferings of the frustrated homemakers. The subject matter is often considered superficial compared to the depiction of the replaced and oppressed lives of women. Indian writing in English is now gaining ground rapidly and writers started questioning the prominent old patriarchal domination. They are no longer puppets in the hands of men. They have shown their worth in the field of literature both qualitatively and quantitively and are showing it even today without any hurdle. Today the works of several women writers like Kamala Markandaya's, Nayantara Sehgal, Anita Desai, Geetha Hariharan, Sashi Deshpande, Kiran Desai and Manju Kapur and many more have left an indelible imprint on the readers of Indian fiction in English.

A major development in modern Indian fiction is the growth of a feminist or women cantered approach, that seeks to project and interpret experience, from the point of a feminine consciousness and sensibility. The image of women in fiction has undergone a change during the last four decades. Women writers have moved away from traditional portrayals of enduring self-sacrificing women, towards conflicts, female characters searching for identity, no longer characterized and defined simply in terms of their victim status. A major preoccupation in recent Indian women's writing has been a delineation of inner life and subtle interpersonal relationships. In the galaxy of Indian novelists in English, Indian women writers shown luminously like their male counterparts by their significant contribution to enrichment of Indian English novels. The women novelists, who have risen to celebrity and won global recognition in literature are Cornelia Sorabjee, Iqbalinnisa, Hussain, Santha Rama Rau, Rama Mehta, R.P Jhabvala, Attia Hossain etc. These novelists seem to have derived inspiration and influences from British novelists in respect of art and device in writing novels. They resemble to a great extent Jane Austin, George Eliot, Bronte Sisters, Mrs Gaskell, Dorothy Richardson and Virginia Woolf in the art of characterization and portrayal of psychic mind of women. Like the British women novelists both qualitatively and numerically in exploration of inner mind of women and thereby assert their own identity. They further differentiate themselves categorically from the group of British women novelists in the thematic exploitation of Indian life, scenes and culture and externalisation of interior region of Indian women's mind.

The last three decades has seen the emergence of prominent Feminist in Indian Literature. Sashi Deshpande, an eminent Indian novelist in English, was born on August 19, 1938, in Dharwad, Karnataka. After her schooling in Dharwad, she graduated in Economics from Elphinstone College, Bombay. Thereafter at Government Law College in Bangalore she won two gold medals and after serving briefly as a junior lawyer, she took her master's degree in English Literature from Mysuru University. She took a diploma course in mass communication in Bombay leading to three more medals and then a short career in journalism.

The present paper aims to highlight Sashi Deshpande's attempt through her stories to voice the subsistence of dominant power structures prevalent in the socio-cultural matrix and the female desire to repudiate and defy these structures. Her protagonist registers their remonstrance and oppose whatever is pernicious to the quest of self-identity, self-assertion and self-worth. Their subtle resistance to social, political and patriarchal hegemony has paved a way to bring about a change in their profession. Sashi Deshpande has exploited their skill in projecting connivingly the agonized mind of the persecuted women. Her portrayal of woman characters in the novels invariably bears authencity to her feminist approach, outlook and perspective. Her keen observation of life of Indian women and their interest in the study of their inner mind are evidenced by their vivid and panoramic portrayal of their plight.

Sashi Deshpande, an eminent Indian novelist in English, was born on August 19, 1938, in Dharwad, Karnataka. After her schooling in Dharwad, she graduated in Economics from Elphinstone College, Bombay. Thereafter at Government Law College in Bangalore she won two gold medals and after serving briefly as a junior lawyer, she took a master's degree in English Literature from the Mysuru University. She took a diploma course in mass communication in Bombay leading to three more medals and then had a short career in Journalism. Sashi Deshpande's father, Adya Rangachar, better known as Sri Rangachar, better known as Sriranga, was a highly reputed Kannada dramatist and Sanskrit scholar. His liberal attitudes (he never let the family members identify themselves in terms of caste or religion) had an enormous impact on his daughter. But her fiction cannot claim any influence of her father's works. It is said that Sriranga's plays deal with ideas, whereas Sashi Deshpande could never separate ideas from people, even for artistic purposes. She married D.H. Deshpande, a professor of pathology, whose progressive outlook and unconventional ways equal those of her father. At the end of a year with him in England, when he was a Commonwealth Scholar, she described their term abroad in three articles sent to her father, who in turn sent them to the *Deccan Herald* where there were immediately published. A series of short stories followed, which were eventually published as anthology entitled *The Legacy*. This collection has been well received by both the academic world and the reading public. Since then, Sashi Deshpande has published four other collections of short stories – *It was dark, It was the Nightingale, The Miracle and other stories, The Intrusion and Other Stories.* An avid reader and admirer of Enid Blyton, Deshpande has also written short-story volumes for children-*A Summer Adventure, The Only witness, The Hidden Treasure & The Narayanpur Incident.* They were initially inspired by her need as a mother provide suitable Indian stories for her own children to read. In addition, she has published several essays in books, scholarly journals, popular magazines and newspapers. An edited volume of her significant essays is soon to be published by Penguin India.

Sashi Deshpande's remarkable success with the literary form of the short story gave her the confidence to deal with the larger canvas of the novel. In her short stories, Deshpande had tried some unconventional subjects such as rape within marriage, reversal of gender roles, forbidden love, burden of motherhood and female sexuality. Her novels are obviously concerned with feminist issues. She portrays modern educated and career-oriented middle-class married women, who are sensitive to the changing times and situations. She delineates the middle class educated women to show patriarchal protagonists. Feminism in Indian English fiction has a series of counters and ordeals on the part of woman to strike at the roots, to belong and assert her individuality in a traditional society. Like man, woman is born free, but she is in chains, not always and everywhere. All women do not conform, they rebel, they reconcile and they are both Kali and Durga, symbols of destruction as well as creation. During the Vedic period, Indian woman enjoyed the pride like Gargi, Maitreyi, Lopamudra who walked equally with men. Even Sita, Savitri, Shakuntala and Draupadi, who made their appearance at a later period in history, were not said to be passive, submissive, docile and servile. Sita in *Ramayana* has resisted the demonic aggressiveness of Ravana; Shakuntala in *Mahabharata* proved the strength of her nerves by meeting the challenge of Dushyant; Dushyant displayed the female ferocity by washing her hair in the blood of Dushasana who had attempted to disrobe her in the court of the Kauravas. Freedom for the Indian woman meant freedom from centuries of male-domination and male-ordained social and cultural norms. Though the Indian woman did not have to struggle like her American Counterpart for Universal suffrage, she had to strive to attain recognition for her individuality and acceptance by society, of an existence even beyond her gender-based roles. Patriarchy had compelled the Indian woman to be totally subservient to the male in both the social and economic spheres.

She draws serious attention of her readers, to the dilemmas of women and the choices they make when they find themselves in the whirlpool of complex man-woman relationship. Though her women protagonists are consistently pressured in clumsy, knotty relationships, her women firmly refuse to become prisoners of orthodoxies, fossilized traditions and stereo typically idealized identities. Thereby she casts a very hard look at the structural dynamics of the society functioning against the advantage of the female species. Her novels play out their lives flux and fragility, differences and clashes, sufferings and struggles, societal and interiorized levels and self-reflexivity of these women and her own self.

A woman is always defined in the context of her relationship with man. She is never assigned an autonomous status but is bestowed relative position. Women's roles are primarily kinship roles: daughter, sister and mother. In all these roles it is incumbent on women to accord with the wishes and need of men. Hence, a woman has always been the object of male subjectivity. She has been defined in terms of her relationship to the male needs in society. Her role and position in society are also assigned by patriarchy in terms of popularly available stereotypes of the suffering mother, the agitated wife or the mistress, in all the cases an easily dispensable adjunct to the male counterpart. She is not allowed to speak or act in an autonomous fashion but is spoken to and acted upon. The strife of Indian women to gain equal stature has made them sensitive to socio-culture norms which advocate the inferior status of women. They have started interrogating and re-defining the definition of human being in terms of nationality and have explore the hidden logic behind the barriers of "man" and "woman", "male" and "female", "masculine" and "feminine".

The theme of oppression and exploitation of women is presented by Indian fiction writers palliatively, with black realism and with a deeper sense of involvement. Women have both sustain and questioned the patriarchal pressures and the work of women writers show us the resistances the subordinated ones have put up. They believe that the concept of gender is not merely a biological phenomenon but it has social constructions as Simone de Beauvoir says" One is not born, but rather becomes a woman". In the recent Indian fiction, women refuse to deal with injustice and oppression acquiescently and rather challenges it with fortitude and decisiveness. Women writers like Arundhati Roy, Kiran Desai, Jhumpa Lahari, Sashi Deshpande, etc. have established their credentials in the modern literary world and have contributed in presenting the changing role of Indian women in the modern society. Among the recent Indian women novelists writing in English, Sashi Deshpande's credentials are most impeccable. Her major novels include – *The Dark Holds No Terrors* (1980) *Roots and Shadows (*1988*) The Binding Vine (*1992*) A matter of Time (*1996*) Small Remedies (*2000*) Moving On (*2004*) In the Country of Deceit (*2008*) Ships that Pass (*2012*) and Shadow Play (*2014*)* The primary focus in Sashi Deshpande's short stories is laid on women in different roles-wife, mother, daughter and an individual in her own right.

Sashi Deshpande's short stories sensitively portray a woman's frustrations, despair pain and anguish in a society governed by the rigid codes laid down by the patriarchal social order. A married woman's sense of alienation and frustration in her dull routine life with an indifferent and insensitive husband and her subsequent wish to seek pleasure and fulfilment in the company of another man, not her husband, constitutes the thematic texture of Sashi Deshpande's short story "An Antidote to Boredom". G.S. amur considers it one of Sashi Deshpande's best stories and says that the story "dramatizes the suffering of a woman who makes an unsuccessful attempt to escape from the prison of her fixed role as a wife and live a life of spontaneity". The woman is fed up with the dull routine of her life with a cold, insensitive and indifferent husband and undemanding child. Excitement and happiness return in her life when she suddenly meets a young widower at her son's school who develops an instant liking for her. Their frequent meetings soon develop into a warm and loving relationship between a man and a woman. The husband remains totally absorbed in his rigid schedule of work and fails to take notice of his wife's affair with another man which further disillusions her. The woman is tortured by a feeling of guilt towards her son. She ultimately checks her infatuation and decides to stifle her longing for adventure and settles back as docile wife for fear of disturbing the calm tenor of her life. However, she bitterly regrets her decision soon afterwards as she realizes the authenticity and the value of her experience with her man. She says," I let go of the mirage I and tried to grasp so long and now I realized, when it was too late, the most piercing thought of it all-that it had been no mere antidote to boredom, but the best part of my life. And I let it go."

In the short story "The Intrusion", Sashi Deshpande describes a honeymoon that proves to be psychological rape culminating in a physical one. The story, very artistically, records that pain and humiliation experienced by a newly-married woman whose crass and insensitive husband exercises his conjugal rights by imposing himself on her unprepared body. The young bride is full of inhibitions. Before entering into the physical relationship with her husband, she wants to have some acquaintance with this new man in her life. She says: "But how can I, with a man I scarcely know? It's not fair…it's indecent. He should have given me some time." The honeymoon proves to be an unpleasant experience for the young bride. She undergoes mingled feelings of guilt, shame, fear and embarrassment all along and towards the close of the story; she suddenly wakes up at night to the horrible and humiliating experience of her privacy being intruded upon by a stranger who happens to be her own husband. In her words:

> And it was not the sea that was pounding my body but he, my husband, who was forcing his body on mine. I was too frightened to speak…I could do nothing…I could not move away…his movements had the same rhythm, the same violence as the movements of the sea: yet I could have borne the battering of sea better, for that would hurt but not humiliate like this.

In "*Death of a Child*", Sashi Deshpande records the loneliness of a woman and her experience of grief, guilt and shame caused by an abortion for which she blames herself. The narrator of the story is a woman married to an insensitive and indifferent husband. She has two children and now pregnant with her third child. The woman has a feeling of being trapped. The woman feels that to breed like an animal is not the sole purpose of her life. Overcome by a strong sense of resentment and hostility towards her husband which gives rise to a feeling of rebellion, the woman decides to abort the baby. However, after the abortion, the woman is overwhelmed with a feeling of guilt and feels that the ghost of her dead child would always accompany her.

"It Was dark", the title story in the volume for short stories by the same name, is a moving tale of the rape of a fourteen-year-old school girl. In "Lucid Moments", Sashi Deshpande expresses her protest against the lack of identity of women in a patriarchal set up. She, very sensitively, depicts the pain of an old woman who is on her death-bed and the state of helplessness and despair of her daughter who watches her die. The old woman is not much tortured by the physical pain that she experiences as by the thought that she knows nothing about her own mother looked or what was her name. There was no photograph of her and her father never spoke of her.

In the short story, *"It was Nightingale"*, the protagonist, lovingly called Jayu by her husband, is all said to go abroad for a couple of years to pursue her career. The husband does not like her going away. Jayu too suffers from a feeling of guilt and finally decides not to let go the opportunity go. She justifies her decision in these words.

> "To me our lives are intertwined, yet they are two distinct strands. They are like two lights that shine more brightly together, but to keep my light burning is my responsibility and mine alone".

In "My Beloved Charioteer", Shashi Deshpande depicts the trauma of two women, a mother and daughter, both widows, living together. After, the death of her husband, Aarti comes along with her young daughter to live in her mother's house who reveals to her daughter the traumatic relationship she shared with her husband. Recalling the humiliation and pain suffered by during nights with her husband, the old woman tells Aarti:

> At Night, I scarcely dared to breathe, I was so terrified of disturbing him…I slept there, afraid to get a glass of water, scared even to cough. When he wanted me, he said,: Come here". And I went: And when he finished, if I didn't get out of his bedfast enough, he said, "You can go". And I got out.

A woman's acute sense of loneliness in a foreign land, her alienation from her husband and her yearning for a sense of belonging and for companionship forms the thematic texture of Sashi Deshpande's short story, "Ghosts". The woman is in England with her husband who has come here in connection with his job. The only company she has in her apartment is of her son, an infant. The husband is away during the day and returns only at night. The brief contacts that she has with her husband at nights fill her with bitterness and disappointment. Their sexual relation is purely a mechanical affair.

> And then, when it was over, they turned their backs on each other in perfect unison, as if they had practiced this earlier. he went off to sleep. She could hear his soft steady snores-but she lay in the dark trying to burrow through the silence.

In her desperation the woman passes most of her time sitting in front of the T.V. screen peopled by faces that smile at her and wink at her and make her feel that she is part of them, a real person and not a ghost with whom people looked through.

In *"The Stone Women"* Sashi Deshpande portrays a young woman's attempt to mould her personality according to the wishes of her husband, her sudden realization of it and her final resolve to preserve her identity. The husband and wife visit a temple. In the courtyard of the temple, they find beautiful stone carvings of women in all kinds of pose-looking into the mirror, doing their hair, playing on some musical instruments, dancing and hunting. The wife, in particular, is fascinated by these stone women with lush bodies, high breasts, tiny waists, straight noses and elongated eyes. She recalls how on her husband's disapproval; she had stopped wearing her favourite silver bracelet and how hard she is trying to give up her habit of humming Hindi film tunes only because her husband dislikes it. And now when her husband expresses his dislike for a new dress she is wearing and gazes at her with thoughtful narrow eyes, the woman's mind leaps back to stone women in the temple and she reflects:

> This is how they must have looked. I realize the men who sculpted the women in stone, as they shaped them, from their imaginations… working out their fantasies… creating women with unreal bodies, women who played and sang and danced all day.

The woman is overcome by a sudden fear as if she is "becoming one of them too-women frozen for all the time into pose they have willed into.' And then overcoming her fear and asserting her individuality, she declares: "it's comfortable, I like it". The story ends with the husband somewhat puzzled by his wife's unexpected reply and the wife humming her favourite Hindi film song.

Incipient feminism is the keynote of Sashi Deshpande's short stories. Her protagonists are contemporary middle-class Indian women who are conscious of their individualities and selfhood. They want to defy patriarchy and grow out of their specific roles. They believe in conformity and compromise for the sake of retention of domestic harmony. Sashi Deshpande's short stories, featuring female protagonists, reconstruct aspects of women's experience and attempt to give voice to 'muted' ideologies. Sashi Deshpande's short stories prove the authencity of her claim that, "a world without frightened, dependent, trapped, frustrated women are a better world for all of us to live in."

Works Cited

Amus, G.S. "Preface". *The Legacy and Other Stories.* Calcutta: Writers Workshop, 1978.

Beauvoir, Simone de. *The Second Sex.* Trans. H.M Parshley, London: Vintage, 1997.

Deshpande, Sashi. *Writing from the Margin and Other Essays.* New Delhi: Penguin/Viking, 2003.

Deshpande, Sashi. *Collected Stories.* Vol.I Delhi, Penguin Books, 2003.

Deshpande, Sashi. *Collected Stories.* Vol.II Delhi, Penguin Books, 2004.

Miller, Jane, *Women Writing About Men.* London: Virago, 1986.

Literary Insight (ISSN 0975-6248).

Volume-9, Issue-2 July 2018, pp. 247-251.

Volume-10, Issue-I January 2019, pp. 441-445.

CHAPTER 2

Nonfiction for Prolific Writing: Exploring the Benefits of the Genre

Raja Kumar Tenali

> "Reading literary fiction stimulates cognition beyond the brain functions related to reading, say, magazine articles, interviews, or most online nonfiction reporting."
>
> – Susan Reynolds

If it's literature or not, the fact is that writing is purposive. It sometimes meant for sharing thoughts, feelings, opinions, or sometimes imparts knowledge; it may teach something or gives information to alert, or let people know of something significant; and sometimes entertain and influence to form opinion on important things or persons. Writing plays a significant role to let people to identify themselves with people or acknowledge situations. This can happen in from trivial things to hard things. Writing creates a network and works as a bridge among human brains to know each other. In our life we all write something (whether we are professionals in writing or not –) irrespective of our status in the society. Everyone writes letters, diaries, complaints or applications to the officials, feedback on newspaper content like news, news reports, articles, columns, stories, and so on. Whatever is written is presented in a form.

Every person has a story to tell, secret to divulge, pain to lament, feeling to express, an urge to confess, facts to reveal, experiences to inspire, knowledge to share, show knowledge to attract, knowledge to impart, inspire to revolutionize, secret powers to exhibit and so on. In such cases we choose to *writing* often. Thoughts are boiling in our brain and hearts are overwhelmed with enthusiasm to share every feeling of what he tries to reveal. By sharing orally we reach to the slender. Therefore there is every scope to opt writing. The word 'writing' often indicates fiction writing. When there are so many things that are factual in our lives it is not pertinent to go for fiction writing. There is a much scope to write an account under nonfiction genre. Nonfiction has a wider scope which we fail to accept or understand its prolific beauty and productive usage. For that matter everything we write is somehow a fact though it is fixed in the frame of fiction. We cannot limit the advantages with nonfiction writing as the genre inspires in connotation which leads the readers to action. A brutal murder in fiction is less to be provocative than a man beaten up in the lockup by the police in reality under nonfiction. Real things or happenings evoke feelings much from the deeper inside the heart. Anne Frank won the millions of hearts with her much acclaimed 'The Diary of a Young Girl' as her documentation of Holocaust was real. Anne's diaries and papers were a treasure of history and manifestation of cruelty to the mankind. We need to note that had it been a fiction we would not have remembered the diary till today. That is the prime example of the power of nonfiction writing.

Fiction and nonfiction are two separate directions of unlimited scope and destinations. There are limited numbers of writers who write fiction and their imagination may not reach to everyone's mind; but in case of nonfiction, everyone has to tell a unique story which is not untrue, and caters variety of life dynamics. All writers put together can't reach to the height or the depth of the variety of knowledge, thought or experience of such huge number of individuals. The dimensions of those stories of such heterogeneous individuals include legendary stories through great sacrifices, trifles to adventurous stories, from naïves to criminal nature brats, ethos to pathos (pathetic lives), cunning-lazy to innocent-hardworking ones, urchins to subtle ones, true-politicians to blood-sucking bureaucrats, and the list is unending. These varieties of people throw their lives to influence the people to get inspired with their true account of complete humanness. Topics for nonfiction can be unlimited. Anything the writer wants to tell, reveal, disclose, divulge, counsel, instruct, teach, express, put forth, narrate comes under the category. In terms of mass media, writing profiles, news, reports, reportage, documentation, feature articles, interviews, advertisements, radio talks, news analysis, weather forecast, business speculations, literary reviews etc. come under the nonfiction category. 'Before the Headlines', 'story behind the story', are the phrases we often hear. For every news item or the story, there should be a background on which we put things or facts or incidents together. The list of areas that cover things under nonfiction is exhaustive. *Do it yourself*, for example, elongates the task of the writer.

The difference between fiction and nonfiction is a thin line. Fiction is not beyond facts; nonfiction is not confined to all facts. Some narrative nonfiction stories include their thoughts. In fiction we create facts in real characters; in nonfiction we create beauty in facts. The source of fiction is imagination based on facts; the source of nonfiction is factual based on history, knowledge, information, skill or ant subject which is not fabricated. Whatever the writer proposes to tell by writing emanates from his knowledge, wisdom, or factual information. Whereas fictions emerge from imagination, creative and fictitious thoughts, though facts can be the driving force in the make-believing process.

Nonfiction writers are supposed to choose some established writing styles based on the content and the readers, in other words your audience and writing purpose will determine your style. Firstly, the content of writing is varied under nonfiction – right from personal essays through editorials in newspapers and literary journalistic features. Secondly, the writer needs to understand from which type of writing under nonfiction is apt for the presentation of the content. The nonfiction writer needs to identify the content for the writing. Nonfiction includes – history, philosophy, religion and spirituality, science, popular science, politics and social sciences, essay, self-help, business and economics, health and wellness, crafts and hobbies, travel guides, cookbooks, parenting and family, children's nonfiction, educational guides, text books, language books, humour, art books, memoirs and autographs, biographies, travel literature, journalism, *ekphrasis*, lyrical essay, and flash nonfiction (creative nonfiction written about seven hundred and fifty words). The list is not conclusive in itself and a writer can write any creative style to convey the content. A nonfiction writer normally chooses from these styles of writing which are classified under four major styles – expository nonfiction, narrative nonfiction, persuasive nonfiction, and descriptive nonfiction. In any nonfiction style, elucidation of facts is of paramount importance, clear description of the facts will be enough to extract the readers.

Expository Nonfiction

When the writer attempts to explain certain things or to information the reader about a topic. With expository writing, the reader may or may not have prior knowledge about the topic being discussed but the writer provides information about what it is, who someone is, what something means, how something works, and why something is important. Hence, proper research is essential to successfully executing expository nonfiction. *Bone by Bone by: Comparing Animal Skeletons* by Sara Levine and T. S. Spookytooth (2013) on comparing animal skeletons and how these bones of skeletons play an important role; *Born in the Wild: Baby Mammals and Their Parents* by Lita Judge (2014) on the wild life of baby animals and their parents; *Daylight Starlight Wildlife* by Wendell Minor (2015), reveals the variety of animals that surround us when we are awake and when we are sleeping by an amazing and luminous paintings; *Mysterious Patterns: Finding Fractals in Nature* by Sarah C. Campbell and Richard P. Campbell (2014) is an elegant introduction of fractals through examples that can be seen in parks, rivers, and our very own backyards; *The Street Beneath My Feet* by Charlottw Guillian and Yuval Zommer (2017) is on our fascinating journey down through the layers of the Earth and layers of the rock and the planet's molten core; *With a Friend by Your Side* by Barbara Kerley (2015) on sweet thoughts about the value of friendship and *An Egg is Quiet* by Dianna Hutts Aston and Sylvia Long (2006) etc., are the examples of expository nonfiction.

Narrative Nonfiction

Also known as creative nonfiction or literary nonfiction is a true story written in the style of a fiction novel. It presents the contents in a compelling way and the facts are told as a story. The reader feels as if reading a fiction as it uses the techniques and style of fiction *viz* characters, plot, conflict, and scene-setting. Books under this genre can cover about any topic of interest to have a great reading experience. *Behind the Beautiful Forevers* by Katherine Boo explains life in a Mumbai slums: *Without You, There Is No Us* by Suki Kim writes about a reporter goes inside a school for the sons of North Kores's elite; *The Secretary* by Kim Ghattas was an inside account of Hillary Clinton's term as Secretary of State by a travelling journalist; The Lonely War by Nazila Fathi was an Iranian journalist's account of the struggle for reform in modern Iran; *Galileo's Daughter* by Dava Sobel was a look at the relationship between Galileo and his oldest daughter, a nun named Maria Celeste, are the examples of narrative nonfiction. Narrative fiction deals with the topics like history,

Science, global issues, social and contemporary issues. Some narration is stuffed between the facts, as in sandwiches, in nonfiction.

Persuasive Nonfiction

It is a form of nonfiction writing that aims to convince the reader of a certain point of view. In persuasive nonfiction the writers use the facts to support his arguments and convince the readers of the story. Newspaper editorials in such a way try to support their arguments by providing proper evidence to persuade the readers. The purpose of the story is to persuade the reader about something. Advertisements newspaper columns academic essays, reviews brochures campaign flyers contain good persuasive write-ups with careful word choice, logical arguments, diligent reasoning rhetoric questions, emotive and metaphorical language, facts and statistics, expert's opinion and analysis, and cohesive summaries. This technique persuades the reader to trust the writer. *The Diary of a Young Girl*, a collection of diary entries by Anne Frank; *A Brief History of Time* by Stephen Hawking; *In Cold Blood* by Truman Capote; *The Colour of Madness* by Samara Linton and Rianna Walcott; *The Yoga Manifesto* by Nadia Gilani, are some of the examples on persuasive writing.

Descriptive Nonfiction

The writer uses figurative language, rich details and sensory language to help readers understand the information. Travel Guide is the perfect example of descriptive nonfiction. Travel guides focus on describing places to visit, cultural and historical significances of the places keeping in view of the travel themes such as relaxation, adventure or culinary experiences. The descriptive writers plant the scene, or image in the minds of the reader. It usually involves descriptions of senses – sight, sound, sense, touch etc., to make the travel more alluring or tempting. *The White Album*, *Slouching Towards Bethlehem* by Joan Didion, *Changing my Mind* by Zadie Smith, are some examples of descriptive nonfiction. In nonfiction we need not narrate things to attract the readers; and clear description of the facts will be enough to extract the readers. Nonfiction writers, however, sometimes use all the above techniques in a single book depending on the need.

Majority of the share in literature is nonfiction in different modes or genres as its unlimited nature permeates in every corner of our lives as well as literature. C. Toni Graham says "Writers create impressions that inspire, stir emotions, evoke questions and sprinkle seeds of awe". Maybe obsessed that nonfiction has some limited scope to write on; but fiction has certain limitations, though it has the option to imagine anything. Nonfiction seems to be like fiction loaded with reality.

When there are too many bitter facts which the author is unwilling to write directly, or not willing to face risk or pressure, he will surely go for fiction writing. Of course, it doesn't happen always. Khushwant's *Train to Pakistan* was a fiction based on fact and on his personal experiences. The concepts expressed are based on true and real life situations. This may be termed as 'nonfiction under disguise' with a disclaimer. The stories with disclaimer in most cases touch the lives, incidents or day-to-day happenings of lives of someone with no imagination, concoction, or fabrication. Sometimes the writer tries to convey messages with fiction. However, it sometimes lacks the desired effect as it claims the story is fictitious. In case of nonfiction genre the reader acknowledges the truth to accept the reality. Therefore, nonfiction is a much sought after genre to penetrate into the hearts to reach beyond fiction. There is a need to write more in the genre to inspire the readers more.

The following quotations may help us understand more of nonfiction as a writing genre.

> "Poetry is a way of coming to know the realness of things; fiction is a way of coming to know the world of relationships; nonfiction is a way of coming to know the world of the mind."
>
> – Kelly Cherry

> "Writing nonfiction means I tell people's stories for them, not because they're special but because we all are."
>
> – Jo Deurbrouck

> "There are things we can say in nonfiction that cannot be said outright in fiction. And there are truths that can be conveyed in fiction that the constraints of nonfiction would never allow."
>
> – Anaik Alcasas, Sending Signals: Amplify the Reach, Resonance and Results of Your Ideas

> "Fiction has a burden which nonfiction does not: it must seem life-like."
>
> – Unknown

> "Without ACTION, reading nonfiction is a waste of time"
>
> – Oran Kangas

> "It's always seemed odd to me that nonfiction is defined, not by what it is, but by what it is not. It is not fiction. But then again, it is also not poetry,

or technical writing or libretto. It's like defining classical music as nonjazz."

– Philip Gerard,
Creative Nonfiction: Researching and Crafting Stories of Real Life

"I write horror because I'm a writer of nonfiction."

– Et Imperatrix Noctem

"There is a difference between fiction and nonfiction deeper than technique or intention. I value both but genuinely believe that fiction can tell a larger truth."

– Dorothy Allison, Bastard Out of Carolina

"You know what I love about writing non-fiction? The story is already there. I just have to write it down."

– Oliver Markus Malloy,
Inside The Mind of an Introvert

"Nonfiction is a form of literature that lies halfway between fiction and fact."

– F. Scott Fitzgerald, The I.O.U.

"Fiction is entertaining. Nonfiction is epic."

– A.D. Posey

"I read nonfiction for information, fiction for truth."

– Michael M. Thomas

"Most nonfiction writers have a definitiveness complex. They feel that they are under some obligation – to the subject, to their honor, to the gods of writing – to make their article the last word. It's a commendable impulse, but there is no last word. What you think is definitive today will turn undefinitive by tonight, and writers who doggedly pursue every last fact will find themselves pursuing the rainbow and never settling down to write. Nobody can write a book or an article "about" something. Tolstoy couldn't write a book about war and peace, or Melville a book about whaling. They made certain reductive decisions about time and place and about individual characters in that time and place – one man pursuing one whale. Every writing project must be reduced before you start to write. Therefore think small. Decide what corner of your subject you're going to bite off, and be content to cover it well and stop."

– William Zinsser,
On Writing Well: The Classic Guide to Writing Nonfiction

References

1. Ann Abramson, *Who Was Anne Frank?*, by Grosset & Dunlap (2007), eISBN: 978-1-101-09965-0
2. AYN RAND, *The art of nonfiction: a guide for writers and readers*, First Plume Printing, February 2001, eISBN: 978-1-101-13729-1

3. Brenda Miller and Suzanne Paola, *Tell It Slant: Writing and Shaping Creative Nonfiction*, 2019, ISBN: 978-1-26-045460-4 MHID: 1-26-045460-6
4. Elissa Washuta and Theresa Warburton, *Shapes of Native Nonfiction*, University of Washington Press, Seattle, 2019
5. Jell Talbot, *Metawritings-Toward a Theory of Nonfiction*, University of Iowa Press First Edition (2012)
6. John Steinbeck, *America and Americans and Selected Nonfiction*, Viking Penguin (2002), eISBN: 978-0-142-43741-4.
7. John Warner, *The Writer's Practice: Building Confidence in Your Nonfiction Writing,* Penguin Random House LLC, ISBN 9780143133155 (paperback), ISBN 9780525504931 (ebook), 2019
8. Michal Stawicki, *Slicing the Hype – A Simple Formula for Finding Great Nonfiction eBooks* (2015), visit www.michalzone.com
9. Stephen Harrod Buhner, *Ensouling Language: On the Art of Nonfiction and the Writer's Life* 2010 eISBN-13: 978-1-59477-900-8
10. Thomas C. Foster, *How to read Nonfiction like a Professor: Critical Thinking in the Age of Bias, Contested Truth, and Disinformation*, Harper Collins India Publication, Digital Edition MAY 2020 ISBN: 978-0-06-289588-2
11. William Zinsser, *On Writing Well: The Classic Guide to Writing Nonfiction* – 30th anniversary ed. HarperCollins Publishers Inc., New York, NY 10022, ISBN-10: 0-06-089154-8, ISBN-13: 978-0-06-089154-1, EPub Edition © SEPTEMBER 2012 ISBN: 9780062250506
12. https://www.10differences.org/difference-fiction-nonfiction/#comparison-chart-fiction-vs-nonfiction
13. https://www.10differences.org/difference-fiction-nonfiction/#differences-between-fiction-and-nonfiction
14. https://www.10differences.org/difference-fiction-nonfiction/#what-is-non-fiction
15. https://blog.reedsy.com/guide/nonfiction/
16. https://jerichowriters.com/non-fiction-what-is-creative-writing-in-non-fiction/
17. https://dontbignorant.in/category/benefits-of-reading-nonfiction/
18. https://dontbignorant.in/category/benefits-of-reading-nonfiction-books/
19. 10 Types of Nonfiction Books and Genres | Writers.com

CHAPTER 3

Positioning of Letters in Fiction and Non-fiction: A Comparative Study

Jipsa Maria Joy

Until a few centuries ago, letter writing was the only method of communication between people living in far-flung places. Letter writing play a major role in ancient history of literature. Letters are of different types. There are personal letter, official letter and business letter. These letters are written for expressing different matters, experience, needs and aim of life. The pattern or the method of writing too differs from one type of letter to another type of letter. Personal letter is written to the known person in an informal manner whereas the official and business letters are more formal. They are written to the people who are not known or who are officially known. Whatever the letter is, Letter-writing is a part of literature. It requires a command over language and fluency in it. A good letter comes out of one's good language and writing skills.

Letters do not play merely a role of medium for communication, rather expresses the sociological, political, cultural perspectives of the particular period. Letters have long been an important source of biographical information and a powerful tool for historians of all kinds. They allow the reader to look behind the scenes, and this intimacy can provide intimate knowledge of historical subjects, even if borrowed or stolen. The letter takes on a unique liminal status when the writer's main historical contributions are literary. Letters from poets and other writers allow their readers to straddle the line between contextual research and artistic interpretation.

The eighteenth century is generally known as the great age of letter writing: postal routes developed rapidly and the epistolary novel emerged as a very popular genre. Letter writers of the time used the form to describe and explore personal, everyday experience. The Romans and Egyptians passed messages this way. In 1653 Devalayar, a Frenchman, established a postal system in Paris. He set up mailboxes. Letters placed therein shall be forwarded if he uses envelopes supplied only by him. Later, a schoolmaster from England Rowland Hill invented the adhesive post Stamped in 1837; Through his efforts, the world's first stamp was issued in England 1840. Hill created the first uniform postage rates based on weight Size Hill's stamps made prepaid postage possible and practical. Since then, letters were sent from different parts of England and then it was used in all the countries which were ruled by the Britishers, little by little all nations accepted this method and started following this. In this paper I will be exploring the evolution of letter to a part of literary genre and different usages of letter forms in English literature. There are novels that are written in epistolary or letter form, whereas letters themselves exists as a genre.

This paper does a comparative study of positioning of letters in fiction and non-fiction with respect to Samuel Richardsons *Pamela* and *Letters to Felice* which comprises the letters written by the writer Franz Kafka to Felice Bauer from 1912-1917. These letters were acquired by Schocken from Felice Bauer in 1955, in addition to roughly half of Kafka's letters to Grete Bloch, Bauer's friend.

Samuel Richardson is an English writer known for three epistolary novels, namely *Pamela; or, Virtue Rewarded* (1740), *Clarissa: Or the History of a Young Lady* (1748) and *The History of Sir Charles Grandison* (1753). The novel *Pamela; or, Virtue Rewarded* was first published in 1740. It is Considered as one of the first true English novels. Writing in a new form, the novel, Richardson attempted to both instruct and entertain. Richardson wrote *Pamela* as a conduct book, a sort of manual which codified social and domestic behaviour of men, women, and servants, as well as a narrative in order to provide a more morally concerned literature option for young audiences.

> And the next day I was very sad, and began my long letter. He saw me writing, and said (as I mentioned) to Mrs Jervis, 'That girl is always scribbling; methinks she might find something else to do'; or to that purpose. And when I had finished my letter, I put it under the toiler, in my late lady's dressing-room, whither nobody comes but myself and Mrs Jervis, beside my master; but when I came up again to seal it, to my great concern, it was gone; and Mrs Jervis knew nothing of it; and nobody knew of my master's having been near the place in the time: So I have been sadly troubled about It. (Richardson 58)

Samuel Richardson delivers the entire narrative of his epistolary novel Pamela through the emphasis on letters and their use. Even though the work belongs to genre of novel its form and narrative stresses more on letters. Pamela is the story of a young women who works as a housemaid for an upper-class woman. She is made servant of the mistress's son after her death, who is an evil knight with negative intentions. The letters written by the protagonist to her parents serves as narratives of the novel with a few responses. It is these letters that tells the story to the readers. The male master is another character who provides more information through his interference in the letter. "…you ought to be wary what tales you send out of a family. Be faithful and diligent; and do as you should do, and I will like you the better for this." (44) Writing in the story is also dangerous. Master's interception of her letters is a constant threat, and because of them he is better equipped to take advantage of her. Pamela needs writing to communicate and ask for help, which is a tool for her enemy. Considering the previous fate of her letters, it is doubtful whether her fears described in letter 14 (pp. 61-65) did not lead her to further misfortunes. Indeed, given the ease with which the Master took away one of Pamela's letters, one wonders if her family receives any letters containing sensitive information. His command of the household is absolute and neither female can disobey their master. All they can do is hope that "he will give over all attempts: And that [they] shall better know what to do [later]" (65). Postponing the inevitable, hoping against all hope – the servants in this text have no method with which to defend their innocence and honour.

In the beginning, the letters written by Pamela to her parents describes her working condition as happy. After the death of the mistress Pamela fears that she would have to go back to her village life of distress and poverty. She expresses her joy in the letters when the Knight announces her as his servant. The novel constitutes seven volume of letters Pamela wrote to her parents and others. Though each of the letters, the readers come to know more about the characters and the letters becomes intense as the story moves on. The narrator of the story is Pamela herself and the narrative mode is epistolary. This is what makes the novel stand different. First, the letters are a symbol for privacy and bodily ownership. Specifically, they help Richardson make the radical point that even a servant has the right to control over her own body and her own thoughts. Secondly these letters provide some good moral lessons along with lots of solid examples of Pamela's virtue, empathy, and kindness.

These letters are the source of narratives. Character herself becomes the narrator. The author conveys to the readers through the letters. Even though the novel belongs to the genre of fiction, its narrative style bestows on non-fiction. There exist letters that are a part of literature which belongs to non-fiction. One such work is *Letters to Felice*. *Letters to Felice* is a collection of letters sent by Franz Kafka to Felice Bauer from 1912 to 1917. These letters were taken over by Schocken Books from Felice Bauer in 1955. There were also letters sent to Grete Bloch, Bauer's friend. Additional letters to Bloch were acquired at a later date. Kafka and Bauer were engaged twice during this time period and Kafka wrote some of his most famous works, including *The Metamorphosis*, *In the Penal Colony,* and his first attempts at writing *The Trial.*

These letters are originally published in German in 1967 as *Briefe an Felice*, the collection was first published in English by Schocken Books in 1973. The translation of these letters was produced by James Stern and Elisabeth Duckworth.

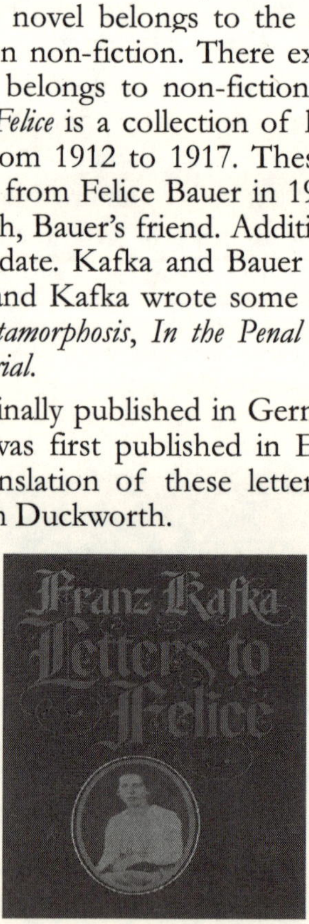

"This extraordinary biography fills the empty spaces between Kafka's own writings of friends, family and conteporaries with so much empathy and imagination that one can't put it down".(Rundshau) Kafka is one of the fascinating figures of world literature. However, even after eighty years of his death no concrete history of his life was available. Only after the publication of these letters, Kafka's life came to day light. Even though letters are included in non-fiction, these letters have a lots of stories to tell. It includes the thoughts, imaginations and emotions of the writer. As it is addresssed to someone intimate to the writer, it has the heart of the writer.

Franz Kafka and Felice met in Prague on 13 August 1912, when he visited his friend. A week after the meeting, on 20 August, Kafka entered in his diary:

> Miss FB. When I arrived at Brod's on 13 August, she was sitting at the table. I was not at all curious about who she was, but rather took her for granted at once. Bony, empty face that wore its emptiness openly. Bare throat. A blouse thrown on. Looked very domestic in her dress although, as it turned out, she by no means was. (I alienate myself from her a little by inspecting her so closely ...) Almost broken nose. Blonde, somewhat straight, unattractive hair, strong chin. As I was taking my seat I looked at her closely for the first time, by the time I was seated I already had an unshakeable opinion.

The letters he sent her after the meeting expressed his disappointment if she did not respond as frequently. His short story *The Judgment* written on the night of 22 September 1912 was dedicated to her. They met again for Easter of 1913, and he proposed marriage in a letter at the end of July that year. Their engagement took place ON Sunday 31 May 1914, but was broken a few weeks later in August.

Their communication was mostly through letters. They spend ten days together in Marienbad. Their second engagement took place on 12 July 1917, planning to marry soon and live together in Prague. But fate had other plans. Kafka broke the engagement again in December that year because he Suffered from symptoms of the tuberculosis that was to lead to his death. They got separated on 27 December. More than 500 letters which he sends to her were saved by Felice which were published as *Letters to Felice.* But the letters send in response did not survive. His letters to Felice are very much literary affairs, just as Kafka used his personal problems as the basis for his fiction. It is often eloquently romantic in his early letters as if he is courting her. A letter written three months after he initiated the correspondence is remarkable in its intensity and displays the literary stance of an earnest lover. In his recollections of the suffering he caused her after first termination of their engagement, he waxes eloquent about his guilt. He uses the letters to converse with himself, just as he does in his fiction.

Kafka's correspondence with Felice is also literary in a deeper sense. The letters are a communication of images, of poses. His first letter to her reads like a casual introduction from an urbane young man. He later confessed to Felice that it took him ten days to write the letter; he revised and polished it in order to give it the impression of casualness. In his later letters to her, he makes a virtual fetish of asking about the everyday details of her life: what she did, what she ate, whom she saw, and so on. Yet Kafka began to write intimately almost from the beginning. In his letter of November 1, 1912, he uses a less formal salutation, and on November 11, he employs the informal (intimate) German form of address. Tellingly, however, he informs her in the same letter of his unfitness for marriage and fatherhood; such ambivalence must certainly have confused Felice. He began writing to her more and more frequently; at times he composed two or three letters per day.

The letters apparently were potential substance for Kafka's fantasies about her as well as about himself. These fantasies ultimately concerned the ideal bourgeois existence, which his father and society at large seemed to champion and which he believed was beyond his grasp. Felice, a name which means "happiness" in Latin, was in many respects less a living person than a fictional construct or a projection of Kafka's desire. The anguish that Kafka felt over the "happiness" he sought with Felice makes the letters at times rather painful and poignant. In his letter of November 26, 1912, he acknowledges to her the contradictions that plague their relationship and expresses his very real concern about his health.

It is not certain what Kafka meant by that, but some scholars, Ernst Pawel, for example, suggest that his morbid aversion to sexuality and the act of intercourse – quite clear in Kafka's diary entries – made him realize that the physical intimacy of married life was beyond him. On March 6, 1913, he wrote to her that she would never be able to live with him, not even for two days. His letter of April 1, 1913, mentions his fear that he would never be able to possess her, that he could only kiss her hand. Kafka desired marriage but lived in mortal fear of it. He hoped that his relationship to Felice might help him overcome his inner difficulties. The letter of May 23, 1913, speaks of the miracle "cure" that he believed might result from their marriage. But finally, their marriage didn't happen.

A joint analysis of the use of letters in literary genre places it in different positions. On one hand letters themselves become a literary work whereas in some case different genres gets mixed up. Taking Pamela into concern, even though it is a fictional work, a part of it is built in a non-fictional mode. That is, the genre of letter writing is combined to form the narration. The author communicates with his readers through the letters written by Pamela. It is these letters that introduces the characters, plot and events. The story moves on with a stream of consciousness technique that uncovers through the thoughts recorded by Pamela In her letters. The role of letter is independently represented in Letters to Felice. Here the letters itself is literary genre. It belongs to the genre of non-fiction and includes the actual life, experiences and thoughts of Franz Kafka. This shift of position of letter in literary canon uplifts it from mere mode of communication to a literary work.

Works Cited

Frempoutzakos, /. "Letters and Their Importance in Pamela." *Riseofthenovel*, 3 Apr. 2015, https://riseofthenovel.wordpress.com/2015/04/03/letters-and-their-importance-in-pamela/.

Kafka, Franz, et al. *Letters to Felice.* Schocken Books, 2016.

"Letters to Felice." *Enotes.com*, Enotes.com, https://www.enotes.com/topics/letters-felice.

"Pamela; or, Virtue Rewarded." *Wikipedia*, Wikimedia Foundation, 22 Nov. 2022, https://en.wikipedia.org/wiki/Pamela;_or,_Virtue_Rewarded#Conduct_books_and_the_novel

Richardson, Samuel. *Pamela.* Dent, 1978.

CHAPTER 4

Transformation of Warli Artwork: Conventional to Contemporary Art

Nivedita Thakur and Dr. Avdhut Atre

India is a country where we find diversity in culture. This diversity in Indian art always narrates power pack variations of Indian folks like we have a huge collection of music, songs, paintings, theater, performing arts, rituals and many more…

The Indian folk are an integral part of Indian culture. And our identity is directly or indirectly associated with our art. Because folk art is directly connected to the people and their spirituality. This folk is handed down through generations. This is like the storytelling of our life stories…

Village artists always render their expressions in Folk Paintings. These paintings have deeply emerged in the community's tradition and culture. They share their values, perceptions and express their cultural identity mainly.

India has many folk painting styles that always represent their region which are thought to be as classic as our renowned epics Ramayana & Mahabharata. These paintings narrate stories from Ramayana, Mahabharata, Bhagwat Purana along with their village life, nature – animals, birds, sun, trees, moon etc.

This article will explain Warli Painting's Evolution from traditional style to contemporary art form.

Introduction of Tribe

Warli Tribe is the utmost tribe of Western Maharashtra. According to Wilson – WARLI word is derived from the word "VARAL" which means piece of land (small patch of land). Warlis are dominantly found in Thane-Palghar district of Maharashtra. Some of them are scattered in Nasik, greater Mumbai, Gujarat-Maharashtra. They speak Warli language, a sub-type of Marathi language.

History of Warli Art

One of the oldest tribal painting styles is WARLI PAINTING which is practiced by the Warli tribe. This painting style is very popular all over the world. This art is rooted in Maharashtra and still being practiced in their region. (1)

Warli painting is an ancient art form stretching back to 2500 or 3000 BCE as per Yashodhara Dalmia's book – The painted world of the warlis.

This is a very ancient and popular painting style among Indian folk art.

Some also suggested that this tribal art style is said to have its presence from the 10th century A.D and got recognition in the 1970s. Most tribes consider Nature as their mother. With the same belief, Warli culture is centered around mother nature and dominantly depicted in their paintings.

Primarily warli paintings were done on the walls of the huts (mud coated walls) to decorate their homes. Also was part of the rituals during marriages. This reminds the practice where stone age people paint cave walls as their painting canvases.

This art form is dominated with geometric shapes like circles, triangles, squares, types of lines, dots etc.

Warli painting has received cultural intellectual property of tribal community. The tribal non profitable organization "Adivasi Yuva Seva Sangh" initiated to start registration process in 2011. Now Warli painting received intellectual property rights under geographical indication.

It usually takes 15 minutes to 2 months to complete one warli painting. It depends on size and detailing of the painting.

Material

These masterpieces appear on the walls of huts or houses by village artisans with pure intentions. Traditionally, this style is done on the mud wall with white paste. They clean walls and coat them with mud (Geru) and make their canvas ready to paint. Later on these canvases are covered with various themes with white paste. White paste is made with rice, water and gum that acts as a critical catalyst. Bamboo sticks are chewed to make paint brushes.

Themes of Paintings

Warli paintings are deep rooted in their beliefs, day to day life, forest scenes and many more. If we observe closely, we notice humans are celebrating their festivals, rituals along with nature and Animals, birds are also making a blast.

The central motif in each ritual painting is the square, known as the "chauk". Mostly Chauks are of 2 types:-DEVCHAUK & LAGNACHAUK

Devchauk is a square-shaped motif which represents Goddess (goddess of fertility).

In between chauk artisans draw images of Dev along with offerings.

During festivals like Holi, Diwali, during harvesting, rituals (marriages), these paintings are done on Warli houses. The main subjects for the paintings are their daily routine, nature, god-goddess, animals, birds, etc…

Warli paintings are very geometric in nature. They resemble elements to basic geometric shapes like for sun, moon depiction they use circles, for mountain and pointed trees depiction triangles…. Together they make a sacred piece of land in painting…

Some main mural painting themes are as follow:

Ritual Based

Each ritual painting has a square shape motif called as "chauk". Chauks are of two types – a) Devchauk b) Lagnachauk. (3)

Suvasini (married women) draws this painting. Warli marriage is mainly a five days ceremony. The painting is done just one day before marriage. This kana or chauk protects the bride and groom from evil spirits, to bless them in terms of long life, fertility and a prosperous married life.

- *Lagna Chauk* – Lagna Chauk is rectangular motif based painting focussing on Palghat Devi figure in the center. This devi (goddess) is said to bring blessings to the bride and groom. This is painted on the walls of bride's and groom's houses. This typical chauk consists of diverse geometrical patterns. Warli people believe that this chauk is jewelry of the goddess. For this reason the lagna chauk is with intricate geometric patterns.

- *Dev Chowk* – This pattern is drawn at the time of wedding. This pattern is drawn just next to Lagna Chauk. A panchsiriya – panch means five & siriya means head is painted either standing or riding a horse. This painting protects newly married couples from bad luck.

Kanna

Kanna is a Warli layout sample. Generally this sample is drawn with the aid of using Suvasinis. This is an image of virginity and drawn within side the bride's residence as a ritual. Vulva of a virgin warli bride is represented with the aid of using the image of kanna. This sample is included on partitions with the assist of rice paste (white), Kumkum (red), turmeric (yellow), sindoor (orange).

Tarpa Dance

Tarpa is a widely recognized people's dance of Warlis. This dance shape is finished with the aid of using the men & girls at night. It's a kind of gathering. Tarpa is a kind of device that's performed withinside the middle and surrounded with the aid of using dancers. This dance shape is sharp and complete of pleasure and expression.

Marriage ceremony

In this kind of portray, usually the groom takes his spouse to his residence on a horse observed with the aid of using dancing visitors and musicians. In Hindus, the bride constantly sits at the back of the groom and in warli way of life the bride constantly sits in the front of the groom.

Festivals

Holi, diwali – In those varieties of artwork are with plenty of a laugh and joy. Festivals inclusive of holi, diwali, harvest gala's together with dance scenes are very famous.

Birds, animals, bushes

Warli tribe revolves round Mother Nature. And they cognizance at the factors of Mother nature in every and each portray. They admire mom nature and contain varieties of bushes, birds and animals of their canvases.

Human Figures

The principal focusing motif of the portray is constantly surrounded with the aid of using the various human figures. Hunting scenes, fishing & farming, gala's, dances are different subtopics of the primary artwork. Human our bodies are depicted with the aid of using triangles joined together. Upper triangle represents the trunk and the decrease represents the pelvis.

As warlis are farmers, animal motifs like Cows, Bulls, Cocks, Hens, Sheep's, puppies are utilized in portrays as those are home animals. Bird motifs like peacocks, sparrows are occasionally visible, snakes, frogs also are visible. Peacock is a countrywide lovely chook depicted anywhere in conventional textiles, embroideries and artwork in India. Frogs are depicted for heavy rainfall; scenes of harvesting or farming are proven to develop grains in enough quantities and prosperity.

Painting Technique

Warli portray is likewise recognized for its simplicity. Warli artwork are quite simple to attract and include mere outlines with only a few info or nothing. Basic geometric shapes like circle, triangle, rectangular are used to create enthralling warli artwork. Previously Warli portray turned into executed on dust partitions with white rice paste. Today artisans do artwork on hand-crafted paper or on canvas with white paint.

These magical extraordinarily simplistic artwork have a completely particular conventional scheme i.e. brown and white.

Characteristics of Warli Painting

They use herbal or synthetic colours. Most of the artwork has a border with easy geometric shapes like triangle, circle, rectangular.

Motifs of sun, moon, birds, bushes accompany the principal subject.

Faces of human figures are in a circle and frame with triangles. Female bodies are recognized with the aid of using sticking out curve strains symbolizing ponytail. Figures of deities, bride and groom have unique attributes.

Role of Warli Artisans

Traditionally those artwork have been practiced with the aid of using Suvasinis (married girls) as a part of their customs together with their songs (Dhawal Geet). But present day situation has changed. These artwork are practiced with the aid of using each adult males and females. Warli is reached in each residence of our us a and globally additionally as a part of their domestic decor.

The first Warli artist who added warli portray in limelight is JIVYA SOMA MASHE. Until then it turned into only a ritual withinside the warli community. He converted this historic artwork into creative practice. His excellent artwork are regarded and proudly selected with the aid of using artwork lovers, creditors and investors. Mashe is likewise regarded as the daddy of Warli Painting. He turned into venerated with Padma shri in 2011. Warli artwork has received recognition over time and now nearly anywhere we discover warli artwork on ornamental items, saris, mugs, t-shirts and on international structures that we can speak afterwards...

After getting this artwork famous, it has now no longer remained constrained to the dust partitions covered with cow dung, it has crossed diverse mediums of portray like canvas, paper and obtained a standing in residence decorations. It isn't always simplest shifted to the partitions of flats, Diwankhana of Bungalows however it's far followed proudly for beautification of Five supermegacelebrity Hotels. It is likewise visible on family articles like, Coffee mugs, Files, Wallhangings, Paperweights. Main diversification of this artwork is its access withinside the fabric world. Simple & aesthetic in apparel, warli artwork portray is back & gaining plenty desired fame. Recently warli tribal artisans are becoming publicity with city way of life and a brand new era of warlis are adopting motifs like town buses, heighten Buildings, Railway, Ships etc. But nonetheless today, motifs like Warli marriage ceremony, Tarpa dance in circle, Indian farming style, Birds and animals life-style to be had in surrounded nature, those motifs are retaining the lifestyle of Warli. In this Global generation of remix and fusion way of life, even supposing this artwork is diversified, warli artisans are following this modification with the aid of using now no longer seeking to smash conventional originality of portrayal.

Today's Warli

This is the oldest people's artwork. It has its beginning in areas like Palghar & Thane district of Maharashtra. With all geometric info and simplicity, those artwork have grabbed the eye of viewers. They are becoming preferred throughout India and throughout the world. Nowadays those artwork are becoming generated with the aid of the use of cutting-edge printing strategies and additionally introducing cutting-edge shadeation schemes with city motifs on them, inclusive of bicycles, roads and different city surroundings. Even fabrics, cushions, wall hangings, work of art are becoming included with the aid of using the use of warli motifs. This globalized artwork shape is getting famous day with the aid of using day. This enthralling artwork shape additionally regarded on marketing and marketing campaigns, style outfits, on airports and lots of more….

Depiction of Warli paintings on Global Platform

Traditionally warli is a part of warli's house's wall. Warli paintings not only adorn the walls of the houses but also adorn building exterior. The best example is Lodhi Colony. The walls of the Lodhi Colony are covered with mesmerizing Warli art… On the walls artists successfully express their tribal stories. This project was organized by Start India Foundation. This foundation always focuses on Indian folk Art. Artist Tushar and Mayur explores and does experiments in folk but at the same time he pays attention to the traditional sense of that particular art form.

Fig: 01.1

One more example of wall mural painting in Warli style is Hisar Airport's Wall. This wall is decorated with warli paintings. 'Hamara Pyaar hisar' is a group of school and college students and some elderly persons. Their mission is to beautify the walls and open space of Hisar by painting them with beautiful paintings. As a part of their campaign, they painted walls of Hisar airport (Maharaja Agrasen International Airport). This activity was led by Artist Harish Chandra. This group painted the boundary wall of the airport. It took only 3 hours to complete the task.

We can see Warli painting's one more "Avatar" at the International Airport, New Delhi. This art is made with stainless steel and size is 14 feet X 28 feet.

Fashion shows, fashion weeks are the best opportunities for designers where they showcase their talent to larger audience groups. The world looks up to these designers and their collections for the latest and upcoming trends in garments, style!

Warli art has made an impression on the fashion world also. Fashion Designer Archana Kochhar launched her garments at the New York Fashion Show (September 12 2018). The entire collection was in black and white. The hand painted warli was the main attraction which was done by warli artisans. This collection was a very stylistic expression. It's a perfect blend of comfort and creativity into one.

Purvi Doshi is a label which brings sustainability in clothing and fashion. Purvi Doshi also showcased warli on garments in Lakme Fashion Week Jan 2016.

She express her designs and patterns through warli prints on garments.

Fig: 01.2

Fig: 01.3

This fascinating warli art has many world records in her hand. Art Club of IISER Pune organized one event where 470 students came together to create a history in the warli art world. On 1st November 2014, They created a warli about 2600 sq ft, nearly the size of a football field. This entire event was sponsored by Pidilite Industries. This movement was accepted by the LIMKA BOOK OF RECORDS.

Fig: 01.4

Another world record had been registered for organizing a warli painting marathon. Artist Shruti Tiwari is artist from Mumbai who organized Warli Marathon to support corona Warriors. She made 200+ paintings in just 21 hours. She started this marathon on 4th May 2021, 10am and ended on 5th May, 2021 at 7 am. This activity has gone for New World Record at Bhayandar, Mumbai, Maharashtra.

We saw the appearance of warli on walls of buildings, on clothes, and in different warli experiments. Advertising world is also mesmerized by warli paintings.

The coca cola advertisement campaign (2010) was launched in 2010. The theme was "Come home Diwali"

According to Anand Singh, Director, Marketing (Colas), Coca-Cola India, "Coca-Cola appeals to our optimism, to our belief in goodness and stands for celebrating togetherness. It is about enabling and acting as a catalyst in making connections. Much like the brand – Warli – the traditional art form is also about togetherness and simplicity and symbolizes our connection to our roots. The Coca-Cola Deepawali Campaign ties all this together. It is a tribute to the youth of today. It captures their emotions and their desire to remain close to their roots as they step out in search of new opportunities."

This campaign appeared on television as well as in print media.

Conclusion

Warli painting is a decorative art form created by creative minds of warli painters who are deeply rooted in their culture and tradition. Traditionally they do these paintings on the walls of their houses on particular occasions like weddings and for decorative purposes.

Education is the only key which helps a person to grow in many levels and platforms. Many warli artisans have started completing education in arts and many teams. This helps artisans to develop their creativity and skills and this results in their designs and art form.

Due to globalizations artisans are exploring their art in different media as well as on different canvases. It has become the commercial activity of warli artisans.

Because of growing popularity and demand we need to encourage entrepreneurship and educate them through education so they can explore their art with the same time they can earn more.

Works Cited

""It's the Warlis Who Make These Paintings."" *People's Archive of Rural India*, 5 Mar. 2019, ruralindiaonline.org/en/articles/its-the-warlis-who-make-these-paintings/. Accessed 30 Nov. 2022.

"Largest Warli Composition Ever? – News." *@IISERPune*, 11 June 2014, www.iiserpune.ac.in/news/post/largest-warli-composition-ever/52. Accessed 30 Nov. 2022.

Limited, Alamy. "Warli Art Made in Stainless Steel and Installed at International Airport New Delhi. The Wall Size Is 14 Feet X 28 Feet Stock Photo – Alamy." *Www.alamy.com*, www.alamy.com/stock-photo-warli-art-made-in-stainless-steel-and-installed-at-international-airport-78889980.html. Accessed 30 Nov. 2022.

Longest Warli Painting Marathon by an Individual Artist. www.worldrecordsindia.com/2021/05/06/longest-warli-painting-marathon-by-an-individual-artist/. Accessed 30 Nov. 2022.

Service, Tribune News. "Haryana Diary: Hisar Airport Wall Decorated with "Warli" Painting." *Tribuneindia News Service*, www.tribuneindia.com/news/haryana/haryana-diary-hisar-airport-wall-decorated-with-warli-painting-319937. Accessed 30 Nov. 2022.

Vilhat, Anand. "The History And Origin Of Warli Painting." *Medium*, 12 Feb. 2019, medium.com/@anandvilhat75/the-history-and-origin-of-warli-painting-9f6e9ae182f2.

"Warli Painting – the History of a Tribal Art Form." *ExclusiveLane*, exclusivelane.com/blogs/handmade/warli-painting-the-history-of-a-tribal-art-form.

"Warli Painting – a Timeless Folk Art Form of India." *Caleidoscope | Indian Culture, Heritage*, 17 July 2018, www.caleidoscope.in/art-culture/warli-paintings-a-timeless-folk-art-form-of-india.

"Warli Painting Adorns the Wall of Lodhi Colony; All about the Artists and This Maharashtrian Folk Art." *The Indian Express*, 12 May 2022, indianexpress.com/article/lifestyle/art-and-culture/warli-painting-lodhi-colony-maharashtra-tribal-folk-art-mayur-tushar-vayeda-7912783/. Accessed 30 Nov. 2022.

"Warli Paintings, Different Types & Styles." *MeMeraki.com*, www.memeraki.com/blogs/news/warli-paintings-different-types-styles.

CHAPTER 5

Significance of Ecocritical Elements in Indian Writing in English

Nathiya. M. and Dr. V. Rema

Ecocriticism as a postmodern literary approach posits high stress on eco-consciousness. "Eco-criticism might succulently be defined as study of the relation between literature and environment conducted in a spirit of commitment to environmental praxis (Buell, 1995: 138)". In the modern literary world, eco-criticism plays an essential role in upholding literature and environmental ethics. It also synthesizes human being with physical environment. Garrard (2004) view it as "the relationship between humanity and nature is best described as asymmetrically co-independent" (155). Eco-criticism not only studies nature as depicted in literature but also renders human being to have a broader view of nature.

Theory Ecocriticism, a concept first arose in the late 1970's at the meeting of Western Literature Association (WLA). It began developing in 1990' s which focuses on the relationship human and nature, which tells us man belongs to the earth in much the same way as animals and plants do. The term eco-criticism was first coined by William Rueckert in his critical writing Literature and Ecology: An Experiment in Ecocriticism. Rueckert (1978) defines "eco-criticism as the application of ecology and ecological principles to the scholarly study of literary works" (72).

Introduction

Ecology means the scientific study about the relationship between air, land, water, animal while ecocriticism considers human as a part of environment and studies interconnection between man and nature. The word 'Eco' comes from the Greek word 'Oikos', which etymologically means household or earth and 'critics' means judge. Cheryll Gloytfelty is considered as the pioneer in ecocriticism. In

1990s ecocriticism had become a recognized field of literature. In 1996 it was officially announced by the publication of the seminal work: The Ecocriticism Reader which was edited by Cheryll Gloytfelty. Glotfelty (1996) defined in The Eco-criticism Reader – "Eco-criticism is the study of the relationship between literature and the physical environment" (xviii). Peter Barry (1995) writes,

> "For the eco-critic, nature really exists out there beyond us, not needing to be ironized as a concept by enclosure within inverted commas, but actually present as an entity which affects us, and which can affect, perhaps fatally, if we mistreat it". (Beginning Theory: 114)

Aim of Ecocritical Movement

Ecocriticism is considered as the youngest movement of recent times. Though the term was first coined in 1978 by Rueckert but the root of this movement was in Vedas and Upanishads. Rigveda appeals not to cut trees because they remove pollution. Ayurveda refers man not to disturb the sky and do not pollute the atmosphere. In view of present environmental scenario, the eco-critics want the earth to be kept in good order for mankind. There is no single dominant worldview defending eco-critical practice as it is being defined and redefined everyday by actual practice of thousands of literary scholars round the globe to find out the solution to the contemporary environmental crisis through literary study. So, eco-criticism is a branch of science that creates awareness among readers. In order to meet with the present environmental crisis, the ecocriticism plays an important role in building up the eco-consciousness among the readers.

Ecocriticism in Indian Writing in English

Indian Authors

In Indian writing the writers also showed a great concern towards nature and natural objects. They remained very conscious about nature and depicted nature very well. The authors like Amitav Ghosh, R. K. Narayan, Manohar Malgonkar, Raja Rao, Kamala Markandaya, and Anita Desai have invoked Nature and nature-elements for expressing their thoughts for social environment. R.K Narayan is one of the famous novelists in Indian writing in English, who created imaginative world Malgudi for the creation of his novels and short stories. R. K. Narayan is one of the most outstanding regional novelists highlight the natural village atmosphere in his works. His imaginative world Malgudi became the backdrop for his novels. His novels revolve around the Malgudi and used nature as a sitting for his works. His noted works are Malgudi Days, Man Eater of Malgudi, The English Teacher, and The Guide etc. nature and natural objects became the prime issue in English literature. Authors focused on natural objects in order to save the natural environment. Colonialism also played a key role in the destruction of environment throughout the world. Man changed his attitude towards nature and tries to protect the natural objects. In Indian Writing in English the authors also highlighted the theme of ecocriticism in their works through different ways.

Nectar in the Sieve: Representation the Elements of Rural Life

Kamala Markandaya holds a high place in Indian writing in English. She wrote about the traditionality verses modernity. Her novel *Nectar in a Sieve* depicted the family who are deeply rooted with the rural life. Rukmani's the leading character of the novel is deeply attached with her land along with her husband Nathan. They both are working hard in their field for their survival. There is close association between the Rukmani her land and environment. "While the sun shines on you and the fields are green and beautiful to the eye, and your husband sees beauty in you which no one has seen before, and you have a good store of grain laid away for hard times, a roof over you and a sweet stirring in your body, what more can a woman ask for?" (Nectar in a Sieve 8) Nathan and Rukmani always worked together in the field and Nathan her husband admires her beauty. She was too much linked with the nature. They are poor but they never blame on nature though due to draught they did cultivate their properly. Modernity keeps away man from natural environment and ultimately destroys the natural environment. The tannery symbolizes of modernity. It transforms both, the environment and the economic conditions of the village. It also brings about a drastic change in the relationships between the villagers.

The God of Small Things and Natural Environment

Arundhati Roy is an activist and noted novelist in Indian writing in English won booker for her master piece *The God of Small Things*. As an activist she visited many places where she found some natural destruction by the human beings for their benefit. She exhibited the nature and natural elements in her novel. People exploited the natural objects in the name of modern technology. People who live in villages are more connect with nature but people call them tribal. To protect nature is very important in the contemporary era where technology bow there seed very deeply in order to spoil the natural environments. In her novel *The God of Small Things* she highlighted the issues of nature through the character of Velutha. She gave the description of the river Meenchal in her novel. She has used nature images not only for describing the beauty or glorious atmosphere of the region and landscape but also for exposing the polluted atmosphere of Ayemenem. After twenty-three when Rahel returned to native place Ayemenem, "greeted her with a ghastly skull's smile, with holes where teeth had been and a limp hand raised from a hospital bed" (p. 124).

Though it was June and raining the river was no more than a swollen drain now. A thin ribbon of thick water that tapped wearily at the mud banks on either side, sequined with occasional silver of a dead fish. It was choked with a succulent weed, whose furred brown roots saved like thin tentacles under water. Bronze winged lily–trotters walked across it. Splay-footed cautious (p. 124). The modern technology created population in the area and destroy the natural environment and its greenery. Roy frankly highlighted the dark sides of modernization which creates problem in the lives of local inhabitant. She exhibited the image of Ayemenem with greenery as well as the polluted Ayemenem.

Amitav Ghosh's The Hungry Tide

In the 20th century ecological issues are main issue in Indian writing in English. Authors start thinking more about environment and project the shortcoming in their works. Amitav Ghosh is one of the important figures in Indian writing in English. He achieved great admiration from his readers. His master piece *The Hungry Tide* is considered the first work in Indian English fiction who boldly raised the ecological issues first time in India and tried his best to protect the environment. He depicted the association between the people, the fauna and flora, and the physical environment, and in doing so this work depicted both the calamity and the duplicity that were inherent in the conservation efforts in the Sundarbans. In the novel *The Hungry Tide* the novelist revealed the tension between human beings within the same communities and their ties with natural environment. The chafing between the land and sea in the Sundarbans generate.

The chafing between land and the sea in the Sundarbans generate an unvarying rasping between the plant and animal life. Mans regular infringement of the ecosystems of the Sunderbans only rationalize the chaos and strain between the natural elements. The setting of the novel *The Hungry Tide* is Sunderbans Island in Bay of Bengal, the outlook of this island is not only beautiful but also very fascinating. Disturbances and deportation are the common threat on this place and even the attack by tigers are most common in this place. Tidal floods devastate the steadiness the common the life on the island without any admonition. Amitav Ghosh's *The Hungry Tide* continuously talks about the clash between man and nature in the perspectives of the Sundarbans in India and Bangladesh. Amitav Ghosh always raised his voice against the mistreatment with nature and natural objects. "At no moment can human beings have any doubt of the terrain's hostility to their presence, of its cunning and resourcefulness, of its determination to destroy or expel them. Every year, dozens of people perish in the embrace of that dense foliage, killed by tigers, snakes and crocodiles" (Ghosh 7)

An Ecocritical Perspectives in Ruskin Bond's stories

Not only Arundathi Ray, Amitav Ghosh many have explained the beauty of nature and its downfall widely and explicitly in their writings. In this context, we can reminisce the contribution of Ruskin Bond who is called the Wordsworth of India falls under the category of 'nature writers' or 'environmental writers.' Bond who has Wordsworthian sense of belief in nature has accurately depicted such views in his short stories, "Birds Life in the City", "The Leopard" and "My Father's Tree in Dehra" which are the parts of his collected anthology Delhi Is Not Far: The Best of Ruskin Bond.

Bond who has explored the beauty of nature and the destruction of nature unequivocally in these short stories has an enormous effect on the ecological study. He has good romantic sense for nature which is revealed in his writings cannot be denied. He has vividly depicted the environmental issues through the natural scenic hills of Dehradun and Mussoorie as he has seen and experienced them from very close. In his short story "My Father's Trees in Dehra", Bond has talked about his absorption for a small rocky Island which was fully covered by different beautiful plants situated in the middle of a dry river-bed in Mussoorie. The dry river-bed "...was one of those river-beds, so common in the foot-hills, which [were] completely dry in the summer but flooded during the monsoon rains" (Bond 45). Due to such off-putting seasonal effect, the grass remained short in size and brown in colour, while Sal trees appeared emaciated in shape particularly in summer season. The grass, despite such insalubrious appearance, was being grazed by the skinny cattle at the edge of the jungle.

Ruskin Bond who used to visit the island regularly with his father in his childhood had assisted him with great enthusiasm in his tree-planting like tamarinds, laburnum, and coralsaplings plantations etc. They "spent the day planting them on the island, then ate [their] lunch there, in the shelter of a wild plum" (Bond 44). His main aim behind such activity was to maintain the 'weighing scale' of nature.

After long time when he returned back again to visit the island, he saw the same infavourable seasonal changes which created a kind of qualm in his mind regarding the survival of trees planted by him and his father in his childhood. He asked himself, "Could our trees have survived? Will our island be there, or has some flash-flood during a heavy monsoon washed it away completely?" (Bond 44). In spite of such dry river-bed in summer and excessive flood during monsoon, Bond was very buoyant regarding the growth and survival of the planted plants in the island. As he looked across dry river-course, his eyes are caught by the spectacular red plumes of the coral blossom in the island, where he also noticed a number of parrots which had come to live in them. The beautiful planted trees had multiplied in numbers and grown up beyond their limits over the years. When he was thoroughly looking at the planted trees and its scenery, he observed that different wild plants and grasses have also sprung up under the protection of these planted trees. In this small forgotten corner of the world (island), he observed how his father's dreams were becoming true through the growing of the plants in its full length. Bond who has immense poetic sense imagined that the trees were whispering among themselves and beckoning him near. So, it seemed that the trees knew him. In this way, Bond garishly explores the "...ecological theory, environmentalism, conceptions of nature and their depictions, the human/nature dichotomy and related concerns" (Glotfelty and Fromm xviii) in his short story "My Father's Trees in India".

Conclusion

Thus, it is very necessary to protect the nature and natural objects. The paper mainly talks about men's disparaging activity like incessant deforestation, one of the leading causes of global warming or climate change, is making the earth too hot for all living beings. Besides it, the paper also warns us about its unstoppable future repercussion. If we still destroy the nature and its beauty, we will too be in very danger like the birds and animals. So, we need to go for reforestation in order to mitigate the pollution from air as well as to medicate the poisoning human life. Hence, the government and we as human beings have to take prime initiative in tree plantation program with great enthusiasm if we don't want to live on a treeless moon and polluted environment. Conclusively, we can say that it's not the scientist or conservationist or government who can give the best protection to birds, animals, and trees living around us rather it is 'common man' who can give the best protection to them in the long run.

Works Cited

Barry, Peter. *Beginning Theory: An Introduction to Literary and Cultural Theory.* (3rd Edit.). New Delhi: Viva Books Private limited, 2010.

Kamala Markandaya. *The Nectar in a Sieve.* New Delhi: Penguin Books, 1954.

Roy, Arundhati. *The God of Small Things.* New Delhi: Indian Ink, 1997.

Kaur, Rajender. "Home Is Where the Oracella Are': Toward a New Paradigm of Transcultural Ecocritical Engagement in A mitav Ghosh's The Hungry Tide." *Interdisciplinary Studies in Literature and Environment.* 14.1 (2007): 125-141.

Bond, Ruskin. *Delhi Is Not Far: The Best of Ruskin Bond.* New Delhi: Penguin Books India (P) Ltd, 1994.

.... "My Father's Trees in Dehra". *Delhi Is Not Far: The Best of Ruskin Bond.* New Delhi: Penguin Books India (P) Ltd, 1994.

https://www.researchgate.net/profile/ElectronicJournals/publication/340771877_Ecocritical_Concerns_in_Indian_Writing_in_English.

CHAPTER 6

Travelogues: An Innovative Genre of Literature

Ms. Sarika

Abstract

Travel writing or Travelogue is an old canon of literature, dealing with nature writing, adventure writing, exploration writing, guide books etc. Even the picaresque form of novel had elements of travel writing in it. It's a herculean job as one has to be an effective user of language and at the same time be a keen observer to portray and display analytical data. This paper focuses on the real need, utility, relevance and importance of travel literature in today's rapidly changing tourism sector and globalised society as people try to see a new world through the writing and impression of a writer who serves to be a informer, advisor and guide. The canon of travel writing has acquired the centre of importance now rather than being in the periphery it also focuses on the changing paradigm of travel writing today, well-illustrated by surveys and questionairies.

Keywords: Travelogue, Credible, Authentic, Tourism, Hyberbole, Periphery, Culture, Emigration, Paradigm

Introduction

Travel Writing is a genre of Literature which deals with nature writing, adventure writing, exploration writing, guide books etc. Travelling has always been a basic human urge. Men have travelled with various motives – out of curiosity, adventure, on personal and political errands, on diplomatic missions for pilgrimage and spiritual satisfaction, on voyages, for business and trade and now days as a part of multi-cultural immigration and emigration in bobs. Some travellers with alert and methodological minds recorded their observations and experiences and facts of history, as appeared to them in a Kaleidscopic view of the world, which came to be known as a travel writing. In olden times people were familier with travel books of Chinese pilgrims like Fa Hein and Huen Sang, Marco Polo, Batuta etc. In modern times interesting Travelogues have been written by such literary celebrities such as Aldous Huxley, Graham Greene, V.S Naipaul etc.

The Picaresque form of novel was also a type of travelogue, where the author tried to showcase different places and its culture, through the protogonist's travelling journey and adventure, example the Adventure of Tom in Fielding's "Tom Jones". Last but not the least it's a communicative interaction between a writer and the place and its people.

Travel Literature and its Features

For most of the readers travel book is an escape to an imaginary land which is far from the reality of this mudane world. It is a way to get transported to a forlorn land with all safety in their homes. For the writers themselves, it is often somehow a way of preserving a present for themselves and a past of posterity. In an era of modernisation it helps to preserve the natural landscape of a place and also feels its atmosphere. It is a dimension of the recorded part that does not exists in history books. It also gives an account of the culture, history and geography of a place.

A good travel article's style should first of all be readiable and lively, which should be able to sustain the reader's interest. If possible personal experiences and anecdotes can be included in it, which makes it more authentic and credible. Therefore personal record with universal touch and appeal should be the aim and strategy.

Travel writing involves a multi-dimensional role of being a narrator, observer and reporter. Therefore, a good travel writer must have the following characteristics.

- A good travel writer is the assimilation of a reporter, novelist and also a researcher. A person who lives in the past as well as the present. He/she should have visual imagination and creativity, with a capacity to communicate a picture of a place.
- Have a completely open mind, well informed and free of subjectivity and culture.
- He/she should read about a place, its history, its geography, its politics and culture.
- Writing informative article, involves reading a lot about places and putting the information in a factually correct form and is an informative way. Information on a particular place can be available in pamphlets, brochures, tourism booklets etc.

- Creative Travel Writing is a class by itself, creativity is inborn: it cannot be inculcated but can be just fine tuned.

Travel Writing Should be

Travel writing doesn't need to be a descriptive essay now, but editors and readers expect much more now. The expectation are: –

- Concrete rather than abstract
- Facts rather than description and opinion.
- Knowledgeable explanations of the culture, craft, cuisine, customs etc.
- Combinations of visual truth with a formidable array of useful facts.

Example of Travel Writing

From Literature

"An Area of Darkness" is a book written by V.S. Naipual in 1964. It is a travelogue detailing Naipaul's trip through India in the early sixties. A classic of modern travel writing "An Area of Darkness" is Nobel Laureate V.S Naipual's profound reckoning with his ancestral homeland and an extraordinary perceptive chronicle of his first encounter with India.

"AN AREA OF DARKNESS" is an account of a year that he spent in India. Not just an account, a way sordid account. When he says "An Area of Darkness" he really means it.

Style of Travel Writing

Style is the most important asset of Travel Writing. It should not be a mere description and poetic phrases which would carry away the reader, which would be in vain at the end. A travel writer needs to blend fact and creativity to make a place come alive to the readers. So a writer must be very simple, short and plain English, use appropriate and deemed adjectives and avoid exaggerations and hyperbole as much as possible. One has to be like a reporter with keen and observant eyes along with being an efficient communicator being successful to portray people, places, customs and festivals. A travel writing which is written for a magazine allows a writer greater leeway in terms of style and context.

The main purpose of writing travelogues was to note down proper and accurate information about the places to be visited. In this way, one can pen down historical places, traditions and the political and economic outlook of that specific country.

One should we either pictures or illustrations but never both and it should be relevant and to context more impressive and catching.

Conclusion

With tourism sector spreading its legs in all modes of life, people now travel for short periods, covering long distance and large areas comprehending as much as they can. People try to see a new world through the writing an impressions of a writer who serves to be an informer, advisor and guide. The canon of travel writing has acquired the centre of importance now rather than being in the periphery.

Works Cited

Indira Gandhi National Open University (1988) *SoH-Feature writing* – 2003 reprint Delhi: Prakash Printing Press.

https:// www.travel writing world.com

Rowse, Darren and Garrett, Chris. Pro Blogger.

Zobel, Louise Purwin – *Travel Writer's Handlook.*

Mc.Bride, Kelly and Rosenstiel, Tom. *The New Ethics of Journalism.*

CHAPTER 7

Life Narrative from the Margins of 19th Century Bengal: A Reading of Rassundari Devi's Autobiography *Amar Jiban*

Dr. Saradashree Choudhury

In the nineteenth century Bengali society, the issue of women's education occupied the forefronts of ideological dialogues and debates. On one hand, the nineteenth century is the period of the Renaissance in Bengal which witnessed the interrogation and critiquing of many societal and cultural traditions, conventions, customs and values. As part of reformist issues, there were debates and disputes among the upper caste Bengali men on the evils of such practices as child marriage, sati and the pros and cons of women's education. The upliftment of the status of women was a matter of key concern that occupied the Christian Missionaries in India as well as the Indian reformers of the 19th century. The low status accorded to Indian women became one of the justifications of the British rulers to perpetuate colonial rule in India. The Hindu religious social customs and conventions were seen by the British as dehumanizing and derogatory, so far as the treatment of women was concerned. The sub-human status accorded to women was pointed out as one of the main reasons of degradation of the Indian society. Sir Herbert Hope Risley points out his views with reference to India, "A society which accepts intellectual inanition and moral stagnation as the natural condition of its womankind cannot hope to develop the high qualities of courage, devotion and self-sacrifice which go to the making of nations" (Risley 171). The category of the Bengali '*bhadralok*' which is a product of the western system of education in India, did not, of course, include women.

On the other hand, although prominent reformers like Swami Dayanand Saraswati, Ishwar Chandra Vidyasagar, Raja Ram Mohan Roy Keshab Chandra Sen, among others in Bengal championed the dual cause of women's education and widow remarriage, the society in general was reluctant to let the women read and write. In spite of the support and efforts of the Christian missionaries and the government towards female literacy, the society was disconcerted as a literate woman was seen as a kind of threat to her family. Such notions were generated by the stereotypical cultural values and social codes that accorded impropriety to certain skills, if practiced by a woman. William Adam, in his "Report on the State of Education in Bengal" (1836), wrote: "A superstitious feeling is alleged to exist in the majority of Hindu families, principally cherished by the women and not discouraged by the men, that a girl taught to read and write will soon after marriage become a widow" (Adam qtd. in Nurullah, p. 21). The Bengali woman was completely dependent on her father, husband, and later, sons, for survival. Geraldine Forbes observes:

> If learning to read and write would lead to a husband's death, then pursuing knowledge was tantamount to suicide. This was a sex-segregated world; men and women did different work and occupied separate spaces. Women interacted primarily with women and it was women who enforced the prohibition against female education. Many of the women who learned to read before the 1870s have reported hiding their accomplishments from other women. (Forbes 33)

Geraldine Forbes' observation makes it amply clear that there was lack of solidarity among the women, even if, they belonged to the same household. The elderly women of the house were highly critical of the younger women, especially of the new brides, if they violated any decorum of the patriarchal household. Women, in the nineteenth century India, occupied the margins of the social structure. It was a time when women's education was still considered as a taboo by the society. As a result of the reform initiatives undertaken by the aforementioned people, educational institutions for women were opened, but, in reality, very few girls attended these schools when compared to the mass of deprived women. The status of a woman was limited to her successfully playing of certain obligatory biological roles, that of mothering children, in addition to managing and performing of household tasks. It is therefore a pleasant surprise that the first autobiography in the Bengali language is written by a woman – self taught, in a clandestine manner, within the household and away from the eyes of her family members, so as to avoid customary scorn, loathing and disrespect.

Rassundari Devi, in the 19th century scenario of Bengal, emerges as a voice of transgression, subtle yet powerful. Her voice articulated through her autobiography, *Amar Jiban*, is one of the earliest records of a woman's experience in a conservative Hindu Bengali upper caste family. Rassundari's autobiography was published in 1876, when she was eighty-eight years of age as she narrates her life in an honest and frank tone. The confessional mode in which she narrates, informs the readers of her day to day life within the household – which is the only terrain where women operated in her times. It contains very less of the social issues as the world outside is not readily or immediately accessible to her. It was not until two decades later that the second autobiography in Bengali was penned by the eminent writer Debendranath Tagore. *Amar Jiban* consists of two parts. The first part comprises of sixteen compositions and chronicles the life of Rassundari; while, the second part, comprising of fifteen compositions is dedicated to Lord Krishna and Chaitanya Mahaprabhu – the savior of Humankind. Thus, Rassundari's act of writing, though a transgressive deed, is imbued with a religious fervor. This kind of structuring of her autobiography could also be seen as means of keeping God as a witness to her achievements.

Virginia Woolf in her ground breaking feminist treatise, *A Room of One's Own* drives home the necessity for women of having a separate space and arrangements for herself if she were to practice her vocation as a writer. In case of the Bengali woman, the room of one's own for practicing writing could not even be dreamt of. Within the household, in the days of Rassundari, it would be impossible for the Bengali Hindu woman to think of having such a space exclusively to herself:

> One needs a lot of things if one is to write: paper, pen, ink, ink pot, and so on. You have to set everything before you. And I was a woman, the daughter-in-law of the family. I was not supposed to read or write. It was generally considered as a grave offense. And if they saw me with all the writing paraphernalia, what would they say? I was always afraid of criticism. So I gave up the idea of writing and concentrated on reading (*Amar Jiban* in Tharu, p. 202).

Rassundari turns her primary area of operation, that is, the kitchen (and the only space she was allowed to have on her own), into a secret classroom where she is the teacher as well as the taught. Thus she turns the virtual prison into a liberating space of discovering her selfhood. Throughout the autobiography, there runs a reiteration of her faith and devotion to God which her mother had nurtured in her as a child. It is her staunch belief in the benevolence of God which makes it possible for her to read and later, write, "I never thought I would be able to read. It seemed an impossible task in my situation. The little that I have learned was possible because God guided me" (*Amar Jiban* in Tharu, p. 202). In fact, it was her desire to know God first hand that instilled in her the urge to read. She struggled to read not because she wanted to be recognized for her pioneering efforts, but, because she wanted to read a Holy Scripture – the *Chaitanya Bhagavata* and enhance her knowledge of God. Therefore, Rassundari believes that there is a divine intervention and design behind her success in learning how to read.

Quite contrary to the expectations of her times, Rassundari narrates her bodily experiences related to childbirth, the rigours of dressing, and the unending drudgery of the household. A woman skilled in managing the household is idealized and romanticized as a paragon of love and sacrifice. Rassundari was in charge of managing the household at the age of fourteen, on account of the ailing health of her mother-in-law. She writes, "People used to insist that women were meant for domestic chores. Newly-wedded girls had to be especially hard working and quiet. They had to work behind a long veil and then they would get to be known as good wives" (*Amar Jiban* in Tharu, p.199). The urgency and priority of replicating the conventional roles within the family was so strong that it makes Rassundari conscious and sensitive to her identity as a woman and daughter-in-law:

> My only effort was to please people through the work I did in the house. My only regret was that I was not able to read and write because I was a girl. Women of today are so lucky. Many parents educate their daughters. I think this is a good practice (*Amar Jiban* in Tharu, p. 196).

Amar Jiban also raises serious concern over a woman's health and nutrition and makes an unabashed statement about the health hazards and neglect faced by the womenfolk in a conservative family. As for Rassundari herself, she mothers her first child at the age of eighteen and the process of birth-giving and bearing children continues till the age of forty-one. Rassundari conceives twelve times and gives birth to eleven children. In a crisp understated manner, she contains the pangs of childbirth, "God only knows what I had to go through during those twenty three years. Nobody else had any idea either"

(*Amar Jiban* in Tharu, p. 196). There was no provision of post natal care during those days and she gave birth at an average interval of two years. Through her experiences, Rassundari also points out that the random eating habits, worsened by the meager intake of food, affected the health of women. Married women were encouraged to eat the leftovers from their husband's platter and ritualistic fasting was considered a virtue. Sutanuka Ghosh Roy observes that, "It was the women who produced food but it was carefully confiscated from them by intricately designed politics. Women were trained and tamed into patriarchal ideology" (Ghosh Roy 66). Moreover, the discomforts caused by dressing up in coarse clothes also lay bare the discomfitures of women who are irretrievably circumscribed within the rigorous hold of rituals and customs. Rassundari narrates how the long veil over her face prevented her from seeing anyone else. She was thus shut away from looking and speaking to other people. At a time when obeisance and unquestioning surrender to patriarchal customs were the only responses women were conditioned to, Rassundari Devi chooses to narrate the harsh realities of unending domestic labour in a very candid manner in her autobiography.

Early in the narrative, Rassundari, a child bride of twelve years of age, describes her condition of a wedded girl as 'the sacrificial goat being dragged to the altar', 'the caged bird'and 'the fish caught in the net'. These metaphors of the 'net', the 'cage' and the 'sacrificial altar', portray the societal structures of the 19th century Bengal as a trap for women that are regressive and reduce them to mere nothing. They are forced into unquestioning surrender to the patriarchal norms that demand complete submission and internalisation of the system. The institution of marriage in the orthodox Hindu society was such that the woman could not exist outside it. The woman is compulsorily made to participate in it, which would later determine her fate either a widow and thus subject to general loathing or as a wife and human machine running the endless tasks of the house.

Rassundari's journey from her ancestral home in Potajia to her in-law's home in Ramdia, at one level, captures the essence of her transformation from innocence to experience. Her sense of selfhood is grounded in her idea of being her mother's daughter. Therefore, at this stage, very naturally, she sees the in-law's family as the 'Other' – a group of people who cannot be identified with:

> Strange are the ways of God! Your laws are so wonderful! You have taken me from my dear mother and from others I love so much and have

> brought me to this distant place. That night we landed. We arrived at their house and saw different people taking part in all sorts of merry making (*Amar Jiban* in Tharu, p. 194; emphasis mine).

Rassundari also gives a physical description of her husband, whom she calls the *Karta* – the Master of the house. Customary propriety refrained a woman of her times from speaking to her husband during the day. Therefore, Rassundari's attempt to give her readers a brief description of her *Karta* in *Amar Jiban* could be seen as a daring act of transgression. Her voice of protest, when denied permission to visit her dying mother, though not overtly extreme, is unmistakably evocative of searing pain and agony:

> They never sent me to her because the household work here would suffer....When my mother lay on her deathbed, she wanted very badly to see me. I have caused her sorrow, hateful sinner that I am. I tried my utmost, but could not go....Why was I ever born a woman? Shame on my Life!...if I were a son in would have flown directly to my mother's bedside. But I am helpless. I am a caged bird (*Amar Jiban* in Tharu, p. 199).

Tanika Sarkar in *Hindu Wife, Hindu Nation: Community, Religion and Cultural Nationalism* writes of the scornful attitude of Indian patriarchy towards a bride visiting her parental home for long periods. Sarkar critiques such attitudes and laments the condition of married women whose happiness is dependent upon the whims of her new authorities. Sarkar says, "The wife who spends a large slice of her time with her own parents, is a woman who deprives her new masters of valuable labour time" (Sarkar 86). Seen in retrospect, Rassundari might appear to some readers of the twenty-first century as the epitome of the safe-effacing wife and daughter-in-law who held her family obligations above anything else. Yet, she is the one who made a much louder attempt than the other women of her times could dare to think of, in depicting her situation. Moreover, one must make allowances for the conditions in which she learnt the medium of protest, that is, writing.

Although she started out with the aim of reading the *Chaitanya Bhagavata*, Rassundari ended up writing her life narrative which is a treatise on the quality and kind of life women in nineteenth century Bengal were subjected to. Her particular account is a representation of the general condition of women who were denied a voice by the prevailing strictures of decorum and propriety imposed upon them. Rassundari makes no attempt at hiding the grueling experiences of domestic labour. The issues that she touches upon in *Amar Jiban*, such as, identity crisis as a child bride, experiences acquired through the body, humiliating treatment of women and widows, denial of space and agency – all form the crux of later Indian feminist discourse. Although Rassundari was no inaugurator of any women's movement, her efforts at reading and writing on her own, is in itself, a strong gesture of resistance against the dehumanizing myths of a patriarchal society that fails to fulfil the dreams of its women. Had Rassundari not tried to move beyond her allotted space, an entire section of the nineteenth century Bengali Hindu society would have remained unrepresented.

Works Cited

Devi, Rassundari. *Amar Jiban (My Life)*. Trans. Enakshi Chatterjee. Calcutta: Writers Workshop, 1999. Print.

Forbes, Geraldine. *Women in Modern India.* Cambridge: Cambridge University Press, 1996. Print.

Ghosh Roy, Sutanuka. *Amar Jiban (My Life): A Comprehensive Study.* Kolkata: Books Way, 2021. Print.

Nurullah, Syed, and J.P. Naik. *History of Education in India: During the British Period.* Bombay: Macmillan, 1943. Print.

Risley, Sir Herbert Hope. *The People of India*, 2nd edn. Ed. W. Crooke. Delhi: Oriental Books, 1969. Print.

Sarkar, Tanika. *Wife, Hindu Nation: Community, Religion and Cultural Nationalism.* Indiana: Indiana University Press, 2001. Print.

Tharu, Susie, and K. Lalita, eds. *Women Writing in India.* Vol.1. New Delhi: Oxford University Press, 1991. Print.

Woolf, Virginia. *A Room of One's Own.* London: Hogarth's Press, 1929. Print.

CHAPTER 8

Nonfiction Writing and Innovation in Hindi Literature

Dr. Vedprakash Borkar

Introduction

Generally, literature is understood to mean story, novel, poem or drama writing etc. But at present, various forms of literature are coming to the readers. As fast as the time is changing today, with the same speed changes are taking place in each field and this is the reason why the literature also looks different. However, non-fiction is not like literature or more literature today. Along with giving a new app to the literary writing going on in the traditional way, it also gave a big sky. The author's character thrived in the form of new genres, which we know as innovations. Through these new modes the reader gets acquainted with the life experiences of the author, his knowledge and different perceptions. In this research, new genres will be introduced keeping non-fiction writing and innovation in the core.

Nonfiction Writing and Innovation: An Overview

India corrected the slavery of English for a long time. Most of the feudatories and the Nawabs had made a treaty with the British and the British gradually established their suzerainty over India with their trade and military power. Despite all this, the people fought against the British rule. He did the work of public awareness through many mediums and made him aware by showing the face of exploitative power to the Indian society. This awareness is called the renaissance of Dr. Ramvilas Sharma in Hindi.

To create awareness in the society, there is a need of education. Literary writing is the medium which inculcates the power of thinking and reasoning in the people. Great literature has been produced in India since ancient times. In ancient times, many epics,

Vedas, Puranas etc. were composed and society got benefited from it. In the modern era, stories, novels, poems etc. were written for a long time, but other than these genres, new genres also took birth and made their own place in literature.

The literature also prospered by coming in contact with the western country and new themes emerged. Today we are into the technology world and can't ignore the internet connection with the literary world. In this unit, the topics of non-fiction writing and innovation will be discussed. The description of various non-narrative genres in this context is as follows –

Essay

The word Nibandh means 'to bind'. Essay is a modern way of writing, which is called Essay in English. Acharya Hemchandra Suman writes in his book 'Sahitya Vivechan' that 'Essay is the mode of work in which the author reveals, in a limited size, his emotional and thought reactions to this diverse world.' Whereas the great English author Lord Bacon calls it 'scattered picture'. Be that as it may, the essay mode has an important place in literature and is a popular genre.

Bharatendu Era

The beginning of the Hindi essay is from the Bharatendu era. This was the time when the voices of four more social and cultural reforms were being heard. Social, economic and political movements dominated. They were raising their voice for their identity, culture and language. This was called 'renaissance'. At the same time, the author expressed his thoughts in a very powerful, fearless and methodical manner. In this period, the consciousness towards social evils, the opposition to the British rule and the development of language and culture.

There was a worry for him. Essays related to this subject started being written in newspapers and they were widely popular. Writings like Bharatendu Harishchandra, Pratapnarayan Mishra, Badrinarayan Choudhary Upadhyaya 'Premghan', Ambikadatta Vyas and Balkrishan Bhatt in developing the literature of the then era. Contribution is being made. In the Renaissance period of Hindi, the important emerged and replaced as a literary genre.

The 'Essay' mode became the most suitable mode for writings on the subject of history, culture, knowledge, social concerns etc. with language. Bharatendu Harishchandra made the problems of the times as the subject of his essay. He himself was known as a social worker. His thoughts are reflected in his essay. In addition to social discrepancies, history, religion, language and literature were also subjects of his writing.

Women's consciousness is mainly visible in these essays. Women's service method, feticide, the convention of the assembly in heaven, why Indians do not get the life of Indians from the British, etc. are the famous essays of Bharatendu. Bhartendu's essays satire along with subtle observation. He was adept at saying great things in an interesting way. Bhartendu mainly adopted emotional and reflective style in writing.

Balakrishna Bhatt has been the most effective essayist of Bharatendu period, Dr. Laxmisagar accepts Pandit Balkrishna Bhatt as the first essay writer of Hindi. Bhatt composed serious essays on political, literary, social and psychological subjects. He has also looked at social problems. Through essays written on serious topics like women and their education, women wisdom, child marriage, English education, the reader gets acquainted with their sentiments and language arts consciousness. Along with writing reflective essays, Balkrishna Bhatt also wrote essays like hope, self-pride, faith indicating emotional, descriptive and mental disorders.

Badrinarayan Choudhary Upadhyay Premghan was an essayist on social concerns. Essays like National Congress ki Daurdasha', 'Bhartiya Praja ke dukh ki duhae' and 'Thithae par government ki kadae' are the result of the pen run on political movements. He also composed essays in poetic style. Apart from this, Pratap Narayan Mishra who is considered to be the essayist of the soul expression. He was one of the leading essayists of this era, both flirtatious and serious in his essays. 'Khushamad', 'Tath', 'Dhoka', 'Balak' are his flirtatious essays, then 'Aap', 'Bat', 'Nari' come in second grade essays.

In this way most of the essays were composed in the Bharatendu era and this genre got new heights. This essay, written about different subject matter, is embellished with many styles. The specialty of these essays was that they were easily associated with the public.

Dwivedi Era

In the Dwivedi Yuga, this mode progressed as a mature mode. Even in this era, almost the same styles of essays were developed, whose seed had been planted in Bharathedu Yuga. Essay writing on language and grammar is more in the Dwivedi era. The essay writing tradition which Mahavirprasad Dwivedi himself nurtures through Saraswati, differentiates it from Bharatendu Yuga.

The main essayist of Dwivedi era is – Mahavirsad Trivedi, Balmukund Gupt, Govindnarayan Mishra, Sardar Purnasingh, Chandradhar Sharma Guleri, Babu shyamsundar Das, Babu Gulabrai etc. In this era, mainly literature and language, scientific invention, archeology and history, life cycle, spirituality, geography and other useful social subjects. An essay was written on you.

The essay writers of the era expanded the mentality of the public, due to which the social concerns of the Bhartendu period developed a new knowledge, scientific approach, a vision towards new inventions.

Shukla Era

The third phase of Hindi writing after the Dwivedi Yuga is called 'Shukla Yuga'. This was the time when the First world-war had ended and its results were being seen on a global scale. In India too, independence was in turmoil. Foreign influence was making way for new genres in literature. The essay was covering a new topic with its ability. At such times Shuklaji was associated with this tradition but he was different from other restrictions. His essay had its own characteristics. The essays of Acharya Ramchandra Shukla gave new dimensions to this method. While their essays are linked with traditions, they also establish new thoughts and feelings. 'Chintamani' is a collection of Shuklaji's essays, in which the essence of the essay is the highest. Greed, greed, enthusiasm, anger etc. are the essence of their mental disorders.

In this era, with the help of development, in which new appearances of practical character, language-style, theme and craft etc. appear. Emotional, narrative, critical, thought. Fine essays were composed with impunity, with verbal, incidental, descriptive, etc. essays. Acharya Nandadulare Vajpayee, Ramdhari Singh Dinkar, Jaishankar Prasad, Elachandra Joshi, Jainendra, Prabhakar Marchve, Dr. Bhagirath Mishra, Dr. Ramvilas Sharma, Dr. Vidyaniwas Mishra, Kubernath Rai, Dr.Sampurnanand, Paldey B. Sharma, Vishnu Prabhakar, Ramruksh Benipuri, Yashpal etc. are a list of the rights of the modern times, In whose essay the qualities of deep thinking, whole thinking, life activity as well as imagination, sweeping consciousness, culture, vision and quality are visible.

Criticism

Due to which the writing of essay-writing in almost the same circumstances, this method also emerged. As a result of the lack of literature on Hindi literature during the Bhartendu era, Hindi literary writing got acquainted with new concepts and on Changes started taking place in the 'traditional literary culture'. Many genres of literature flourished. They started appearing in more sophisticated forms. Criticism writing is also one of them. Criticism writing is a source of intellectualism as well as a scientific point of view. In the Bhartendu era, Hindi criticisms were published in magazines. In these periodicals, literary critics used to write reviews of the book, in which he published the introduction of the book as well as its various aspects. Used to put In fact, the literature of this era had its beginning with intellectual conflict, new consciousness, and debates. Seriousness started coming in this mode.

In his book 'Hindi ka Gadya Sahitya', Dr. Ramchandra Tiwari specifies the major trends of the Hindi review field as follows:

1. Classical Criticism
   i. Poetic discussion in the tradition of ritualistic character texts.
   ii. Establishing principles from a new perspective
2. Comparative Evaluation and Judgment.
3. Development of a new practical method of review, explanatory criticism
4. Innovation, Research and Review.
5. Ancient or Practical Criticism Innovative or Commentary.
6. Reading and research.

Among the critics of the tradition of ritualistic character texts, Lala Bhagwandin's 'Alankar Manjusha', 'Kalash' by Ayodhya Singh Upadhyay 'Hariaundh', Sitaram Shastri's literary theory is prominent. Acharya Ramchandra Shukla was also a supporter of new review theory. Seeing it in its original form, created a sympathetic critic.

At present, the app of the society that we see in front of us today has been created after so many acclaims and sacrifices. His cultural attitude was lacking in the criticism of Dwivediji. He used to consider the collective welfare of man as the goal of creation, then at the same time modern science is also seen in his criticism. The Dwivedi era was the time when the reader was getting introduced to many Indian and foreign languages and was also developing comparative evaluation and judgment. At the same time, there has been a trend of comparative criticism in the creators.

In this region the names of Padmasingh Sharma, Mishrabandhu, Lalla Bhagwandin etc. are specially mentioned. After the establishment of the Pragativadi lekhak Sangh in the year 1936, the dynamic criticism which was influenced by the Karl Marx thought began. In the year 1935, the writings of Shivdan Singh Chauhan started a dynamic criticism of the need for progressive literature in India.

In 1940, Elachand Joshi started the method of psychological criticism by writing literary works. Critics like Dr. Nagendra, Elachand Joshi analyzed the compositions in a psychological way in their critical works. After this it was enriched by Ramvilas Sharma, Muktibhodh, Namvar Singh, Shivkumar Mishra etc.

The main works of this time are 'Nirala Ki Sahitya Sadhna' by Dr. Ramvilas Sharma, 'Ek Sahittik ki Dairy' by Muktibodh, 'History and Criticism' by Ramvir Singh, 'New Paradigms of Poetry', 'Kahani Nai Kahani' etc.

After the series of literary theories and discussions started in the magazines. Issues of women and Dalits were raised in a magazine like 'Hans'. Problems like postmodernism, post colonialism, fragmentationism, structuralism, existential crisis, self-exile, new symbolism etc. were discussed.

Satire

Satire is a mode in which the satirist, with his sharp writing, attacks the discrepancy, which is totally unfair to the society. Often he is the one who cleans the mess of the society. His job is to clean the mess of social distortions. Kabir did the same thing through his work.

Acharya Hazariprasad Dwivedi says that Satire is the one where the speaker is laughing in the loop and the hearer trembles. Yet answering the one who says it is to make oneself more ridicule. The satirist Harshankar Parsai says that "self-realization of life, criticizes life, exposes discrepancies, adultery and hypocrisy does." In fact, self-consciousness is such a method that is an infallible means of fulfilling a social cause.

As an independent genre, the tradition of writing satire was recognized only in the modern era. Ridiculed all the evils which were weakening the society. In this context, it would be expedient to remember a "Ek Adbhut Apurva Swapna" written by Bharatendu Harishchandra. This is an important satire of that era. Similarly, Radhacharan Goswami's 'Budhe muh muhase' is also a famous satire.

In the Dwivedi era, little work was done on this genre, yet GP Srivastava, Bechan Sharma Ugra and Badrinath Bhatt, etc., wrote satire in the novels of Premchand, the primacy of satire is visible. When he talks about social concerns, it is a genre that came with its entirety in other genres of literature, such as satire story, satirical poetry, satirical drama etc.

In the shadowy period, Nirala composed a satirical poem like a 'Kukurmuktta'. He also wrote novels like "Kulli Bhaat" and "Billesur Bakriha" laden with social anomalies. In 'Kukurmuktta' he explicitly and explicitly attacks capitalism by saying –

Khun chusa khad ka tune ashishta
Dal par etra rha hai capitalist!

In modern times, satire got acceptance and prestige too. Harishankar Parsai's 'Jiva of Bholaram', 'Vaishnav's Slippery', 'Jwala aur Jal" (novel), "Raag Darbari" (novel) by Shrilal Shukla, 'Jeep par sawar elliya' by Sharad Joshi, etc. Gave new dimensions to it and made its special place among the readers.

Sharad Joshi and Harishankar Parsai also gave height to this genre through literary forums, poet meetings etc. The satirical works of Shrilal Shukla are also very interesting, his novel 'Raag Darbari' is a very important satirical work. The names of Narendra Kohli, Prem Janmejay, Gyan Chaturvedi, Gopal Chaturvedi, Harish Naval, Shankar and Suryabala are notable in the writing of satire.

Surybalaji's collections "Dhritarashtra Times", 'Desh Seva Ke Akhara', 'God had said' etc are prominent. When the number of satire writers is small, she says – Women are forbidden to speak, otherwise the taunts of women are skillful. Along with them, politics, literary devaluation, middle-class mentality and the contradictions of the media do not leave anyone, Similarly, the names of Sushil Siddharth, Alok, Girish Pankaj etc. are also important among the new satirical writers.

Today satire has become an important literary genre. It is flourishing as an interesting and effective mode which has the ability to speak deeply in a great manner. The satirical genre is an important achievement of literature. Many magazines like 'Vyang Yatra' are doing the work of making satirical writing flourish.

Sketch

Sketch means drawing through lines. It is also called word picture or 'sketch' but a natural question is what can be the use of sketch in literature. In fact, if the creator gives shape to the expressions of the works related to literary genres in the form of words, then the reader receives it in exactly the same way as the picture of a painter.

Basically sketch is a picture which the writer gives shape not through lines but through words. The sharpness of the drawing makes it unique. Professor Ramchandra Tiwari writes that even in the drawing, any person, object or reference is marked. This painting is done completely without being neutral. The lines in the sketch speak.

When the painter is giving a description of an object, person or place, then he definitely has an emotional attachment to it, but does not keep that feeling in the center, but by keeping that character in the center, moves forward his creation with a neutral sense and it. It is portrayed as it is and presents it to the reader in such a way that the characters, events and context add a deep introduction to the reader. This is clearly visible in the drawings of Mahadevi Varma.

All the characters of 'Atit Ke Chalchitra', whether it is 'Rama' or 'Binda', 'Sabiya' or 'Bitto' or 'Lachma', forced to live a cursed life in a remote mountainous and lacking area, come alive and ask the reader Somewhere deep down.

Look at an example: 'A face scorched by the sun looks as if someone has cooked a raw apple over a fire. Dry eyelids have liquid eyes as if floating in the bottomless waters of tears.' And the laughter above has dried up from the sun. The blueness that spreads on the lips with the cold, becomes even more evident from the whiteness of the teeth." The sketches of Mahadevi are so powerful that 'Lachma' stands in front of us exactly as she is.

Memory is the base material of the sketching, the detail of these memories, the subtle marking and the vivid description is the sketch. Mahadevi Verma's statement about the sketch was given by Prof. Chauthiram Yadav quotes in 'Hindi ke shreshtha Rakhachitra'. He says that "When the painter puts in front of him an object, person, or colorless picture in some lines in such a way that his particular posture can be recognized, then we call it a sketch. Even in literature, the writer puts such a picture in some words, which can introduce that object or person, but there is a difference in both.

The main features of the sketches are as follows –

i. It is mostly person-oriented and to reveal that central character. The focus is on the subtlest points.

ii. There is a lot of sense of sensibility in the sketches because the writer is directly emotionally attached to those characters. Apart from Mahadevi Varma, Ramvriksha Benipuri, Prakashchandra Gupta, Vishnu Prabhakar and Harishankar Parsai etc. also present them in their sketches by connecting with ordinary characters on the level of sensation.

   Another feature of this mode is memory originality. By recalling a familiar character, place or object, it can be seen the most in the writings of Mahadevi. They present such a picture of memories of animals and birds that they become immortal.

iii. Authentic experience, neutrality, close supervision and clear objectives are its other characteristics.

Dr. Bhagirath Mishra writes that "The main purpose of the vignette is to make the character vividly clear, to awaken the spirit of sophistication, change of perception, development of generosity, creation of public heart, awareness of justice, consciousness, compassion towards the afflicted etc. Thus to establish the ideal of a loving and sympathetic life and to delve into the real forms and experiences of life is the main aim of the vignette.

Memoir

Remembrance means to remember. In fact a person does not forget his past. These memories are the link of his present. He shares those memories with others which is a kind of 'Mansik Virechan'. What the writer himself sees, what he himself experiences, he describes in his memoirs. His feelings and sensations remain in his description. Memory is a form of remembrance. According to the Hindi Sahitya Kosha, the memoirs are always factual.

It does not contain exaggerated facts because it is an account of its own memories. At the same time, the events are the same characters which the author has cherished from the past.

Banarsidas Chaturvedi says, "Memoirs, sketches and autobiographies are so closely related to each other that it is difficult to decide where the boundary of one meets the other and where it separates." (Memoirs, page 4)

Memoir writing in Hindi started in the twentieth century. Mahavirprasad Dwivedi wrote memoirs like 'Anumodan ka Ant' and Sabha ki Sabhyata', while Balmukund Gupta wrote famous memoirs related to Pratapnarayan Mishra. In this era, many memoirs were printed in 'Saraswati' magazine, in which there were memoirs of many important writers. This in itself was a great achievement. Apart from 'Saraswati', 'Vishal Bharat', 'Sudha' and 'Madhuri'. Memoirs were published prominently in magazines. Premchand Smriti issue of 'Hans' magazine is also a heritage of memoir literature. Banarsidas Chaturvedi, Kamtaprasad Guru, Vrindavan Lal Verma etc. were prominent memoir writers who have written memoirs related to other writers.

Mahadevi Verma also played an important role in writing memoirs. He has written memoirs on Rabindranath Thakur, Maithilisharan Gupta, Subhadra Kumari Chauhan, Prasad, Pant and Nirala in the composition 'Path Ke Saathi'. Rahul Sankrityayan – Memoirs of 'Bachpan ki Srumtiaya', 'Jinka mei krutadya hu' and 'Mere Asahyog ke sathi' are prominent.

In fact, memoir is a relatively new and popular genre, which not only sheds light on the personality of the writers and top personalities, but also brings the reader to the places and events where the writer reaches through his memories and brings it down from his pen.

Biography

Biography has an important place in the non-fiction writing tradition. In biographical writing, a particular person is depicted, who with all his shortcomings and qualities emerges in front of the reader in a complete way. The entire account of life is biography. In this mode, both the internal and external aspects of one's personality are discussed.

Biography is a new genre in Hindi literature. Although this tradition has been in Sanskrit literature for a long time. Harshacharita, Buddhacharita, Dashcharita etc. are life stories. In these charitable writings, along with the kings and emperors, the lives of great men were in the center.

Any person can write biography, even if he is an ordinary person, but writing a biography must have a purpose. By reading the biography, we get acquainted with the personality and creativity of the person as well as his surroundings and society and the inspirational-episodes related to his life and his lifestyle etc.

Biography is also significant because it is not fiction but reality. It is a document related to the life of a real person, so the information based on it itself is considered reliable and authentic. The biographer portrays all the aspects of whose biography he is writing together, so it includes both merits and demerits. While writing the biography of Dr. Ramvilas Sharma 'Nirala', along with his goodness, his awkward behavior was skillfully engraved.

The Hindi biographical writing tradition is also believed to be from the Bharatendu era. This was the time when all the new disciplines took birth. Bhartendu also wrote biographies like 'Charitavali', 'Bundi ka Rajvansh', 'Udaipurodaya' etc. Although the Bharatendu era was the infancy of biographical writing, yet a considerable amount of biographies were written during this time. It flourished in the Dwivedi era and biographies of Dayanand Saraswati, Gandhiji, Madanmohan Malviya, Dadabhai Naoroji, Ahalyabai etc. were written which became very popular. But the biographies written on Gandhiji, especially written by 'Roma Rolla and translated into Hindi 'Mahatma Gandhi: Vishva ke adwitiya purush' are very popular.

Rahul Sankrityayan has an important contribution to biographical literature. He was proficient in many languages. His field of experience was very wide. He had traveled to many countries and met many people. He introduced them to Indian society by writing biographies of 'Karl Marx', 'Lenin', 'Stalin' etc. Written on Sharchandra Chattopadhyay 'Awara Messiah' (Vishnu Prabhakar), 'Kalam ke Sipahi' (Amrit Rai), 'Premchand ghar mei' (Shivrani Devi), the first indentured (Giriraj Kishore), Nirala's literary practice (Ramvilas Sharma) etc. there are famous biographies.

Biography writing has developed into a rich genre. Biographies of people related to social, political, religious, literary, scientific, sports and film life are being written continuously. Through these biographies, we get to know the untapped aspects of their lives with people from different fields. These historical documents are not only made, but we are also given some lessons. While reading the biography, the reader unintentionally enters the area with which he does not have a distant relation. In fact, biography is the best way to understand the individual, society, environment and the time.

Autobiography

Autobiography means a statement about yourself or your story. Autobiography, biography and memoir are almost similar genres, but they are different genres with subtle differences. When a person tells his story it is called an autobiography but when another person writes about someone else it is a biography.

Since someone else authors the biography, it may not be as authentic as the autobiography. In autobiography, the author writes about himself, so whatever he says about himself will be true, it can be assumed that. Autobiography is never complete because the autobiographer cannot present the details of his last day in it whereas biography is the details from birth to death.

Writing an autobiography is a difficult task, it requires courage and integrity. When the autobiography writer sees himself from a critical point of view, only then will he be able to give a true description. The author has to be neutral in this. It is not an easy task to present your success-failure, merit-defect, weakness and strong side to the readers.

Babu Rajendra Prasad writes his autobiography in a hierarchical manner in which he tells about the events of that time and his participation in the movements etc. Acharya Mahavirprasad Dwivedi has written the personal things of his life very clearly in his life story. The condition of writing an autobiography is that the writer should record the events with great neutrality and honesty while remembering the memories of the past, only then it will be authentic. Autobiography is a literary genre in which the reader continues to learn. Therefore it is also necessary to have values in it.

Autobiographies have the voice of an era and their reading touches us. Autobiography is a cultural history through which the reader is able to understand that period. The autobiographer may be speaking about himself, but history, experiences, entertainment, information and feelings are also embedded in him. With which the reader automatically establishes an identity.

Innovation in Hindi Literature

Innovation means 'new experiment'. From time to time new experiments are being done in the literature. Bharatendukal can be called the era of innovations. New genres were born in that literature. Some old genres entered literature with new colors and flourished. Since then it has been used continuously in literature. The era of a new story, a new poem, etc. has begun. Innovative crafts and themes, even the language of writing also changed. There was an atmosphere of controversies and arguments, but together they enriched the literature.

At the same time new non-fiction genres were born in literature. In the modern age of the Internet, literature is easily accessible to everyone. Along with prose-song, short story, new story, other genres come in which diary, travelogue, reportage, letter, interview etc. are prominent. Monologue writing would also be called innovation. Although these were not written extensively, but still this use has been done in the literature.

Writers resorted to such methods or invented these modes to shape their expression. He went on getting acceptance in the literary world. It also happens that sometimes the writer goes on writing in which he covers many subjects like his experience, pain, social pain, discrepancies, morality, values etc. but he is not able to keep his writing under any genre. In fact, there is a fine line between almost all the genres of literature, which separates these genres, but their movement in each other remains constant. The author does not write in any one genre, rather he gives form to his expression. It is the author who chains the genres.

Reportage

This word reportage, which came from French, can be seen as an innovation in Hindi literature. In modern Hindi literature, 'reportage' has been accepted as an independent genre. 'Reportage' is the broad form of 'report'. In 'report' the matter or event is kept as it is, whereas in reportage, detail is given with some interesting analysis. Due to the interestingness generated in it, it becomes readable. No report can be written without being present at the scene of the incident because there will be neither credibility in the details written on hearing from somewhere nor the joy of direct vision. Reportage is effective only when the creator is an eyewitness to the incident and is able to relate his feelings to it. Creators like Dharamveer Bharti, Phanishwarnath Renu etc. visited the site of the incident and associated themselves with those facts, incidents and created special works.

Important events like famine, natural calamities, revolution, movement and war etc. have been written in 'Reportage'. Dharamveer Bharati's Reportage 'Yudh Yatra' contains reports related to the Bangladesh war, which he himself wrote during the war in Bangladesh. Phanishwarnath Renu's 'Rrunjal Dhanjal' was also written in a similar way in which he has given a live depiction of the Bihar drought of 1966 and the devastating floods of 1967.

In fact, reportage is a discipline related to journalism, but it is not a short-lived genre because in it the reporter becomes the creator and by creating elegance with the information in it, makes it a genre of literature. The reportage is a reality seen and experienced in which the sentiments of the author are also included. Continuous writing work is being done in the reportage mode in Hindi literature.

Diary

Diary is a new genre of modern Hindi literature. Diary writing was prevalent in Europe for a long time. In fact, the diary is very personal in which the writer mentions his everyday happiness, sorrows, life experiences and incidents etc., which he does not want to make public. It is possible that in the diary, the author has written many unpleasant or even sad incidents in the heart of others.

Most of the places and days are also mentioned in the diary along with the accounts given by the author, which makes it believable. Although there is self-writing in the diary, but still the information about the circumstances, interests, lifestyle etc. of that period is contained in it like Mohan Rakesh's diary contains his conflicts, but the glimpse of the literary conditions of the time is also embedded in it.

Dhirendra Verma's 'Meri College Diary' is divided into four volumes, in which apart from the personal life experiences of the author, the sound of the movements for freedom at that time is also heard. Both literary and social references are found in Dinkar's 'Diary'. Along with literature, Dinkar had a considerable infiltration into the political environment as well. He was associated with both politicians and litterateurs, so it is natural for him to have both backgrounds in his diary.

Harivanshrai Bachchan wrote a diary during his stay in Ireland, in which he described his life there, England. The activities of the university, English literature and literary activities there have been described.

Diary writing is an important genre of literature, which contains authentic information along with truth. In the beginning of his diary, Harivanshrai Bachchan writes that diaries are often not written for the purpose of publication, but when they are published, they have the quality of naturalness, truth, simplicity and liveliness for which conscious literature blinks. The vitality and vitality that the direct contact with life gives to expression is not achievable by any literary technique.' In fact, in today's era when life has become multicolored, in such a way, diary writing is the only way to get closer to the truth.

Interview

Usually, when we read the work of a litterateur, somewhere a glimpse of his personality is visible on him but it is not clear. There is a difference between assessing an author or creator through reading his works and through interviews. Interview brings us face to face with the creator and we get to know the creator more closely. Interview makes us fully aware of the thoughts of the person.

Letter Writings

Letters have been playing an significant role in everyone's life. Although letters continued to be written for a long time, it was accepted as a genre in literature only in the modern period. Letter is a medium of communication of ideas or information, so it is important in private life as well as in government or non-government work. Personal letters have special significance because they are close to the feelings of both the writer and the reader. In a personal letter, expressions are spontaneous and naturally expressed. Letters are beyond artificiality. This is the reason why letters of distinguished persons have been accepted as a genre in literature.

Hindi writers did correspondence with other litterateurs. They spontaneously described the literary environment, compositions and other situations with each other through letters and these letters proved helpful in understanding their vision. Letters of many writers like Maharishi Dayanand, Jawaharlal Nehru, Premchand' Nirala,

Muktibodh Hazariprasad Dwivedi, Ramdhari Singh Dinkar, Girija Kumar Mathur, Trilochan etc. were printed and became famous.

Ramvilas Sharma presented letters in a collection titled 'Kaviyo ke Patra'. He collected correspondence with famous poets of Hindi. This collection is momentous. Ramvilas Sharma believes that letters are also important for the history of Hindi literature. Letter-literature has emerged as an innovation in literature. Today many universities and publishers are involved in archiving the letters of old authors so that they can be published and made accessible to all. With this, the readers will be able to get information about the creation process of the creators, their vision, culture and their life.

Works Cited

1. Hindi Sahitya ka Itihas, Ramchandra Shukla
2. Hindi Sahitya ka Itches – Dr. Nagendra
3. Hindi Sahitya, Laxmi Sagar Varshney
4. Hindi Sahitya Kosha, Part 1 and 2
5. Gadya ki Pahchan, Arun Prakash
6. Hindi Sahitya ki Bhumika, Acharya Hazariprasad Dwivedi
7. Rachnatmak Lekhan, Harish Aroda, Anil kumar Singh
8. Lekhankala aur Rachna Kaushal, Parikalpana Prakashan, Lakhnau
9. Vartman Sandarbha mei Hindi, Mukesh Agrawal
10. Rachnatmak Lekhan, S.RAmesh Gautam
11. Srujnatmak Lekhan, Rajendra Mishra, Takshshila Prakashan, New Delhi

CHAPTER 9

Think!!! Where are we going?

Dr R Sujatha Rani

Marriage has a strong definition. It is the strong bond and relation between not only two members but also two families. To maintain a good relationship spending more money is nothing important to doing marriage. The couple maintains a good relationship and continuing their relationship in their lifetime is important. In ancient days parents married their children too early. Even the bride and bridegroom don't know the meaning of the marriage at that age. Bride is dependent on the bridegroom and her in-laws' family. This is the main reason the girl had not opened her mouth though she suffered at in-laws home. The reason behind the suppression stage of the girl is she doesn't have education, financial support, a job for her secure position, age for questioning, and not having support from the government. But they continue their relationship until the end of their lifetime.

Born as a *Girl* is cursed in ancient time but boon in present. Illiteracy, sati, child marriages, and slavery has been changing. The mindset of the parents started to change. But this did not happen easily. It takes years and years. Many were fighting for the rights of girls. First step is Girls need education. Girls' education started after that they slowly improvised their financial independence. These are the signs of the strengthening of girl position. The second step is everywhere and in the field they get reservations. Due to reservation, girls also get good positions in all fields. As Gandhi said, when a girl can walk on the road at midnight, we will have complete freedom. Due to software jobs that one also proved the girls. As per history the reason for many wars and disturbance might be a girl. Saving culture and tradition are also in the hands of girls. So that everyone thinks if the girl got financial independence automatically the other development will happen. With the support of all evidence at present girls are also covering not only the earth but also the sky. They are showing their ability in all fields. They are rushing forward to be nothing less than men. This change is something to be proud of. And after this development, what we hear and see more now-a-days is divorce immediately after marriage. Why is this happening? What does our development teach us? Who is responsible for this? Is it due to their education? Their financial independence? Is it a job? Is it due to development? A heightened thought process? Or Parents?

In the past, the issues of divorce happened abuse, infertility, and financial problems. But the present scenario is totally different from the past scenario. Ego is also included. Both girl and boy are working hands and educators so that if any issue runs between them due to ego simply chooses divorce. What does our education learn, our development and our technology? The meaning of education is to improve our knowledge in all aspects, respect others, and live happily with adjustment. Taking care of both parents is another issue. If a couple discusses their responsibilities before the marriage they should accept the pros and cons in their relationship.

As much as a girl needs education and financial independence, it is equally necessary to control certain desires and habits so that they do not go out of their control. It should be used to advance her studies and her family in every possible way. Family traditions and culture depend on the behavior of a girl child. But if today's youth thinks that it is old fashioned and does not consider gender differences, then where is the value of the girl who is the source of this life. Not only the parents but also the government these days are providing all kinds of opportunities for the development of the girl child. With faith in their children, parents support their child to stay in hostels and give them the opportunity to study and do jobs. Children should use it as an opportunity for their higher growth. Due to getting more liberty some of the girls are crossing their limits and questioning the culture and tradition of India. So some newly entering girls also question why they should not follow the same path if their fellow sister is walking in the wrong way? Then mom and dad's honor and manners, and the career of those who have a thigh bag, do not care about anything.

Being modern does not mean getting used to a vagrant life. Every day we read or hear something in newspapers or news channels. Today, in some financially developed districts, it is seen that girls smoke more than boys and do not take care in the matter of clothing. If you ask for something, it is not correct to say that it is a foreign culture and that the way of looking should be changed. If that is true then why do foreigners follow Indian culture? Why do all the countries of the world respect our sarees? Our food? Our family relations? There is nothing wrong with wearing a modern dress that is not obscene. We should not forget that clothes are worn to cover the body and to enhance beauty. And when it comes to family matters, our children learn everything from our behavior. Things that don't seem wrong before marriage and age can get us into trouble in many ways later in life. Life changes after marriage, especially when every family development is in the hands of a girl. That is the greatness of a girl. High earning and financial independence at a young age has become another problem. The way of thinking of parents has changed in the way of choosing a suitable groom for a girl. Some parents buy a plot, car, luxury items with the girl's earnings and postpone the marriage due to lack of desire to repay the debt. When looking at a boy, one should see whether he comes from a family with good values, not like an ATM. If both are educated and doing good jobs, it is a small matter to provide for themselves. But if it is sent to a family whose values are not known, the value of money is not given to the girl on the other side, but not to the boy on the other side, so it does not take long to get divorced. Even marriages that cost a few crores are not given the importance given to divorce and to maintain the relationship.

Apart from this, love affairs in corporate offices, dating culture and family conflicts are the cause. All these things done in the name of development are hindrances and difficulties after marriage. Even if you know all this before marriage, boys should avoid showing masculinity after marriage. Applause when both hands join together. Also, love and dating only happen if both are willing, so boys should know the girls' mind and act accordingly. Good behavior and manners are essential for both girls and boys. When one does not understand this sensitive matter one starts showing arrogance and doubting. Whenever they ask questions, they do not hesitate to divorce because of financial independence. Then the court steps!! So when choosing a life partner it is better to discuss your previous relationships beforehand. Because through education you learn to think higher. The meaning of development is not separation, it's the meaning of togetherness and understanding. If you think you are telling the truth by telling it first, there is no need to question it later.

Education should teach adjustment in life only then that education will have value. Girls should stop looking at boys like an ATM machine. Parents of girls should look not only for property but for a family with good values. Parents of boys should see property and beauty in a girl but also modesty and tradition. Only then the daughter-in-law can accept the in-laws as parents. The family system is strong because the girl thinks higher than the boy. When the girl is happily accepting the responsibilities in the family, then the girl's education and financial independence become the foundation of everything.

CHAPTER 10

Reviewing Don DeLillo as a Representative of Contemporary American Culture

Shweta Chauhan and Dr. Tanu Gupta

An incredible technological boom has occurred in the last few years and it is marked by globalisation. When we talk about globalisation, we're talking about a system with the capacity to work as a whole on a planetary scale in chosen or real time. Here the capacity refers to the technological, organisational and institutional capacity. Current information and communication innovations, such as the use of computers and faster long-distance communication, international networks can easily link up with people and resources from all over the globe. What is meant by "institutional capacity"? The liberalisation, privatisation and deregulation of the regulations and the conduct followed by a nation, state to restrict the activity within its jurisdiction. Organization capacity denotes the ability to use networking as the borderless interactive and mode of activity saturation that is both adaptable and effective. Not everyone or everything is globalised, yet the global networks touch everyone and everything that structures the planet. This is due to the fact that all social, economic, and communicative pillars of society are cultural spheres that have gone worldwide.

Manual Castells's trilogy *The Rise of the Network Society* (1996, 1998, and 2000), *Power of Identity* (1997) and *End of Millennium* (1998) discuss a new form of network society, a new type of civilization spawned by the digital revolution. He characterises the network society as a worldwide behemoth of groups, corporations, population and regions that are interdependent and interrelated. Connectivity in the network is an information, matter and energy through a system of channels. The network society is a network-based communication and microelectronics-based information fuel the social structure of this future society. Network definition: a group of related nodes that make a network. Connecting individuals in a network, these nodes serve as the can be human being themselves, for example, individuals within a group who are bothered about their government or the technologies employed by the populace. The Network organisation serves as a cultural glue that holds communities together. With a network, you can change the weight of individual nodes. Since they take in more pertinent vital to the network and they may swiftly and effectively process information and accelerate handle it. For the performance of the network all nodes are necessary. Given that when the it reorganises the network, adding new nodes and removing old ones.

The globalised world is built up of networks. The networks of computer networks form the internet. The electronic networks developed global financial markets. It facilitates efficient processing of monetary transactions. The network of communication is formed comprised of linking numerous media in local or worldwide connections-production studies, computerised information system news room, computerised information system and increasingly interactive receivers and senders. The global economy consisting of a web of exchanges, marketplaces, factories, and pools of labour propelled by the convergence of data, capital, and corporate structures.

Three factors led to the rise of the network as the dominant organisational structure: principal features of networks that have benefited from current technical environment. They are flexibility, survivability and reliability of the networks. They are scalable and can decrease or expand in size when there is any disruption. They are survivable in the sense that, they have no centre and can work in a broad combination. There's a wide variety of possible setups. In the past, they had a poor track record when it came to managing their resources effectively. The process of bringing together and focusing these assets to achieve a specific goal task. New forms of communication and information technology, however, have avoid the pitfalls of previous network designs. This metamorphosis technologies relaxed the power of networks at the basis of the change in technology, which was founded on the revolution of tiny electronics that arose during the '40s and '50s.To put it simply, it laid the framework for the new technological paradigm, established mostly in the United States in the 1970s and rapidly disseminated anywhere around the world, launching the modern era of information.

Technology all throughout history can be regarded as a method of augmentation and growth of the human mind and body; the method in which early twenty-first century is marked by the explosion of portable devices with built-in computing power of pervasive wireless communications. The results of these aid the people or organisations, the social units that can talk to one another wherever they are. The boundaries between machine and human existence are blurred with the emergence of nanotechnology, and the meeting point of biological and material processes using miniature electronics to improve the synergy between us and our networks on a deep level to the unrestricted arena of human endeavour, where boundaries of space and time are transcended.

The network society causes a reorganisation of physical space. The geographical contiguity desists to be a prerequisite for the consensus of interactive cultural norms. Space is altered via remote, interactive communications, a new form – "the space of flows". It is constructed of information systems and electronic circuits, and it is also built up of real-world locations and areas whose symbolic or the networks themselves, but on the functional meaning derived from those networks particular features as locales. The space of flows are built of parts of places, rapid transit, sophisticated data networks, and cutting-edge communication systems characterised by spaces of intermediation and symbols. In other words, the locations do not disappear but their significance and reasoning are absorbed into the system. Thus, locations become hubs or nodes. There has been substantial debate in recent years over the global city emergence. It is not just a metropolitan hub that is prominent in the global geography of information and financial management. For such cities, the term "global city" was first proposed twenty years ago. Cities like New York, Tokyo, London, Paris, etc. are included. Using the most rigorous of analytical standards, the global city is not an unusual metropolis, and it slowly expands to encompass the areas in places all throughout the world. The global city is established with areas that in diverse locations secure the management of the global information networks and worldwide economic networks. For instance, most of New York and a few streets in Parts of Manhattan are considered part of the world's most populous and influential metropolis, although the vast majority of the island is not global, thus the global city is a non-contiguous territory linked by the network, it is reconstructed with the mission of controlling globalisation through the use of networks transcend location. When these different social and spatial elements interact, a new social and spatial structure is created. Disjointed and geographically varied network of spots.

A Postmodern American literary canon is Don DeLillo. His talk was about, topics covered range from the popular media and consumer habits of today to sports of the present day, nuclear war, the cold war, digital age, emergence of the technologies and innovations, etc. DeLillo's first novel is *Americana* (1971) is followed by *End Zone* (1972), (1972), Movies like *Great John Street* (1973), *Ratner's Star* (1976), *Players* (1977), and *Running Dog* (1978), *White Noise* (1985), *Libra* (1988), *Mao II* (1991), *Underworld* (1997), (1997), *The Body Artist* (2001), *Point Omega* (2005), and *Cosmopolis* (2003) (2010). He has won the National book award for *White Noise* in 1985 and Faulkner Award for *Mao II* in 1991.

In America's history, progress has always accompanied with a development in science and technology. This is very important in the modern world evidently more so given the pervasive nature of phenomena like consumerism. As it turns out, this idea has spread widely in the postmodern era. At this point in history, it's easy to see that humans are nothing more than the hostage. Consumerism, the ravenous spawn of technology. As a postmodern author DeLillo provided an intensive consideration to this subject of consumerism and technology in his works. The advent of modern manufacturing helped set many people free. Simple production methods and the widespread use of raw materials that date back to the Middle Ages has made machinery and technology significant in the lives of man.

The development of science and technology has effectively increased the divide between superstitious notions regarding life and led scientific understanding and technological progress as proper. The development of an embryo in the idea of industrialization was reflected in the construction of machines and technology, that solved the problems and decreased the pre-eminence of irrational beliefs in religion and the supernatural that stifled scientific progress. Over time, thanks to a plethora of innovations and widespread implementation of such innovations in the technology is a very recent development in the history of human civilization. Emerging technologies changed become the standard against which all other global powers are measured, countries with the booming technology have its right to conquer or dominate other countries which are technologically underdeveloped. In a consumerist society, we are driven to a world where ownership of commodities are indispensable and encouraged by others. Then important component that identify consumerism is its concentrate upon consuming the elementary similar to a magnificent banquet in terms of wants and ownership of conspicuous commodities and a life of plenty. The final decades of the twentieth century saw a correlation between class and trajectory of globalisation and introduced the consumerist philosophy openly. 20th Century, post-World War II, post-modernism, post-Fordism supported the growth of consumer ideology. Zygmunt Bauman, a famous sociologist, helped develop the idea of consumption. He had analysed the conflict of modernism with ambiguity of post-modern ethics, post-modern arts and a critique of liquid modernity.

According to his theory, in the post-industrial period, a consumeristic society means people yearning to be updated with the new style packets in every possible area. That is to say, the people are doomed to eternal rejection and isolation. People have to make peace with their purchasing habits again.

DeLillo's novels, especially *Cosmopolis*, deals with this issue of materialism. It wanted to emphasise on the impact of consumerism on a person in the contemporary times. The twenty-first century is an information and knowledge era. Networks society with the new technologies that has impacted the full element of our lives. We have stepped into a sphere of cyberspace in which the individuals are shrunk into information or information transformed into human beings computerised. In cyberspace, we have switched from capital to cyber-capital by the computer screens, which have reduced our rights of passage. That's why it's so important to dissect how modern technology affect society and have also, affected human life in the twenty-first century.

The United States of America is a land of gun violence, terrorist attacks, conflicts, and the stifling of daily life due to its overwhelming size and population. DeLillo represents a country with a lot of people living in it. His protagonists struggle mightily in his works since they aren't given any moral direction. They live a good, quiet, and enlightened life that is something one should strive towards. In his view, this postmodern culture is influenced from a society that does not care about ecological imbalance. As a whole DeLillo's is the territory of shopping malls and supermarkets, the temples of market structure based solely on customer demand, as espoused by the new consumerist ideology.

DeLillo has dealt with man's lost consciousness of both cultural and the natural setting for his fiction. In an effort to better understand what it means for man to be a main source of ruining the beauty of the area and generating an ecological unbalanced state of the world now. In some ways, the cultural divide may be the most important cause of all of man's internal shifts in perspective. His characters may be placed in the neutral territory it has been said that his vision borders on paranoia because of the connections it makes. About every facet of his culture and society. His novels provide a window into a specific time period, which is highly recognised as belonging to the postmodern era and now, as he keeps penning, the flow of time frame is designated as automobile modernism. Most of his books are classified as postmodern.

Postmodernism is a vague and all-encompassing movement in the visual and literary arts, studies in history, philosophy, and other fields. Books written by DeLillo since 1985 have focused on the ambiguities and inconsistencies that characterise postmodern society. The 'global postmodern' becomes a topic of interest in books. That is a world map crisscrossed by the unending stream of signs and messages resurging forms of nationalism and religious fundamentalism, as well as the bloodshed they've sparked, terrorism on a global scale.

DeLillo has an unhealthy preoccupation with the development of technology, the impact of images, and the omnipresence of today's media. The famous, the cultish, the cultural icons: for DeLillo, they represent powerful tendency of postmodernism in America's contemporary culture. It's admirable that people are responding culturally and intellectually to technology so early to the late stages of globalisation and industrialization. Every cutting-edge gadget features economic growth and democratic hope. As the norm and a cornerstone of modern life, technology limits people in important ways. They can't help but influence their natural surroundings because of how they have to live in this technology world. Technological drives humankind's uneasy place in nature. One of the goals of postmodernism in literature is to increase man's horizons so that we may all work together to improve the level of living. But the postmodern lifestyle has offered some detrimental effects on the environment.

Dr Tanu Gupta and Ramandeep Mahal in "Consumerism in Edward Albee's The American Dream" (2015) mention that people in the consumerist culture are influenced by commercials every day. They make purchases that they cannot afford. They also discuss that some opponents contend that consumers' purchases serve as stand-ins for wholesome interpersonal connections. These things cause differences in human interactions.

According to DeLillo's philosophical musings, reality is what is identified as "here" in his novels. It not only unachievable, but also the truth being ever-evolving and relative. They also create an infinite web of interdependence, making the aforementioned conclusion exceptionally tricky to reach. Writers like Octavia Butler and Margaret Atwood take a different attitude to the world, one in which nature plays a central role. Simultaneously, the authors like Don DeLillo, Karen Tei, Umberto Eco, and Jean Baudrillard focus on nature as no longer existing as a domain independent of human agency. Without a question, everyone can relate to the devastating impacts of a catastrophic failure or shared destruction, faster than the speed of success. According to socialist physician Cyrus Edson, "sickness binds the human race together." like a chain that can't be broken (34). The characters in DeLillo's novels share Edson's point of view.

Topics that DeLillo has chosen to explore in his writing include conspiracy theories, cold conflicts and cultural upheavals of the present day. The current human fixation on visuals and data is a prominent theme in his fiction. flitting over TVs and phones. DeLillo uses satire to poke fun at man's dim wittedness authentic from phoney. World War II, the Cold War, the atomic bombs, the rise of consumerism, and the tensions between different cultures in the 1960shave given the vast majority of authors a stage upon which to present the risk and cruelty meted out by humans in a credible fashion in their writing. Their writings are a scathing indictment on those who would destroy the old ways of accepting the risks of modern life and adopting an irresponsible lifestyle that is bad for your health. DeLillo is the prominent representative of mainstream modern American literature. He has focused his writing on the darker aspects of American culture, creating a portrait of the broken, the ill, the demented, and the suicidal.

Works Cited

Abrahamson, Peter. "Review Essay Liquid Modernity: Bauman on Contemporary Welfare Society." *Acta Sociologica*, vol. 47, no. 2, 2004, pp. 171-179.

Baudrillard, Jean. *Simulacra and Simulation*. University of Michigan press, 1994.

.... *The Consumer Society: Myths and Structures*. Sage, 2016, pp. 25.

Bauman, Zygmunt. *Liquid Modernity*. Polity Press, 2000.

Derrida, Jacques. "Structure, Sign, and Play in the Discourse of the Human Sciences." *A Postmodern Reader*, 1993, pp. 223-242.

Gupta, Tanu, and Ramandeep Mahal. "Consumerism in Edward Albee's The American Dream."

Research Journal of English Language and Literature, vol. 3, no. 2, 2015, pp. 218-224.

Jameson, Fredric. *Postmodernism, or, The Cultural Logic of Late Capitalism*. Duke university press, 1991.

Patterson, Matt. "Zygmunt Bauman, Consuming Life." *Canadian Journal of Sociology*, vol. 33, no. 2, 2008.

Marx, Karl, and Friedrich Engels. *The Communist Manifesto*. Progress Publishers, 1969.

Nel, Philip. """A Small Incisive Shock": Modern Forms, Postmodern Politics, and the Role of the Avant-Garde in *Underworld*." *MFS Modern Fiction Studies,* vol. 45, no. 3, 1999, pp. 724-752.

Wilcox, Leonard. "Baudrillard, DeLillo's "*White Noise*," and the End of Heroic Narrative." *Contemporary Literature,* vol. 32, no. 3, 1991, pp. 346-365.

CHAPTER 11

The Commercial Social Media: An Insight into the Commercial Side of Social Media and its Impact on the General Population

Aswin Mohan

Social media in the post-pandemic world has become an unavoidable element for all as it comprises a medium for entertainment, e-commerce, skill learning, and many other features for a community that had been blocked out from society for over a year. Social media platforms like Instagram, Snapchat, Twitter, etc. experienced a boom during the pandemic times as more people started engaging in these platforms for entertainment and social connections.

These trends are seen to continue even after the pandemic that too even after social restrictions are lifted. Most people only see one side of social media, the entertainment side where people post pictures, dances, funny memes, vlogs, etc. but there is another commercial side to social media that most don't see. Social media is not merely made for the entertainment of the user but to make users engage in a community where people sell and buy things. During the pandemic when people started engaging in social media platforms more and more there can be seen a sudden jump in sales through social media platforms as most people had only the online way to purchase things. The interesting thing is that even with the brick and mortars shops opening after the COVID restrictions these online purchase trends seem to be still on the rise.

According to a recent study, Instagram generated an estimated $47.6 billion in revenue in the financial year 2021, accounting for almost 50% of the Meta platform's total revenue. In this context, social media can be considered a commercial space where goods are bought and sold. According to Economic Times, Over the last three years, Instagram has introduced several add-on features for businesses to facilitate commerce on the platform, estimated to be a global market worth $10 billion by 2021, according to a Deutsche Bank analysis. Besides the Shop Now button seen at the end of a few sponsored posts, the platform allows businesses to use Shoppable Tags for regular posts and Insta Stories. Users can tap on a tag in a picture or a video to buy products directly from a brand's site.

When companies and sellers set their roots in social media platforms there must be something that assists companies in making their customers aware of their products and features. So to fix this gap they move on to using advertisements to promote their products and services. There is a saying in business that goes "If you try to sell to everyone you will end up selling to no one". So finding a target population to sell the products is a hard task for an ordinary seller without many resources, this is where social media platforms come in and this is where our personal data comes to use. Whenever an ordinary person thinks about the term personal data the first thing that comes to mind is that of bank details, private photos, phone numbers, account details, passwords, etc.. but that is not the case for social media platforms.

Social media is filled with advertisements targeted to people that are specifically in tune with the individual's interests. So every photo we upload, every reel we see, every photo we like, comment on, and every hashtag we follow to act as data for these social media platforms to target advertisements to us that cater to our own interests. So we can only see advertisements for the things we like on these social media platforms. This is the same reason we can observe advertisements for the things or services that we search for on E-commerce platforms like Amazon, Instagram, or Facebook. There are instances where a simple google search of a product or service can haunt the users with pop-up ads all over our social media spaces. In addition, these social media platforms have the user's live locations, who our friends are, what our favorite topics are, what music we like, what artists we like, what movies we like, and how long will we use social media in a typical day, so on and so forth. So in a way, we can see social media as a knavish salesman who knows almost everything that a best friend of ours would know.

In the post-pandemic, world fashion and the trends associated with it are seen to have taken a different trajectory. According to a survey conducted by Shopify, a popular e-commerce website, Brands like Zalando reported a 32% to 34% growth in gross merchandise value (GMV) during the second quarter of 2020. Fast-fashion brand Shein saw its valuation double to $30 billion, making it the world's largest online-only fashion retailer. Fashion brands with an e-commerce store maintain a stronghold in athleisure, like Nike and Lululemon, and have reported incredible growth over the course of the pandemic.

The influencer culture has also been the main factor that pushes the sales of these websites. Social media influences and celebrities have an immense fan base that supports their content but there are several people that idolize these influencers as well. So a product advertised by them is more likely to drive up sales for the company. Another thing to note is that these influencers mostly don't advertise directly but rather the company pays these influencers or celebrities a certain amount of money to use their clothing or cosmetics in their social media posts. These create a desire in the audience to buy these products to be liked or to imitate the influencers. This can be observed in the recent trends of anime-based items of clothing, K-pop clothing, movie-based articles of clothing, musical band-based products promoted by popular bands, and so on and so forth. A recent example from Kerala can be seen in the T-shirt from the Malayalam Movie "Minnal Murali" which was trending on Instagram for some time as well as The 'Malayali' T-shirts with Malayalam comments supported by actors from the Malayalam Film Industry. These specific examples also serve another purpose as these shirts or clothes in the above-mentioned example as not so common now as they were then because they have gone out of trend on social media.

The term trend implies an outlook or a fashion that is opted by or is considered fashionable by a social circle. Trends can change according to new ideas, or pop cultural references or can be because the influencers or celebrities opted to wear or dress in a particular way. After the pandemic the shift from clothes as something to wear to wearing things as a way to express our own self is predominant. Fashion itself defines itself as a way to express self and to establish autonomy at a particular period or place in a specific context. Thus the trend culture influences these social media users a lot to avoid being seen as outdated, to stand out, or simply to cater to the fear of missing out. The fact that should be considered is that these trends are not a unique way to express our own unique identity as these trends are usually manufactured as a mass commodity by the corporates for making the customers more so as to increase their profits.

These trends in fashion can be observed on college campuses as it showcases the pulse of youngsters. After the pandemic according to studies, the use of trendy outfits from online stores has increased. The youngsters during the pandemic had access to or had only social interaction via social media, thus creating a new peer group for themselves. The use of cosmetics has also seen a boom in the post-pandemic space thus re-establishing the 'fairness' craze of Indians. Tik-Tok gurus and Instagram influencers are seen giving makeup routines for youngsters and promoting and advertisement of fairness creams, lipsticks, face masks, straighteners, and cosmetics in the process. The very act of following these influencers target advertisement of the promoted products in our social media feeds The use of cosmetics in the age group of 18-30 has increased according to studies. These trends in the post-pandemic space that are supposed to create a unique identity to express self-have a dark side as well.

These trends in fashion that itself defines as a way to express identity or self have a major disadvantage as they can also create mental health issues as well. According to a study conducted in universities across the United States and England, the most common disease among campus students is anxiety and depression. Studies have directly linked these diseases with social media, as it mostly arises due to comparison, inferiority complex, and the fear of missing out. A person who may not be able to follow these trends on social media whether it be clothing, lifestyle, or any other factors is more likely to compare oneself to peers who follow the same. Clothes are also considered a way to establish social hierarchy as well. There exist a short story in India where a man got more attention due to his expensive clothing as opposed to when he was wearing cheap clothes, he then during the party started to feed his clothes to express the opinion that it was due to the clothes he gained attention so he should feed it well. It can be observed that these factors can create a sense of insecurity out of which the corporates commercialize, this can be observed in the fairness craze of India and the booming sales of cosmetics in India. These insecurities and hierarchy caused by social media don't simply exist on the basis of trends or items of clothing but are also directly associated with the number of likes, comments, and shares of the posts or advertisements. These social validating factors are referred to as social currency in contemporary times.

Social currency is just like the dollar and we attribute value to it in the form of likes, comments, shares, etc... These currencies act as a form of value factor by which the viewers may or may not choose to view or even trust the authenticity of the post on social media platforms. People are more likely to trust a post or advertisement with hundreds of likes and comments as compared to a similar advertisement with fewer likes. In marketing, it is called the economy of attention, which is like an attributed currency. The funny thing is that these likes and comments can be bought with money through several websites as means of promotion, there are even hundreds of YouTube videos providing instructions on how to do the same. This should not be considered as a question of the authenticity of social media advertisement posts but rather how corporates can act on our minds to gain trust.

While taking a look at the post-pandemic Kerala, an advertisement that struck me was one by the online store Ajio. Ajio during the Onam season opted for a different kind of advertisement as opposed to the traditional clothing that every other brand promoted during the Onam season. Starring the South Indian celebrity Kalyani Priyadarshan, Ajio used swag clothing and the clothes that are trending among youngsters and social media asking a question as their slogan 'Keralam Mario?' which translates to "Has Kerala changed?" This begs the question of whether the advertisement is implying that the change in clothing habits due to online promotions, sneaky advertisements by influencers and celebrities took an impact on the past culture of Kerala again begging the question "Has Kerala changed?" or do corporate advertisements have the power to change Kerala?

The change of advertisement strategies from a united cultural level to a specific individual level can be observed from the times before the pandemic. The famous and inspirational advertisement campaign of Nike during the London 2012 Olympics is an apt example to prove the same. During the London 2012 Olympics while Adidas paid millions to declare an official association with the Olympic movement in its marketing Nike was sidelined to stay away from anything related to the same. Nike was not even allowed to use any of the athletes from the Olympics. During these adversities, Nike took up the challenge to bring out a "find your greatness" campaign featuring amateur athletes "finding their greatness" in places called London across the world. Thus Nike focused on the specific individual and inspired the viewers to find their own greatness to be the hero that they always wanted to be.

These shifts of focus to individuals can be also seen in advertisements of Calvin Klein. Calvin Klein Inc. is an internationally operating, American fashion house. Calvin Klein first used supermodels with size zero bodies for their advertisements, which created an ideal body type due to advertisements. These ideal body types create insecurities in the people who became engaged in these advertisements. However, after a certain period of time, Calvin Klein seemed to revolutionize or redefine body politics by creating body-positive advertisements that looked similar to Kardhasians. These advertisements seemed to connect to a larger audience and created huge discussions among the people. These acts that seemingly create equality and body positivity must be questioned further.

Michael R. Solomon, professor and chair of Haub School of Business at St. Joseph's University department of marketing, said to FashionUnited, a fashion blog that "It's possible to say all this marketing on things like body positivity and self-expression is just another way to selling clothing". While reading this statement in connection to Calvin Klein's body-positive advertisements a question arises whether these advertisements are really aimed to promote body positivity or whether they are used to create a new set of consumers that can connect to their advertisements or create an image as a brand that takes up social issues or a combination of all.

When questioning Calvin Klein one must also look up into new advertisements popping up on Instagram and social networking sites that use Afro-American models that subvert the fair skin stereotype. It should be brought into question whether these corporate structures are really helping to subvert the stereotype or whether these are just publicity stunts to attract more customers.

Thrift culture is the new thing that Instagram has added to its cart, especially in the Indian markets. Thrift culture refers to second-hand clothes that are resold on social media sites. These clothes cater to the trending interest of youth while being economical. Thrift culture is a totally different experience in the Indian markets as one has never thought about using clothes to be a trend. These shops are advertised as being helpful to the environment as they reduce garment wastage which is the main problem that many commercial brands turn a blind eye to in their advertisements. A new trend thus means more waste. If not managed properly, old clothes end up in incinerators or landfills within years of production. Clothes do not biodegrade in a landfill and could remain there for more than 200 years before decomposing. There are some brands that offer to take used clothing to provide new clothes at a reduced rate, and they themselves advertise as eco-friendly brands. This eco-friendly initiative although good is also a feel-good initiative to make the customers buy more to feel good as they feel like they ate doing something for the environment. According to a report by resale platform ThredUp and the analytics firm Global Data, global used clothing sales would rise to nearly $77 billion by 2025. The industry currently sits at a $36 billion opportunity this year.

End of Reason sale, 50% off, The Great Indian Festival, Big Billion day, etc.. are some of the terms related to several "shopping festivals" conducted by e-commerce giants. While shopping for something at exclusive rates, it must be questioned why they provide such discounts to a large population. They have spent money on advertisements on televisions, in newspapers, and even on social media about how cheap you can buy extensive products. The real question to ask is what is their profit in doing the same? These mega shopping festivals usually occur by the end of the year when old stocks must be cleared for the warehouse capacity for new models that come out in the coming year. These e-commerce giants create a specific date to generate FOMO also known as the fear of missing out to generate a high volume of sales so that a reduced margin will yield profit in the long run. Most people buy something from these commercially created festivals thus falling into the better price trap or the FOMO trap. These festivals can thus be considered as mass advertised commercial festivals rather than something that really helps the consumers.

Advertisements whether they be on billboards, on television, on social media, or even through sneaky influencer means yield a common purpose, which is to attract new customers and create new sales. Every marketing strategy, campaign, etc.. is designed by professionals who have many years of experience and is trained to attract the attention of the consumers. Attention Economics treats human attention as a scarce commodity and applies economic theory to solve various problems at a macro level. Attention is not an infinite resource it is a finite one. On average, people are exposed to around 6,000 and 10,000 advertisements in a day. The average human brain is simply not capable of processing such a bombardment of content, so the vast majority of advertisements that are seen are only ignored or forgotten within seconds. So the professionals design advertisements to grab attention in the shortest time possible, thus engaging new and new gorilla marketing techniques which may showcase several trends or problems of the society or individual. The very next time we see an advertisement it must be brought to question why we like it, dislike it, ignore it, or why it caught our attention, thus hoping to understand the corporate tricks that the professional advertisement agencies engage to gain trust or to create discussions in the social space. The influence of money in marketing, especially in social media must also be brought into question when we encounter influencers, advertisement pop-ups, and commercial shopping festivals.

Works Cited

Goel, Prerna. "How Technology Can Solve Influencer Marketing Problems?" *The Economic Times*, The Economic Times, economictimes.indiatimes.com/news/how-to/how-technology-can-solve-influencer-marketing-problems/articleshow/93006564.cms.

Iqbal, Mansoor. "Instagram Revenue and Usage Statistics (2022)." *Business of Apps*, 6 Sept. 2022, www.businessofapps.com/data/instagram-statistics/.

"9 Best Sites to Buy Instagram Followers UK (Real and Active)." *The Economic Times*, economictimes.indiatimes.com/industry/services/advertising/9-best-sites-to-buy-instagram-followers-uk-real-and-active/articleshow/93281000.cms.

Barrow, Paul. "Attention Pays: The Economy of Attention in Advertising." *The Drum*, The Drum, 22 Mar. 2022, www.thedrum.com/opinion/2022/03/18/attention-pays-the-economy-attention-advertising.

Bhalla, Kritti. "Thrifting Is the Latest Trend on Indian Instagram, and It Is a Great One for the Environment." *Business Insider*, 22 July 2022, www.businessinsider.in/tech/enterprise/news/thrifting-is-the-latest-trend-on-indian-instagram-and-it-is-a-great-one-for-the-environment/articleshow/93052837.cms.

Fraser, Kristopher. "The Relationship between Fashion and Mental Health Awareness." *FashionUnited*, FashionUnited, 27 May 2022, fashionunited.uk/news/fashion/the-relationship-between-fashion-and-mental-health-awareness/2022052563287.

LIFE, AJIO. "Onam 2022." *YouTube*, AJIO Life, 19 Aug. 2022, www.youtube.com/watch?v=6_Bi7NKO1pY.

Lin, Yu-Hsuan, et al. "Investigation of the Role of Anxiety and Depression on the Formation of Phantom Vibration and Ringing Syndrome Caused by Working Stress during Medical Internship." *International Journal of Environmental Research and Public Health*, MDPI, 14 Oct. 2020, www.ncbi.nlm.nih.gov/pmc/articles/PMC7602477/.

McLachlan, Stacey. "35 Instagram Stats That Matter to Marketers in 2022." *Social Media Marketing & Management Dashboard*, 22 Aug. 2022, blog.hootsuite.com/instagram-statistics/.

Parnell, Bailey. "Is Social Media Hurting Your Mental Health? | Bailey Parnell | Tedxryersonu." *YouTube*, YouTube, 22 June 2017, www.youtube.com/watch?v=Czg_9C7gw0o.

Parsons, Russell. "Nike Launches 'London' Campaign." *Marketing Week*, Marketing Week, 3 Nov. 2014, www.marketingweek.com/nike-launches-london-campaign/.

Sinek, Simon, and Hye-ri Yun. *Start with Why: How Great Leaders Inspire Everyone to Take Action.* Segyesa, 2021.

CHAPTER 12

The Emergence of African American Literature: An Elaborate Study on Select Non-fictional Writings

Ruth Neyah and Vijayakumar M

Introduction

This chapter takes the readers on an amazing journey through the nonfictional writings practices and thought processes of African American writers. By investigating the genres on which African American authors concentrate, their work enquires into the issues facing the racial category on two continents, exploring both their converging and diverging agendas. Before even the peak of slave narratives, true spiritual narratives ruled African-American literature. In the 19th century, narratives by individuals who had typically been freed from slavery describing their travels to liberation and methods of capturing their lives were described as slave narratives. Slavery, monarchy, and other forms of pre-capitalist social stratification were prevalent in Africa long before the start of colonialism. However, following colonization and fraudulent independence, the majority of the landmass within that region was separated into two distinct societies: neo-colonialist and post-colonialist.

The lives of current African Americans are the main subject of contemporary African American literature. African American fiction spans a wide range of literary subgenres. Black writers have produced a large number of top-selling Western movies, romances, period dramas, detective novels, and quick tales. African American literature frequently focuses on subjects that are of significant relevance to Black people, such as the place of African Americans in American society in general and topics like enslavement, discrimination, and inequality. It's not the same Africa you remember. It examines topics of race, equality, immigration, cultural changes, and more. Some of them are set in Africa, but the majority are spread over many other continents. They are fundamentally personal depictions of family sagas that straddle several cultures and linguistic boundaries. They fundamentally alter how we perceive a new renaissance of African literature because they are loaded with wisdom, knowledge, sensitivity, wars, grief, and tenacity.

There are a few examples out of which I have mentioned a few. Homegoing by Yaa Gyasi is an ambitious book, which is set in Ghana and the US, does what most African novels fail to do: it brings together Africans and African Americans by ingeniously connecting our history in dimensions we could fathom (Gyasi Yaa, 2016).

New-Generation African Poets: A Chapbook Box Set (Saba) by Kwame Dawes, Chris Abani, and the annual poetry chapbook set features a lovely collection of up-and-coming African authors. The scope of this year's collection is no less expansive: Nine introduces poets of exceptional skill who explore themes of belonging while also challenging the lands and oceans that both provide them safety and turn them away. It is especially important to provide emerging poets a platform, and the African Poetry Book Fund does this year after year (Dawes, Kwame, and Chris Abani, 2016).

What Is Not Yours Is Not Yours by Helen Oyeyemi, Helen Oyeyemi's skill with individuals if you have read any of her writing. Characters in this collection of short tales fluidly transition from page to page while immersed in their own personal lives, demonstrating once again Oyeyemi's great talent. Oyeyemi isn't a writer in the usual sense; her personalities are more complicated in nature and have more quirky demands rather than going through a metamorphosis and conquering a series of obstacles. Her skillful writing allows us readers to understand them, leaving us constantly needing extra (Oyeyemi, Helen, 2017).

Characteristics of African American Literature

The immense African diasporic history has formed African-American literature in various nations and has also had an impact on it. It was produced in the broader category of post-colonial writings, but intellectuals make a distinction between the two, stating that "African American literature differentiates from many of the post-colonial writings in that it is documented by members of a minority group who dwell within a sovereign country of enormous prosperity and financial authority. Poetry is prevalent in African-American oral tradition, which also includes religious songs, soul music, funk, and rapping. This oral poetry is also found in the African-American Christian preaching traditions, which employs intentional rhyme, tempo, and recurrence. African-American literature has a long history of embracing all of these varieties of oral poetry, particularly documented poetry but also nonfiction. Not all writings by African-American authors exhibit these traits.

Some academics object to the analysis of African-American literature using Western literary theory. "My desire has been to allow the black tradition to speak for itself about its nature and various functions, rather than to read it, or analyze it, in contexts of literary theories loaned heartedly from other customs, usurped from without," said Henry Louis Gates, Jr., a literary scholar at Harvard. African-American literature frequently uses the device of "exemplifying." A number of additional rhetorical devices, including as metaphor, metonymy, synecdoche, and irony, as well as exaggeration and colloquial expressions, and metalepsis, according to Gates, are grouped under the term "symbolizing." Using other African-American literature as a lens through which to interpret and evaluate their own works is another example of symbolizing.

African American Culture

The term "African-American culture" describes the part played by African Americans to American culture, whether they are integrated into or apart from it. African-American history, especially the Middle Period, is the foundation of the distinctive character of African-American culture. The country has its own culture and has a significant impact on both American culture and international culture in general. The origins of African-American culture lie in the fusion of traditional African civilizations from West and Central Africa with European cultures, which shaped and altered the way they developed in the American South. Considering its place in American society, which means being aware of its ethnographic roots as a huge fusion of West and Central African traditions. Although the practice of African cultural practices was severely constrained by servitude, many customs, ideals, and concepts persisted and throughout time were transformed or combined with other civilizations, including Native American culture.

The Southern American culture has a bearing on African-American culture. They were imprisoned on Southern plantations by

White Southerners, who really affected their diet and dialect. The African-American religious, family, cultural, and financial practices have been influenced by African traditions, servitude, slave uprisings, and the civil rights struggle. Numerous aspects of life bear the mark of Africa, including politics, economy, speech, entertainment, art, performance, styles, spirituality, food, and perspective. In return, many aspects of mainstream American culture have been profoundly and significantly altered by African-American culture. Creolization is the technique of two peoples exchanging their original thinking. The lifestyle of African slaves and their descendants has had a great influence on not just the dominant American culture but also on cultures across the globe over time.

Early African American Literature and Slave Narratives

When researchers approach the early African-American literary collection, they encounter interpretative challenges, as Katherine Faull explains. She examines two memoirs on Moravian funerals written by former Black slaves, each of which addresses genre, modality, polyvocality, and reception issues. Faull demonstrates that the study of African-American signatures as practises is most beneficial. The autograph lacks both the full authority to communicate in her own voice and the passive reception of rules for subjective expression. Nevertheless, the "Speaking subject manipulates meaning via the rhetorical devices of displacement and metalepsis, yet the same subject is also manipulated. The hegemonic discourses of European culture are extended and subverted by the Black signature, yet these discourses continue to determine the process of self-differentiation (Drexler, 2008).

By extending Faull's description of rhetorical techniques, April Langley demonstrates how biblical literacy enabled Black authors to actively engage in exegesis and hermeneutics. The mission of social framework is linked to African-American prose by Phillip M. Richards. This connection between writing and relevance reveals unexpected similarities between the collective tactics used by African-American clerics and later secular Black reformers and those used by white Protestant pietists and their dissenters. Early authors aimed for a "political satisfaction built largely in institutional success," according to Richards, reflecting on the Black elites' development of spectacular credibility and their appropriation of the voices of the "wretched" Black masses. The common interpretation of Black literature as making more general universalist or humane arguments is at odds with this definition.

There is no denying the significance of the slave narrative, and early black novels are unquestionably important for understanding both black literature and American literature in broad sense, but because of our near-obsession with particular narrative types, there are now clear-cut boundaries around what counts as and in black literature. These limits are frequently established in blatantly contemporary and ahistorical ways. Bishop Daniel Payne, a composer and scholarly activist, listed five important categories of literature, including cultural, scholarly, religious, and conceptual, in an 1858 essay titled "On General Literature" in the African Methodist Episcopal Church's Repository of Religion and Literature.

His interpretation of literature managed to draw on concepts that were widespread in the eighteenth century and were still very much in use in the nineteenth century, such as the notions that literature and text – based writ were equivalent, that "the component of literature is to obtain, maintain and distribute to succeeding generations the fruits of intellectual ability, expertise, and acquiring knowledge of the men of all regions and all ages," and that authors of literature should "exhibit in their own native forms, things past, things present, and events to come (Pugh, 2022). Given his didactic view of literature, Payne's reluctant inclusion of novels under "light literature" is not surprising. According to Payne, various genres of writing enable readers to be touched by "the most brilliant conceptions of genius, the most prudent maxims of sages, the most significant findings of empiric philosophy, the prophesies of prophets; furthermore, the very instruction of the embodied Deity." I adopt Payne's concept of literature as a starting point for our analysis, not because I believe it should apply to our bigger projects.

Analysis of the themes in Select Non-fictional Writings

The mere structure of Homegoing, in which each chapter follows a different descendent of a common ancestor, Maame, makes evident the value of family. The significance of family and upbringing may be observed in the characters' personalities and decisions as a result of this framework. The relationships between the individuals in the novel, especially those who are set in the same era in Africa and the United States, also serve to highlight how culture may affect one's prospects and beliefs. For instance, Ness and Kojo, who end up living in the same time period in the United States and are also inherited from a woman from the Gold Coast and a white colonist, are treated as slaves and criminals while Quey and his son receive special rights given that they are associated to a white colonist on the Gold Coast. For many of the personalities, the bonds between parents and children are particularly significant.

When offspring rejoin with their family, as it does with Yaw and his mother Akua as well as with Sonny and his mother Willie, it highlights the value of the link between parent and child. A variant on this theme is when children look to persons who are not their blood relatives as parental figures, such as Kojo looking to Ma Aku who freed him from captivity and Sonny looking to Eli, the happy but erratic father of Sonny's sister. These connections demonstrate that biological ties are not the primary focus of family; rather, love and safety are. For Maame's descendants residing on the Gold Coast as well as those in the US, cultural heritage plays a significant role in the narrative. Parts of Akan culture must be shielded from Foreign interference for the generations who remain in Africa. In Homegoing, Gyasi depicts the lives of Esi's ancestors, highlighting the prejudices and discrimination that black people have experienced and still encounter in the United States. Gyasi demonstrates how misconceptions and overt prejudice prevented persons of African origin, particularly those who couldn't pass for white, from finding employment or just attempting to live free and fulfilling lives after slavery was abolished.

New-Generation African Poets: A Chapbook Box Set (Nane) is a meaningful collection. These poems depicted a world of family, bloodline, frontiers, refugees, and non-borders, as well as the individuals caught in the middle of these events and those who leave, strive, and endure. Poems that deal directly with issues such as adoration, sorrow, faith, rejuvenation, resilience, and naivety that has been lost, stolen, or slain. Reading this book gave me a very intimate feeling, as if the stories were being recounted by friends or family members who wished to document what they had gone through, how they had managed to survive, and how they had been molded and transformed. These poems that are heartfelt, that accurately capture the writers' thoughts and interpretations need to be appreciated whether they are severe or gentle, and that do so in a way that increases the reader's impression.

The themes found in "What is Not Yours is Not Yours," Helen Oyeyemi's debut collection of short stories, are crucial. Sometimes they serve as a key story point, explaining a character's obscure past or revealing the fatal mysteries of an item. They occasionally have a supporting role, contributing to a successful outcome or joining in on a joke. Regardless of whether keys appear frequently in any one narrative, the book's themes involve opening doors, whether real or metaphorical, into all other people's lives and psyches as well as into certain societal conceptions. Every tale in the collection is governed by this principle, which determines whether the reader or the characters are the only ones who benefit from the story. An intriguing and thought-provoking examination of the human urge to discover the truth and the difficulty of ever doing so is "What is Not Yours." The majority of the stories in Oyeyemi's book are about the human experience, but she frequently adds a fantasy element to the mix (Sims, 1982).

The author's extraordinary command of language is evident throughout the book, creating vivid, lasting images with the help of a few simple phrases. "Montse observed that the Seora occasionally became short of breath while having barely moved. In the first tale, "Books and Roses," about an orphan who unwittingly carries the key to a hidden fortune, Oyeyemi characterizes the work of a painter as "a result of stealing pictures out of the air – the air snatched something back.

The book "What Is Not Yours Is Not Yours" is well named because it confirms that no outsider – in this case, the reader – can ever fully understand the enigmas of another being's life and because it celebrates the unbreakable bonds that exist between individuals. Fiction frequently provides windows into the complex inner workings of people, but for Oyeyemi and her most recent work, reality frequently holds more questions than it does answers. The reader learns to understand that we will never completely possess what is not ours.

Conclusion

This chapter brings out the shades of African American literature, culture, background and presents a few non fictional writings written by African American writers. With time, the concept of African American studies has experienced a significant alteration. Writers' tactics and approaches center on the issues of black people's survival in modern society and their hopes for the future. The authors draw attention to the terrible white reality that keeps a contemporary Black hostage and victim. This chapters brings out an elaborate analysis of the themes in select non fictional writings. African American writings are still on focus because of the heritage and the past bitter experiences, it is still a powerful site to pick. One of the goals of postmodern African-American literature is to elicit critical self-reflection on the historical expectations for racial portrayal of black writers. Slave narratives and all black literature have been under pressure to accurately represent African Americans as a race and to discuss their experiences as a whole since the beginning of the 19th century. By satirizing these patterns and exposing them as textual creations rather than accurate depictions of black reality, postmodern African-American writers self-consciously modify the dominant ancient literary modes of black diversity. African-American literature has developed into new scales and forms. The authors' 50 writings, which represent new and evolving ideas and expressions, enrich the tradition. Readers from all across the world have found it appealing. In universities of higher distinction, this is the main area of study.

Works Cited

Farland, Donna. "The effect of historical, nonfiction trade books on elementary students' perceptions of scientists." *Journal of Elementary Science Education* 18.2 (2006): 31-47.

Hathaway, Yulia. ""'They Made us into a Race. We Made Ourselves into a People": A Corpus Study of Contemporary Black American Group Identity in the Non-Fictional Writings of Ta-Nehisi Coates." *Corpus Pragmatics* 5.3 (2021): 313-334.

Hedley Twidle (2012) "In a Country where You couldn't Make this Shit up"?: *Literary Non-Fiction in South Africa*, Safundi, 13:1-2, 5-28, DOI: 10.1080/17533171.2011.642586

Pugh, Sharon L., and Jesus Garcia. "Portraits in Black: Establishing African American Identity Through Nonfiction Books." *Journal of Reading*, vol. 34, no. 1, 1990, pp. 20–25. JSTOR, http://www.jstor.org/stable/40033065. Accessed 4 Oct. 2022.

Sims, Rudine. *Shadow and substance: Afro-American experience in contemporary children's fiction*. National Council of Teachers of English, 1111 Kenyon Rd., Urbana, IL 61801 (Stock No. 43768, $5.50 member, $6.00 non-member)., 1982.

Drexler, Michael J., and Ed White, eds. *Beyond Douglass: New Perspectives on Early African-American Literature.* Associated University Presse, 2008.

Gyasi, Yaa. *Homegoing.* Penguin UK, 2016.

Dawes, Kwame, and Chris Abani. *New-Generation African Poets: A Chapbook Box Set (Tatu).* Akashic Books, 2016.

Oyeyemi, Helen. *What is Not Yours is Not Yours.* Pan Macmillan, 2017.

CHAPTER 13

Building Creative Nonfiction: A Brief Idea and Analysis of Different Works and Broad Map to Creative Nonfiction

Harry B. and Dr. Vijaykumar M.

Introduction

All forms of written communication fall under the umbrella of literature, which is a broad term. Despite the fact that there are numerous literary genres, they can all be grouped into two broad categories, which may be confusing. These fall under the nonfiction and fiction subcategories. Fiction is the umbrella term for all literary works that are made up or invented by the author. This group includes books like short stories, novels, and poetry. Thus, literary works that are based on real-world events are referred to as "nonfiction." Nonfiction literature can help us better understand the world in this way. Let's dive deeper into the characteristics and examples of nonfiction. Nonfiction in the sense just mentioned was first used in writing in 1867. These sample sentences were automatically extracted from a variety of online news sources in order to reflect how the word "nonfiction" is used today. These examples do not represent the views of Merriam-Webster or its editors. In the digital age, it is simple to start a casual and then intimate relationship with someone because texting, e-mailing, and even social media friendships can cross the line and become in-person relationships with just a few keystrokes and swipes on your smartphone. But when reality sets in, it is harder to forget them.

Instead of merely reporting facts, creative nonfiction engages the reader in a way that fosters a deeper understanding of the subject. In-depth research and the capacity to tell a gripping story are requirements for writing creative nonfiction. Just like a good teacher, writers of creative nonfiction need to be able to dramatize the underlying meaning of the facts in an interesting, moving, and instructive way. In the 1960s and 1970s, "The New Journalism" gave rise to the term "creative nonfiction," which refers to reporting that seeks a higher truth than can be attained through verifiable data. Talese (1971) describes new journalism and offers a template for how to present qualitative research. The component The element of surprise is particularly important when writing creative nonfiction because readers should feel like they are getting the true, never-before-reported story. (Cheney, 2001, p. 3)

Non-fiction

Non-fiction is the broadest category of literature and includes writing that's about real people and places as well as fictional accounts of them. Narrative fiction is similar to fiction in that it tells a story and may include the same elements as fiction, such as setting, characters, plot, and conflict. An autobiography is a story that a writer tells from his or her own life and typically focuses on the most important events that happened to the person the author is writing about. Informative nonfiction includes stories and personal anecdotes.

Non-fiction is the broadest category of literature and encompasses so many different types of non-fiction. The story is in first person point of view and typically focuses on the most important events that happened to the author. Some examples of autobiographies include some well-known ones such as Frank Abagnale and Catch Me if you can. Michael J. Fox An autobiography is a story that a writer tells from his or her own life story. There are biographies of Santa Claus, Adam Sandler, The Rock, and many other famous and not-so-famous people. Like an autobiography, a memoir uses first person to tell a story, but they differ from autobiographies because they focus only on one period of the author's life. Memoirs also have an emphasis on the author's relationships and can tell you about the impact of historical events on the author's life. Some of the memoirs include the judge. Greg Mathisone writes about some Mit students who use their smarts to win big in Las Vegas. Lisa Beamer's story about her husband, Todd Beemer's, heroic actions during September 11 Informative nonfiction uses stories and personal anecdotes to elaborate on the subject. This explains topics such as kendo, or Japanese sword fighting. It can promote an opinion or editorial information non-fiction many times.

Although it uses many of the same tactics as fiction, creative nonfiction uses facts to build a tale that is intriguing and emotionally engaging. Creative non-fiction conveys information in a way that leads the reader to a deeper understanding of a subject than merely reporting facts. The ability to tell a compelling story and conduct in-depth research are prerequisites for writing creative nonfiction. Despite frequently reading like fiction, the new journalism is not fiction. The new journalism encourages, in fact, calls for a more creative approach to reporting.

Building Blocks around Creative Non-fiction

In the publishing and academic worlds, creative nonfiction has blossomed since the early 1990s. Nobody genuinely knows who or when the phrase "creative nonfiction" was first used. Although some have said that the University of Iowa, and then Ohio State University, started offering creative nonfiction courses, creative nonfiction workshops were likely offered at colleges and universities across the country in response to the growing interest.

The resource by Richard Terrill gives a summary of the genre and an explanation of the main sub-genres. CNF depends on the writer's ability to accurately recount actual events. Many authors of fiction periodically go over to nonfiction, even if it's just to write pieces about the writing process. Prose in creative nonfiction can take many distinct shapes. Realistic subjects are the main emphasis of creative nonfiction, which uses research to portray events as truthfully as possible.

CNF authors must pay meticulous attention to every last detail. Their work resembles that of a journalist in certain ways, and some forms of journalism can be categorised as CNF. While it's true that fiction writers do their own research (particularly when it comes to historical fiction), An overview of the genre and an explanation of its primary sub-genres are provided by the Richard Terrill page. CNF relies on the author's capacity to properly retell historical events. Many nonfiction writers occasionally switch over to writing fiction, even if it's merely to write articles about the writing process. In creative nonfiction, prose can take many different forms. Creative nonfiction focuses mostly on realistic issues and employs research to accurately represent occurrences.

Voice of creative Non-fiction

The work is based on research to portray events as accurately as possible. CNF, as an emergent genre, is inextricably linked with fiction. A writer uses "personal candour" to entice the reader, like a poet. The voice of creative nonfiction seeks "to engage the sympathies" of the reader, according to writer Richard Terrill, who contrasts the two genres. Kate Bernheimer said that creative nonfiction requires 'intimacy.' According to Jacqueline Leavitt in her book "Nonfiction", creative nonfiction was only beginning to establish its standards as a genre as recently as 1995 and includes writers such as Truman Capote and Joan Didion. In the literary genre of autobiography, a person's life is described in their own words, using it to create a frame that prompts the reader to rethink events in their life.

Kate Bernheimer: "A lifetime of reading is research." Christopher Cokinos: "Such study exposes not just facts of the world, but discloses and moulds the writer's universe." "Reflection, or the second 'I,' is taught in every nonfiction course." This should ideally occur in brief instances, perhaps single phrases, scattered throughout the work.

The story is based on research to portray events as accurately as possible. CNF writers must be meticulous in their attention to detail. Similar to fiction, the length of the works can vary widely; they might be as little as 500 words on a cuisine blog or as long as a book. There are numerous authentic recipes on food blogs, but those in the television series are more representative of the authenticity of their time and place. So, what distinguishes the literary nonfiction genre? Creative Nonfiction includes a wide range of literary styles. A creative nonfiction writer should always be on the lookout for information that may be turned into an essay; the world at large is their subject matter. One of the most important questions to ask when planning to write an essay is, "Who are my readers?" What values do they have? Who are they as individuals? Based on that information, a writer can choose and create an essay topic that has something in common with the reader's values and interests.

A significant part of nonfiction's appeal is the lessons it provides us, the models for how to live; that the writer can endure a tough or unusual experience and benefit from it. "Study exposes not just the facts of the world but discloses and moulds the writer's universe."

"Reflection, or the second 'I,' is taught in every nonfiction course," he says, adding that authors typically struggle to integrate reflection into their work. Reflective nonfiction shows something to the world and teaches something about the writer. The death of the author remains very important and is the foundation of most nonfiction authors, including Christopher Cokinos. Your observation that autobiographical passages in writing often reveal something about the writer (this will be by far the longest explanation): Cokinos has written about the role of nonfiction in higher education for years and about that of autobiography. Other things being equal, if the novel itself is more convincing than a description of that event by an academic nonfiction writer, then the resulting product will be a better nonfiction work. The Girl Across the Road (Lush, 1984), The Problem of Talking to Women (Shorris, 1994), and Coming on Strong: Cross-Cultural Conflicts of Love and Romance in America (Lipsyte, 1992). The Girl Across the Road, a nonfiction account of the defense of a female rapist who was studying law at Georgetown University, reveals in poignant detail the challenges that women face on college campuses today, and it can serve as a guide to all young women who are interested in the field or want to make the most of their lives as college students. The Problem of Talking to Women offers accounts of men and women's relationships with teachers, with the law, and with doctors that illuminate the predicaments in which most of us may find ourselves, or even a description of the whole issue of what it means to be "feminine" and to be a woman.

CNF is one of the fastest growing literary genres. It's almost like a blend of all the other forms; it has the elegance of poetry, the narrative depth of fiction, and the focus of an essay or a piece of journalism. Sienna says creative nonfiction is basically treating factual content in a more literary or literary manner. CNF has a lot of various sub-genres that are all quite different and distinct from each other. If the short story is to the novel, the personal essay is to the memoir. It's like a mini version of a memoir. If you just have one brief event that you want to talk about, you could write a personal essay. It has the same intimacy and first-person focus as a memoir but in a much smaller package, usually something you can read in just one sitting. These kinds of essays are often featured in journals or magazines. So, if becoming a memoirist is your ultimate goal, starting with personal experiences might be a great way to hone your skills as well as start to gain an audience. Number four is literary criticism, which is a piece of literary criticism where the reader shares in your own reading experience. CNF might be based on the facts, but it thrives off the tension that you would get from fiction. It is journalistic, but it's written with more attention to narrative style than an article in a newspaper. A newspaper article is very factual and objective, whereas a piece of literary journalism might have to do a really deep dive into the topic. This genre encompasses a lot of other subgenres, such as travel writing CNF is a really broad format with a lot of different subgenres, and as a way to combine the impact of facts with the narrative impact of narrative tension and style, it's a great way to write about any topic that interests you or your own personal experience. The structure of CNF can be very inventive and very playful. Don't feel trapped in the actual events and instead tell the story in a way that makes sense for you or creates the most tension.

Sienna says creative nonfiction is basically treating factual content in a more literary manner. She says it can be a really difficult form to explain because it has a lot of different subgenres that are all quite different and distinct from each other. A piece of literary journalism is still meant to get the facts across, but with a bit more of a personal touch. For a personal essay, you might need to go back and fact-check your own life or go mining for details. CNF is a great way to write about any topic that interests you, combined with your own personal experience. Before writing a CFN work, do the research and fact check everything before it is possible to be fact checked in CNF. Don't feel trapped in the chronology of the actual events and instead tell the story in a way that makes the most sense for you or creates the most tension.

In Tom Wolfe's creative nonfiction, information and ideas are presented in a narrative fashion, starting with the very beginning of the world in a blend of style and substance. Thomas Wolfe Creative knowledge, also known as individuals in creation or narrative knowledge, has always existed, but until recently, people had only just started to take it seriously as a genre. When you create a creative nonfiction chapter or book, you engage the reader in the narrative. Then you start to teach them the lessons you want them to learn, but you don't just spout them out; rather, you include them in the knowledge you've interspersed between the stories. Building blocks for creative nonfiction are pieces of cork that are also placed together. You just can't take a thousand blocks of a scene or five or six different seeds. The scenes have got to work together. So-called "creative nonfiction" is Reza's approach.

So we try to establish parallels with three or four narratives at the same time, so you have an overall narrative frame for your essay chapter or book, and then you have other narratives. If your readers are not interested in a, then you're really interested in B or C. So, we talk about what they call framing in creative nonfiction: all authors make some kind of argument or a frame for their work.

Conclusion

Creative nonfiction is a combination, as said, of style and substance. Information and ideas presented in a story-oriented manner with the absolute beginning of the world's creative nonfiction people in creating partitions or narrative knowledge have been around for a long, long time but up to now. When you're teaching a reader how to read creative nonfiction, you don't just throw things at them; you give them information. You embed information between stories and try as often as possible to embed information inside the stories. A single article or short story may have four, five, or six scenes, but they are all part of an overall story structure that we call a story structure. A book of creative nonfiction will have chapters that are framed just the way essays are, but the book will also be framed in an overall score of remember the story captures the read. The story always keeps the reader with the information but not the story, so the more stories that you have, the more reason the reader has to stay with what you're doing.

Works Cited

Brien, Donna Lee, and Lee Gutkind. "Creative Nonfiction: A Virtual Conversation With Lee Gutkind." *TEXT*, vol. 4, no. 1, Australasian Association of Writing Programs, Apr. 2000. *Crossref*, https://doi.org/10.52086/001c.35893.

Lee Gutkind. "Creative Nonfiction Immersion Classics by Women." *World Literature Today*, vol. 87, no. 3, Project Muse, 2013, p. 6. *Crossref*, https://doi.org/10.7588/worllitetoda.87.3.0006.

Treat, James. "Imagining Ourselves: Classics of Canadian Non-Fiction, and: Going Some Place: Creative Non-Fiction Across Canada, and: Crisp Blue Edges: Indigenous Creative Non-Fiction (Review)." *Fourth Genre: Explorations in Nonfiction*, vol. 7, no. 2, Project Muse, 2005, pp. 121–23. *Crossref*, https://doi.org/10.1353/fge.2005.0045.

Lee Gutkind. "Why I Chose the Creative Nonfiction Way of Life." *Fourth Genre: Explorations in Nonfiction*, vol. 2, no. 1, Project Muse, 2000, pp. 200–06. *Crossref*, https://doi.org/10.1353/fge.2000.0000.

Dr. Charu Mehrotra. "A Suitable Boy: Blurring the Line Between Fiction and Non-Fiction." *The Creative Launcher*, vol. 7, no. 1, Perception Publishing, Feb. 2022, pp. 37–42. *Crossref*, https://doi.org/10.53032/tcl.2022.7.1.07.

McCrory, Moy. "Primo Levi as Storyteller: The Uses of Fiction, Creative Non-fiction and the Hard to Classify in Levi's Narrative of the Holocaust." *Short Fiction in Theory & Practice*, vol. 3, no. 1, Intellect, Apr. 2013, pp. 85–96. *Crossref*, https://doi.org/10.1386/fict.3.1.85_1.

Robertson, Rachel, et al. "'An Ambiguous Genre': Thoughts on Creative Non-fiction and the Exegesis." *TEXT*, vol. 21, no. Special 44, Australasian Association of Writing Programs, Oct. 2017. *Crossref*, https://doi.org/10.52086/001c.25865.

Richard Terrill. "Character in Creative Nonfiction." *Fourth Genre: Explorations in Nonfiction*, vol. 3, no. 1, Project Muse, 2001, pp. 177–81. *Crossref*, https://doi.org/10.1353/fge.2001.0009.

"Creative Nonfiction." *JAMA*, vol. 282, no. 7, American Medical Association (AMA), Aug. 1999, p. 695. *Crossref*, https://doi.org/10.1001/jama.282.7.695.

"Roundtable: What Is Creative Nonfiction? Two Views." *Fourth Genre: Explorations in Nonfiction*, vol. 2, no. 1, Project Muse, 2000, pp. 191–92. *Crossref*, https://doi.org/10.1353/fge.2013.0378.

Lee Gutkind. "Why I Chose the Creative Nonfiction Way of Life." *Fourth Genre: Explorations in Nonfiction*, vol. 2, no. 1, Project Muse, 2000, pp. 200–06. *Crossref*, https://doi.org/10.1353/fge.2000.0000.

Treat, James. "Imagining Ourselves: Classics of Canadian Non-Fiction, and: Going Some Place: Creative Non-Fiction Across Canada, and: Crisp Blue Edges: Indigenous Creative Non-Fiction (Review)." *Fourth Genre: Explorations in Nonfiction*, vol. 7, no. 2, Project Muse, 2005, pp. 121–23. *Crossref*, https://doi.org/10.1353/fge.2005.0045.

Freeman, Robin, and Karen Le Rossignol. "Clarifying Creative Nonfiction Through the Personal Essay." *TEXT*, vol. 15, no. 2, Australasian Association of Writing Programs, Oct. 2011. *Crossref*, https://doi.org/10.52086/001c.31345.

Hesse, Douglas. "The Place of Creative Nonfiction." *College English*, vol. 65, no. 3, JSTOR, Jan. 2003, p. 237. *Crossref*, https://doi.org/10.2307/3594255.

Freeman, Robin, and Karen Le Rossignol. "Clarifying Creative Nonfiction Through the Personal Essay." *TEXT*, vol. 15, no. 2, Australasian Association of Writing Programs, Oct. 2011. *Crossref*, https://doi.org/10.52086/001c.31345.

study.com: What Is Nonfiction? – Definition and Examples – Video & Lesson Transcript | Study.com. study.com, study.com/academy/lesson/what-is-nonfiction-definition-examples.html. Accessed 30 Aug. 2022.

Nonfiction Definition and Meaning – Merriam-Webster: Definition of NONFICTION. www.merriam-webster.com, 29 Aug. 2022, www.merriam-webster.com/dictionary/nonfiction.

CHAPTER 14

The Immigrant Experiences in Jhumpa Lahiri's Stories in *Unaccustomed Earth*

Dr Tejendra Singh Shiv

Unaccustomed Earth (2008) is Jhumpa Lahiri's second collection of short stories. Stories in this collection deal with the lives of immigrant Bengalis and their American-born children, who struggle with tangled filial relationships and the unending requirement of parenthood. They shuttle between two cultural milieus developing capabilities to negotiate several worlds. The three interrelated stories, titled 'Hema and Kaushik,' which are more emotionally complex and skilfully woven. The stories are beautiful example of Lahiri's insight into the minds and hearts of her immigrant characters. Stories deals with the intricacies of the lives of the expatriates who navigates between diverse cultural groups and the nuances of immigrant psychology. Lahiri interprets the maladies in her protagonists entangled in multiple relationships. The Diaspora experience of the central characters also focuses on their sense of exile, alienation, and uprootedness. All the stories deal with the theme of uprooting and assimilation with the efforts made to establish connectivity among the characters.

In all the stories in *Unaccustomed Earth* Jhumpa Lahiri applies the metaphor based on the epigraph from Nathaniel Hawthorne's:

> The Custom-House which reads "Human nature will not flourish, any more than a potato, if it be planted and replanted, for too long a series of generations, in the same worn-out soil. My children have had other birth places, and, so far as their fortunes may be within my control, shall sterile their roots into unaccustomed earth (Lahiri ix).

Hawthorne suggests that transplanting people into new soil of unaccustomed earth makes them flourish better as they become hardier.

The story '*Unaccustomed* Earth' contains the narrative of the inner conflict of an Indian-American woman, Ruma, who is married and is about to have her second child, when she is visited by her father, an Indian retiree, in her new home in Seattle. The visit brings about a myriad of feelings, bringing back old resentments and a deep reflection on her relationship with her past. As in her previous books, Jhumpa Lahiri's characters are immigrants from India and their American-reared children. As far as first-generation Diasporic people are concerned, they feel like fully grown trees that get uprooted; they are born and brought up in India, and moved to an alien land leaving their homeland, because of some economic, political or marital reasons. There is always a dilemma between their longing for homeland and belonging to the newly adopted land. They want to belong to both the lands. There remains a constant conflict between the two. In the case of second-generation Diaspora characters, they are no way Indian but their Indian heritage captures their psyche to be a part of Indian traditions. They are born and brought up in America; they have to follow the Indian norms inside the house and American norms outside the house. This kind of difference in the condition of first – and second-generation Diaspora people creates a dichotomy in their relationships. It is a well-documented fact among social scientists and migration studies scholars that second-generation immigrants develop a number of ties with the host society that make their experience of their identity utterly different from that of their parents.

Lahiri adeptly scrutinises the minute details of all types of relationships such as father-daughter, grandfather-grandson, sister-brother, and husband-wife. The title of the story 'Unaccustomed Earth' very aptly displays the dichotomous relationship of the immigrant father and daughter. In this story the father tries his best to get the unaccustomed earth, accustomed to his daughter, by renewing the old ties and forging new ties with her and her son Akash; the son's name means 'infinite', it is very symbolic of his multicultural and borderless identity.

Thus, on the surface their relationship seems to be dichotomous but it is also complementary to each other. Both of them feel the same kind of dilemmatic situation while adjusting themselves in an alien land. In the course of the story the father-daughter relationship undergoes a drastic transformation from stranger to very close to each other, and yet again they are depicted as strangers.

The story with the hyphenated title 'Hell-Heaven' deals with the heaven which turns to a hell, just because of the arrival of a distance cousin of Usha's mother. The story centres on a daughter who observes keenly the relationship between her mother and Pranab Kaku, the marriage between Pranab and Deborah, and the break up that happens later. The story presents the struggle between the American way of life, how the parents struggle to preserve the Bengali culture within the family and also within the circle of their family get-together and parties.

The young Usha is the narrator of the story, Usha the child belongs to the second generation of immigrants is in a better position to bridge the gap between the cultural differences of the two worlds – Indian and American. She is in the midst of her in – between life in America is best to bridge the gap of the two homelands.

The story takes place in the early 1970s when Pranab Chakraborty, a Bengali from Calcutta, becomes a family friend of her parents. The familiarity built up in relationship led to great nearness between them. Usha was told to address him Kaku, like her father's younger brother. Pranab in his turn politely addressed Usha's parents Da elder brother and Boudi sister-in-law.

The family has a diasporic existence. Usha's family had been living in the Central Square for the past three years, prior to which they were in Berlin where Usha was born and her father had completed his training in microbiology. After getting arranged marriage in India her parents migrated to the west seeking better job opportunities.

Usha began to become fond of him and looked forward to his visits as he entertained her with his tricks. It was his hobby to take photographs and he took the opportunity to take pictures of the three of them together. In the beginning her mother made it a point to receive him only when Usha was around. But in course of time, he spent time alone with her mother and was developing deep intimacy with him. They shared several interests unlike between her parents, like music, film, politics and poetry. Since Usha's mother and Pranab came from the same neighbourhood in Calcutta, they shared many familiar interests. This indicates that Diaspora yearning in people striving to find affinity in dispersal. Pranab plays the role of a younger brother; he found it easy to draw sympathy from Boudi. Jhumpa Lahiri focuses on the drift in relationships between Usha's parents that gave the intruder his trump card. Usha lists out the differences between her father and Pranab Kaku: "My father was thirty-seven then, nine years older than my mother. Pranab Kaku was twenty-five. My father was a lover of silence and solitude. . . He was wedded to his work, his research, and he existed in a shell that neither my mother nor I could penetrate" (65).

Usha's father was glad Pranab frequented the family and gave pleasing company to his nostalgic wife who missed her life in India. The diasporic predicament is brought to focus very deftly by Lahiri, probing the thoughts of her characters. The development in the emotional relationship between Pranab and Boudi deepened after Pranab bought a Volkawagen Beetle and began to take them out for rides and picnics to Walden Pond. Usha began to notice the growing love relationship between the two as she says, "It is clear to me now that my mother was in love with him. He wooed her as no other man had, with the innocent affection of a brother-in-law" (67).

The happy emotional relationship was growing between Pranab and Boudi was disturbed by the entry of Deborah, the American girl who began to accompany him. The growing jealousy of `Usha's mother is seen in her indifference and finding fault with her spotted face and small hips. Ushas's mother had no good opinion of Deborah and began complaining about the changed attitude of Pranab terming the difference 'hell-heaven' (68). Through the title of the story derived from this statement, Lahiri takes her readers into the core of human emotions and searches for identity in relationships. In contrast to the emotional turbulence and resentment in her mother, Usha began to find in Deborah an intimate friend with whom she could be herself.

The Pranab – Deborah relationship started to grow and by summer he wanted to put a diamond ring on her hand, but Boudi refused the offer. This again indicated that the psychological trauma Usha's mother was undergoing after she felt that Pranab was getting more and more distanced from her. Her frustration in losing his affection is shown in the way she broke the tea cup Pranab used as an ashtray. In the process she also hurt herself cutting her palm. Emotional frustration lets her lacerate herself, finding solace in self-inflicted pain.

Pranab's parents were upset about his marriage to an American girl as they had already arranged a girl for him in Calcutta. Though, he had requested Usha's parents to speak on his behalf about

Deborah as a decent girl. Boudi refrained from doing that Pranab's parents were upset with Boudi for not having intervened and terminated the growing affairs between Pranab and Deborah.

The special dinner Usha's mother prepared only for Pranab a few days before his wedding is noteworthy, and the way she touched him. Usha recalls: "My mother stands beside him, one hand placed on top of his head in a gesture of blessing, the first and last time she was to touch him in her life" (73). In her frustration she constantly told her friends that Deborah would leave him and so he was literally "throwing his life away" (73).

The story moves forward several years when Usha 's parents were invited for a Thanksgiving Party at Pranab's home where all Deborah 's kith and kin were present including her brother Matty with whom Usha had danced and developed some closeness. After grace before meals Deborah's father raised toast to the "Thanks giving with the Indians" (78). The most touching moment came when Pranab stood up to narrate his story in America meeting Usha and her mother who made all the differences in his life. "He walked around the room to where my mother was sitting and draped lanky arm around her shoulder, forcing her, for a brief moment to stand up. . . this woman hosted my first real Thanks giving in America ...If it weren't for that meal, I would have gone back to Calcutta" (79). Emotionally moved, he went to Deborah to tell her that it was such an experience that made him marry her.

Lahiri goes forward in time fourteen years later to tell how Pranab and Deborah divorced as had been predicted by Usha's mother "It was he who had strayed, falling in love with a married Bengali woman, destroying two families in the process" (81).

It is to Usha's mother that Deborah turned to for comfort in her grief. Both of their hearts have been broken by Pranab. Usha's mother had learnt the lesson and her old age drew closer to her husband out of sheer habit. Usha recalled: "I noticed warmth between my parents that had not been there before, a quite teasing solidarity, a concern when one of them fell ill" (81). Usha also got reconciled with her mother who began to respect her identity as a child of America. She had no choice but to accept the fact that Usha dated several American men. One turning point in her mother's life was her taking a degree in library science while in her fifties, to fill the void in her life.

The moving story brings to focus predicament of individuals seeking to establish their identity in Diaspora, seeking emotional fulfilment. A stranger like Mrs. Holcomb, who is far removed from Usha's mother, becomes central to saving her life. Identity is relationship is established in different ways by the various characters.

The story presents that the individuals are caught in between conflicts of family relationships and cultural traditions. They try to establish their individual identities in a new milieu, experiencing at the same time the sense of displacement, alienation, and isolation. These individuals, caught up in the confusion of their migrant lives, need to get connected to family and friends for emotional fulfilment. There is acculturation of the characters in the story in the most cases but some characters remain victims of contra acculturation, longing for their own Bengali culture.

In this connection A. J. Sabastian comments that:

> The story reveals certain facts behind the lives of Indian immigrants in America in pursuits of identity and happiness. Victims of economic exile, they need to live in between the cultures of their homeland and adopted home, striking roots in the unaccustomed earth as they come up with their interpersonal relationships (101).

Work Cited

Agrawal, Beena. "Jhumpa Lahiri's Unaccustomed Earth: Celebration of Indian Sensibility" *The Indian Journal of English Studies* Ed. Suman Bala Vol XLVII, 2010.

Hemlata. "Dichtomy and Dilemma: A study of father daughter relationship in Jhup Lahiri's Unaccustomed Earth" Language in India Oct. 2013. Literature Resource Centre 21 March 2015 Web.

Kakar Sudhir . *Feminine Identity in India* New Delhi: Oxford University Press, 1988.

........., "The Indian Psyche" New Delhi: Oxford University Press. 2002.

Lahiri, Jhumpa. *Unaccustomed Earth* New Delhi: Random House India, 2008. All the Textual citations refer to this edition.

Mukherjee, Subhashree. "Cross Cultural Differences and Cross-Border Relationships in Jhumpa Lahiri's Unaccustomed Earth." *On the Alien A Study of Jhumpa Lahiri and Bharti Mukherjee.*, Ed. Jaydeep Sarangi New Delhi: GNOSIS Publication, 2010.

Sebastian, A. J. "Jhumpa Lahiri Interpreting Maladies" *Dynamics of Culture in Diaspora In Jhumpa Lahiri.* Ed. Nigmanda Das. New Delhi: Adhyayan Publishers and Distributors, 2010.

........., "Interpersonal Relationships in Jhumpa Lahiri's Hell-Heaven" *Dynamics of Culture in Diaspora In Jhumpa Lahiri* . Ed Nigmanda Das. New Delhi: Adhyayan Publishers and Distributors, 2010.

Lahiri . Ed Nigmanda Das. New Delhi: Adhyayan Publishers and Distributors 2010.

Singh, Marjit. *Contemporary Diasporic Literature: Writing History, Culture Self.* New Delhi: Pencraft International, 2007.

CHAPTER 15

Replication of Facts and Imitation of Biblical Allusions in Margaret Atwood's *The Handmaid's Tale*

Rajeshwari S and Meenakshi S

This research seeks to analyse Margaret Atwood's dystopian novel *The Handmaid's Tale* in terms of its actual history and biblical allusions (1985). In this particular study, the researchers employed the qualitative research approach. This study made use of an exploratory research technique to further develop the ideas of the researchers. It helps in the discovery of new knowledge that might lead to a solution to the situation that is being faced. The explorative method investigates novel ideas and contributes to the elaboration of a comprehensive list of potential responses to a challenge. *The Handmaid's Tale* is a story set in a dystopian future that contains important psychological overtones. The only way to properly understand these undertones is through psychoanalysis. The application of biblical concepts to the work under investigation was the primary emphasis of this study. In order to help achieve this goal, relevant passages from the book and the points of view of several other Bible stories have been added.

Margaret Eleanor Atwood is a famous Canadian author. Her father was an entomologist and her mother was a dietician. She chose to become a writer when she was sixteen years old. She went to Victoria College at the University of Toronto and got her bachelor's degree in English. Her first collection of poems, *Double Persephone,* came out in 1961. In 1962, she got her master's degree from Radcliffe College. She was working as an author and teacher. Several awards have been given to her. "Margaret Atwood is known for writing books that are easy to understand." (DiBenedetto) Readers often go to the official Margaret Atwood web pages, which are run by Atwood herself.

The Handmaid's Tale is the story of a woman named Offred who has been captured by the totalitarians and sentenced to a life of suffering in the Republic of Gilead, once known as the United States. Nearly every woman has encountered the same horrors. Atwood talks about how Offred uses her voice to change Gilead, a dystopian future theocracy. The government of Gilead is totalitarian, with the state in charge of everything, even people's thoughts. "... there are no children... doctors, attorneys, university professors... such freedom now seems almost weightless" (Atwood). Offred is one of the women who the government plans to recruit as handmaids in government leaders' houses only for the purpose of child procreation. At the Red Centre, where she is being prepared to be a handmaid (Atwood), Offred learns that "the republic of Gilead has no boundaries."(Shah and Khoso) They are required to alter their names at each new location to "Of" followed by the first name of their new commander. For example, June changed her identity to Offred after approaching the residence of Commander Fred Waterford. Their headgear, which consists of a white bonnet that covers both sides of their faces, and "wings," which are brilliant red robes, make up the rest of their costume.

Research Methodology

The researchers examined the facts and biblical elements in *The Handmaid's Tale* by Margaret Atwood. Researchers did this by using a method called qualitative research. The exploratory research method is used to find out more about a topic that wasn't clearly explained in the last study. For the investigation, researchers used information from a wide range of secondary sources. The exploratory research method was used in this study to help the researchers build on their first ideas. Explorative research helps to find all possible solutions to a problem by coming up with new ideas, which is useful in many situations. Researchers use this method to figure out what their most important parts are. Exploratory research can be done in two ways: primary research and secondary research. Primary research is the first type of exploratory research. When doing primary research, it's important to get information directly from the topic itself. Interviews, observation, focus groups, and questionnaires are all examples of these kinds of methods. Secondary research, on the other hand, usually looks at problems we already know about, such as through literature reviews of published research results.

Results and Discussions

Battle of Infertility

In the book, the handmaids are assigned to bear a child for elite couples. High-ranking men force handmaids to have children after they have been raped in a ritualistic way. They treated it as a ritual ceremony. The children are then raised by the wives and commanders while the handmaids move to another family.

The Rachel and Leah Center in Gilead is where the handmaids learn how to do their jobs. The Rachel and Leah centre is also called the "Red Center." The name was borrowed from the Old Testament.

The stories of Rachel and her sister Leah, who both married Jacob in the Old Testament, are told directly in the middle. Rachel couldn't get pregnant, but Leah had no trouble having children. Rachel was so upset that she gave her servant Bilhah to Jacob as a "vessel" to help her have children. Bilhah had two sons, and Rachel gave both of them names. (Regalado)

The story is the basis not only for the handmaids' job as "breeders," but also for the whole idea of how Gilead came to be. ("Bible Gateway Passage") In Atwood's dystopian novel, Sons of Jacob is the name of the group that took over the government of the United States and set up Gilead. The Sons of Jacob are the men who participated in the effort to establish the Republic of Gilead and who currently hold positions of authority within that nation.

Biblical Phrases

"May the fruit be blessed", "May the Lord Make a Way". These are the biblical lines used by handmaids while greeting one another by using the words from the bible.

The handmaids are forced to say certain greetings to each other and to other people in Gilead. These greetings have become famous because of the show, but they can also be found in the Bible. The words can be found in Deuteronomy 28 as part of the Blessings of Obedience. They are meant to encourage faithful followers to have plenty. The passage says that those who "listen to the voice of the Lord, your God," will be blessed. "Blessed is the fruit of your womb" (Deuteronomy 28:4, New American Bible) and "The Lord will open for you" (Deuteronomy 28:12) come next. (Regalado)

"Blessed be the fruit" is a greeting from the folks of Gilead. It is also mentioned in the Bible as a way to help people have children, which is one of the most important things for commanders and their wives.(Bakkila) The traditional answer to "blessed be the fruit" is "May the Lord open." It sounds like they are requesting God to make handmaids have children. "Under His Eye" is also another Biblical reference meant to be used as a greeting or goodbye (Bakkila). "Praise be" is a phrase that people use when they are happy or appreciative of anything, such as the weather or the news of a pregnancy. (*Old Testament*)

The rise of the Christian right in The Handmaid's Tale draws from American history.

The red robes worn by the handmaids were designed using ideas taken from a variety of sources, such as the clothing worn by puritanical women in the 17th century and the habits worn by Catholic nuns.(Dray)

The reality that religious clothing can and still be forced upon women by authorities in other, more conservative societies is, however, a more significant issue. The Amish, for example, require women to wear long gowns made of dark textiles and head coverings on a daily basis. And the FLDS Church, which is a highly rigid branch of Mormonism, only permits women to wear loose-fitting (and modest) skirts, trousers, or dresses in different colours of blue. Additionally, all of the ladies in the FLDS Church keep their hair in the same kind of ponytail. Atwood utilised history, particularly the Puritan theocracy in America in the 1700s and the political context in the United States in the early 1980s, to demonstrate in *The Handmaid's Tale* how the religious right might be in command.

The United States of America was not established in the 18th century as an enlightened republic. During the 1600s, it functioned as a theocracy at first. In an interview with Indigo that took place in 2017, Atwood said, "This inclination keeps coming back up in America."

She also states that the work was inspired by the emergence of Christian conservatism in the United States as well as the election of Ronald Reagan as president of the United States. In fact, President

Reagan was the first president to make a proposal to modify the Constitution in order to reinstate organised prayer in public schools. This change would allow students to pray in front of the class. This took place in the year 1981. When Ronald Reagan was vying for politics and after he was elected president, he maintained strong relationships with religiously-inspired political organisations such as the Moral Majority and Focus on the Family. When these political factions briefly held power, there was widespread concern that they would make it more difficult for women to get abortions.

It is important to realise that this part of *The Handmaid's Tale* still has an effect on people in the modern world. (Jadwin) Since Donald Trump was elected president in 2016 and conservatives have gotten more power under his administration, there is renewed concern about the Roe v. Wade decision and other rules about abortion. This year, *The Handmaid's Tale* has led to protests against anti-abortion bills in Texas and Missouri, among other places.

The novel by Margaret Atwood is set in a dystopian America of the future, where there is a violent totalitarian regime and women no longer have any rights. (Lambert)In the novel, most of the people have become infertile, so the few fertile women left are taken and given to the higher class men in society as "handmaids" so they can have children.("'Handmaid's Tale' Protest at US Ohio Abortion Bill")

Conclusion

Even though *The Handmaid's Tale* is set in a totalitarian dystopia, it is still science fiction and talks about the present condition of society. The book is full of religious and political history in almost every way. Margaret Atwood has talked at length about how she used real events from around the world to create the world of Gilead and the terrible things that happen there. Its real-life roots are also a big reason why the book is still important more than 30 years after it was first published.

Works Cited

Bakkila, Blake. "This Is What Characters Mean When They Say 'Blessed Be the Fruit' in 'Handmaid's Tale.'" *Good Housekeeping,* 23 Apr. 2021, https://www.goodhousekeeping.com/life/entertainment/a27614328/blessed-be-the-fruit-handmaids-tale-sayings-meaning/.

"Bible Gateway Passage: Genesis 29 – English Standard Version." *Bible Gateway*, https://www.biblegateway.com/passage/?search=Genesis%2029&version=ESV. Accessed 26 May 2022.

DiBenedetto, Tamra Elizabeth. *The Role of Language in Constructing Consciousness in Margaret Atwood's The Handmaid's Tale*. p. 120.

Dray, Kayleigh. "The Handmaid's Tale Was Inspired by These Horrific True Stories." *Stylist*, 1 June 2021, https://www.stylist.co.uk/books/handmaids-tale-true-story/130001.

"'Handmaid's Tale' Protest at US Ohio Abortion Bill." *BBC News*, 13 June 2017. *www.bbc.com*, https://www.bbc.com/news/world-us-canada-40264004.

Jadwin, Lisa. *Margaret Atwood's The Handmaid's Tale (1985): Cultural and Historical Context*. Jan. 2009.

Lambert, Courtney. "Margaret Atwood on What 'The Handmaid's Tale' Means in the Age of Trump – The New York Times." *The New York Times*, p. 9.

Old Testament. https://www.churchofjesuschrist.org/study/eng/scriptures/ot/_manifest. Accessed 26 May 2022.

Regalado, Michelle. "9 Nightmarish Things in 'The Handmaid's Tale' Inspired by History." *Insider*, https://www.insider.com/handmaids-tale-based-on-real-world-origins-history-events-2019-8. Accessed 26 May 2022.

Shah, Sayed Razak Amin, and Muhammad Hassan Khoso. *Freudian Analysis of "The Handmaid's Tale": Analyzing the Defense Mechanisms*. p. 6.

CHAPTER 16

Comparative Study of William Dalrymple and Bill Aitken

Shruti Mishra

Introduction

Abstract

This paper aims to analyse the literary representation of India as an idea in travel writing through the selected works of eminent authors Bill Aitken and William Dalrymple. The paper studies the perception of India among the non-native authors and the outsiders in general. The objective of the paper is to trace the differences in the perception of India for the two authors belonging to a similar ethnic, cultural and academic background (William Dalrymple and Bill Aitken are Scottish nationals who write about India). The authors have their expressed their views regarding various aspects of India, which has been brought into usage to find a pattern in their particular understanding of India as a country, an incomprehensible civilisation and a heavily stereotyped subject of the West. The paper discusses the description of the architecture, sexual minorities, the British imperialism, religion and the ordinary life of Indian people in general.

Keywords: Stereotype, transgender, rep tape, bureaucracy, British imperialism, foreigner, Himalaya, India, Faith and archetype.

William Dalrymple is Scottish historian, writer, art historian, curator, proclaimed broadcaster and critic. He is a prolific writer with numerous works to his credit such as In Xanadu, City of Djinns: A Year in Delhi, From the Holy Mountain: A Journey in the Shadow of Byzantium, The Age of Kali, The White Mughals; The Writer's Eye and The Anarchy: The Relentless Rise of East India Company. The author has t been conferred with the Duff Cooper Memorial Prize, the Thomas Cook Travel Book Award, the Sunday Times Young British Writer of the Year Award, the Hemingway, the Kapuściński and the Wolfson Prizes. He has been five times long listed and once shortlisted for the Samuel Johnson Prize for non-fiction. He is also one of the co-founders and co-directors of the annual Jaipur

Literature Festival. In The City of Djinns William Dalrymple creates a living tapestry of India, which successfully reimagines the surrealistic imagery of a typical Indian scene. The author is a master picture painter who is magical in his vividness and honest accuracy of representation. He constantly makes the Indian reader aware of the inconspicuous details of sundry things that often get lost in the curves of routine and monotonous life. By de-familiarizing the familiar he brings us closer to the ignored object and makes it a new subject of perception. The world, which Dalrymple presents, is not an alien one but the old world in new colors or from a different façade, which only the mind untouched by the native and cultural influences can possibly reach.

The technique used by the author is a unique potpourri of fantastical storytelling, historical facts and personal anecdotes that engulfs the unsuspecting reader into a whirlpool sucking him deeper with every word. The enmeshed reader cannot separate himself from the storytelling. Dalrymple takes an unusual take on narration, which deviates sharply from the conventional travel writing and narration in general. Sheikh Sana Mariyam in her article Treatment of History in William Dalrymple's Works states –

> "City of Djinns is categorized as a travelogue with a tinge of history but it seems to be more of a personal memoir. The complex structure of the book holds together an unusual blend of history and travel experience. Dalrymple's other texts are more confined in their structure and can be neatly categorized as a travelogue or history book."

The author digresses consistently into personal anecdotes, while throwing historical facts in the manner of fictional storytelling often adding his own comments and imagination to the whole. The author is able to present a plethora of descriptions ranging from the failure of the Indian bureaucratic system, the sensational secrecy of the Indian transgender community, British architectural and cultural heritage. The author's hybrid method makes it imperative that he gets ample opportunity to express all his ideas free from the constraints of the conventionalities of travel writing. Monika Jain writes in her article "Imperialist Nostalgia and Orientalist Vision IN William Dalrymple's City of Djinns" –

> *"City of Djinns'* geographical location gives Dalrymple the space for a brief, anecdotal treatment of Indian history. Instead of an in-depth consideration of Delhi as a travel destination, or a concentrated study of its history, Dalrymple opts for an approach that uses elements of both. This hybrid model enables a selective, piecemeal approach. This assists in

> the maintenance of a sense of the positive contributions of the British to India. Despite the work's historical focus, *City of Djinns* is still careful to remain identifiable as a travel book. The text achieves this identification through specific gestures towards typical travel tales, such as William's encounters with Indian bureaucracy and "great glistening cocoons of red tape" regardless of the grounded nature of the narrative."

The author betrays a sense of sympathy to the former British rulers who were rushed into oblivious existence among the unkempt ruins of the architectural British heritage. Although the author tries to keep an unattached manner of characterization the author inevitably and quite naturally slips into the trap of rooting one opinion against the other, one rule against the other and consequently one race against the other. The author mourns the lack of influence the Victorian England could leave on the modern India, which has quickly shrugged off any imperialist imprint of the former rule. The author is unable to comprehend and therefore mourns the inability of the Indians to embrace the wonders of the Victorian England. The imperialist tendency displayed by the author is remarkable. Rebecca Dorgelo in her article Travelling into History: The Travel Writing and Narrative history of William Dalrymple states:

> "Throughout *City of Djinns*, William is represented as a contemporary iteration of nostalgically-portrayed British colonisers. This characterisation, in concert with a number of arguments throughout the text, is an opportunity to representt Britain's imperial relationship with India in a personable, friendly manner. This re-enactment of British / Indian colonial history overlays a complex and conflict-ridden past with an easy narrative of progress, civility and cultural exchange. While such elements form part of the history of the British annexation of India, contemporary texts that exclusively take such a line form a nostalgic, limited representation. These portrayals have the potential to perform their own kind of colonisation, settling in popular (Western) consciousness and impacting on perceptions of imperialism and cross-cultural relations past and present." (Dorgelo, 64)

There is an Orientalist bending is revealed at the borders of Dalrymple's imperialist justification and British reasoning. He is an excellent historian but he cannot help but betray his own prejudices, which are very prominent in certain instances. For Instance he ruthlessly castigates the unlucky genius of Girish Karnad's play Tuglaq. The poignant but unusual intellectual is rubbished as plain, flat character in history only remarkable for his Draconian laws and inhumane spectacle of famous royal persecutions. The author marvels at the remnants of British architecture. He subtly justifies the

British imperialism by showing the disarray of the contemporary Indian administration and corruption of the bureaucracy thus, indirectly suggesting the impact of the loss of the British presence. Indeed the book is filled with nuances, which prove this stance. The author presents the reconciliatory side of the British rule through his description of the British Officer Skinner who he presents as a martyr in the sacrificial fire of British benevolence ruthlessly overlooked by the Indian counterparts.

According to Shodhganga –

> "Dalrymple insists that Britishers have contributed to the progress and development of India by introducing new ideas and building beautiful monuments. He seems to be captivated by the magnificent surrounding of Lutyen's bungalow and gives a detailed account of the British architecture. Thus, indirectly he shows the contribution of British to the architectural development of the country."

Futhermore in his acknowledgement to The City of Djinns he writes-

> "One of the most beautiful legacies of India's colonial past the bungalows of New Delhi designed by Edwin Lutyens – have largely gone: all those in private hands have been destroyed in the welter of demolitions that took place between 1990 and 2000."

He ventures carefully through the Indian subcontinent but not without his own baggage of hierarchy and perception. He infuses humor in his work but sadly most of his wit is lost in establishing the lingual hierarchy of the English language. India always remains an "exotic" land in the eyes of the author. Jan Morris claims Dalrymple to be a voyeur and not an actual participant of the narration. Indeed we rarely witness the author immersed in the story. He always remains an outsider in an exciting story he has been retelling but still not able to grasp it. She says in her Book Review/Swashbuckle and Decay in an Ancient City: City of Djinns –

> "Dalrymple is anything but a voyeur, though. Even his excursions into the worlds of the eunuchs are conducted with courteous and engaging sympathy, and he surveys the multitudinous religious rites of Delhi, so esoteric to alien eyes, sometimes indeed so repulsive, with a grave kind of innocence. He is more a pilgrim than an observer, trying always to understand, and if at the end of the book he seems no nearer enlightenment, perhaps that is the fate of most pilgrims. He rounds the work off with another improbable experience, this time a historico-mythical insight of his own supposed to have occurred to him on the very day he was leaving for Britain; but the suggestion of fiction that attaches itself to this concluding tale, unjustly – perhaps it really did dawn on him

that last morning? – only adds to the effect of an earnest and somehow childlike conquest."

The quintessential meeting with the furtively secretive transgender community, the lecherous Indian Punjabi with the broken English phrases, the description of exotic religious rituals and seductive wordplay when discussing the mythology of India are all what form the outline of the work. However, the author works hard to research and discover the details of the historical artifacts often visiting the site personally and examining for him. The author is to Delhi and India in general a suspicious admirer who is dazzled by the golden brocade of spirituality and exoticism but abhors the blemishes he sees as he moves closer, rushing to know but not able to comprehend the ever ending mystery that is India. The contradictions whirl his wit into illusions he can never make sense of. The smell is addictive, the flavor a bit too strong and the misplaced sense of imperial colonial belonging shattered in the labyrinth of Indian culture.

Bill Aitken was born in Scotland in 1934. He is a naturalized citizen of India since 1972. He has written extensively about India and particularly the Himalayas, which depict his unparalleled love for the mountain range and the countrymen. The author has many a great work of travel writing to his credit. His repertoire include Seven Sacred River, Exploring Indian Railways, The Nanda Devi Affair, Branch line into Eternity, Diving the Deccan: A Motorbike to the Heart of India and Footloose in the Himalayas. The author has investigative spirit by default and an irreparable love for detail, which fall from the brim of his works like a cascade from an eternal water source. Bill Aitken swerves carefully along the edges of the Indian without falling into the hypnotic gorge of the archetypical oriental tapestry, which is abundant in the Indian milieu and almost difficult for the traveller to avoid. It maybe imperative to point out that the balanced writing of Aitken points out to his own tranquility and clearness of mind. Indeed the difficulty of the task can be stretched so far as to say how even the native denizen fails to express India in all its essence without muddling the few instances of true experience with the stereotypes that have been fed them all their lives. The ability of the author as a foreigner to learn without grudges and with an adopted understanding is exemplary. The author puts forward his intent through his Preface where he clears for the reader the true purpose of his writing and his infallible love for climbing and the Himalayas. He says-

> "The aim of recollecting these vintage walks is to try and hint at the timeless sublimity of the Himalayas even in its lower reaches. Perhaps the Himalaya is more important for the peak experiences it delivers than the peaks themselves."

The author writes autobiographically and even being confessional at certain instances. For instance he confesses to being a "callow" traveller, "a jilted lover", and an amateur Indian guest looking for an "exotic truth". However, through the passage of time his journey changes, as does his destiny. The author traveller is floundered by two pathways, which lay muddled before him: either be consumed by the seductive exoticism of oriental imagination or be repelled by the disenchantment with the crudeness of reality. Although the unsuspecting Scottish outsider does surface during intervals of reconciliation with the Indian scenario, these intervals are insignificant and rarely frequent. The author wisely uses Hindi and Urdu phraseology and words to lend legitimacy to his expression but he is cautious not to be consumed by the mystical toxicity of the words. He is warlock who enters the Enchanted but manages to remain unfazed by the vapors of the land. The author says:

> "In the garb of the Himalaya they reflect the Purmananda of the soul reunited briefly with the architect of the universe."

The usage of the words is neither superficial nor shallow. The author is an avid learner who is not preoccupied with getting too much into the meaning of things but tries to accept his surroundings thereby becoming a part of his environment. Aitken is an avid nature and mountain lover, which is betrayed by his detailed analysis of the ecological degradation. The natural beauty of the mountains smites the author. The author becomes an active participant of the narration and doesn't shy away from assisting in preservation of the environment around him. He writes:

> "The City board put constant hurdles in my way and on one occasion fines me two hundred rupees when I removed a dead tree trunk in order to make space for new saplings. The dread trunk had been marked for clearing by the forest department but the clearance to fell from the City Board had not come even as the planting season was due to expire. The babu who fined me seemed delighted at having stopped me planting new trees."

According to Dr Gunmeet Kaur Alhuwalia:

> "Aitken does not like commercializing nature. He is strongly against the modern climbing of peaks for commercial gains and petty rewards. He is disturbed by the rubbish dumped by the dhabas and the people in the forest. He feels:
>
> Responsible Trekking involves keeping our eyes open to every aspect of environmental health and treading with a respect for the ecosystem and the cultural traditions that have grown out of it. Trekker and mountain are both growing together and a sense of this living relationship is what Himalayan travel ideally ought to inspire. (Aitken 249)"

The traveller provides constructive criticism about the surroundings. He comments sharply on the red tape, bureaucratic corruption and the exploitation of the impoverished by the political forces. He states:

> "The degradation was so appalling and then involvement of prominent people so embarrassing that public complaints reached the Rajya Sabha in Delhi. It was reported that even the Commissioner of the division and his family were involved in gattoo plying."

The author displays the tenacity of a traveller and the blunt practicality of a mountaineer. The author works upon his words in a kind of positive transition wherein he begins with a certain instance and late displacing the same with a new acquired understanding. For instance he talks about his first experience with the Indian tea "chai" which is unbearable to him formerly bit gradually he becomes used to its strong flavor as he acquires the correct technique to enjoy it. He says:

> "In those days it came served in a small silvered brass beaker, blisteringly hot and sickeningly sweet. The trick was to hold the beaker in a second looser vessel and allow some of the heat to disperse. When one is tired this chai-found the whole length of the Himalaya-is the best pick-me-up I know of. It affords instant energy and acts like an intravenous injection on the jaded bloodstream."

The author keeps transforming into a pilgrimage, a mountain lover, a foreigner, a native resident, an outsider and a practical statistician as he records the precise details of the distance, length and biological or ecological anatomy of the places he visits. It is heartening to see the humanizing reconciliation of the traveller with his surroundings. He is in love with India and the Himalayas not the mere idea of the India he has witnessed as a wild overgrowth from the western books, media and archetypical ideas in his mind. The India that lives in his mind is not an ancient one with ruins of oriental spirituality but an unromantic one, which reels under overpopulation and pollution but still manages to give a carefree smile. He states:

> "The Himalaya is all about these extremes. Its weather, terrain and ecology switch drastically in a short span. Gentle slopes of inflammable pine end abruptly at a precipice on which the sun's rays hardly ever play. The cold, dank, steep northern face hosts springs in dramatic contrast to the arid southern side. Which of these two sides of the mountain is the true Himalaya? The answer is – both. Along with the glory of the shinning summit we have somehow to square the squalor o the human condition lower on the mountainside."

The author is on a myth busting expedition contemplating, philosophizing and admonishing. He says:

> "A lesson my first trek taught me was how bare and wretched human experience is amidst so much uplifting beauty. The most common perception about Himalaya was exploded for me at the outset the nobility and inspiration the great range has on our psyche is only part of the reality. The full reality includes the crud hovels where one's fellows live, little better than cattle they labor over, feeding, milking and mucking out."

Aitken is excellent at comprehending and correlating the human emotions and honoring the sentimentality of the native as a foreigner. For instance he remarks:

> "Many foreigners find the preoccupation of Himalayan villagers with bhut-pret superstition to be assign of arrested spiritual development but having grown up in a Scottish village where the belief in fairies and other psychic phenomenon is very real (though never publicly acknowledged) O could detect familiar pattern."

There is indeed a certain sense of brooding nostalgia in the lines that smell of home and Scotland. The author keeps going back to his home through the glorification of the pastoral and rustic life. He keeps revisiting the memories by relapsing back in time through the sylvan woods of the Himalayas. The traveller becomes a philosopher and finally a wayward child finally returning home to the familiar memories of rustic simplicity, warm hearth, Scottish practicality and the hardships of survival. Dr. Gunmeet Kaur Ahluwalia in his article "Changes and the Importance of Sustainable Development as Reflected in the Works of Some Famous Writers"says:

> "In his book, *Footloose in the Himalaya* he writes in Chapter One: The Call of the Mountains: "Mountains have always mattered deeply to me. I was born and brought up at the foot of the Ochil Hills in Scotland and was daily ravished by their green and craggy grandeur. I longed to live among such exalted beauty . . ."(1).When he took abode in a house called Oakless in Mussooorie, he felt that his cherished childhood dream had changed into reality."

The author is able to instill humor in the text without belittling the people. In fact he confesses to having become a naturalized inhabitant of the place. He says:

> "I had to accept that having lived for twenty years in Uttarakhand I had become part of the region's culture and judged other cultures accordingly."

Bill Aitken and William Dalrymple share the similar kind of love, attachment and acquaintance with the Indian landscape and its people. However, their experiences differ in multitude, fashion of interpretation and their responses to the challenges thrown by the extreme Indian living conditions. The authors belong to the Scottish fabric of origin and had early acquaintance with the idea of India, which he decided to venture on their own. William Dalrymple has tried to bind the Indian experience through the thread of historical facts and personal anecdotes while Bill Aitken adopts the philosophizing tone of a traveller who ventures into the very being of his existence, the mountains. Both the authors share the same kind of affection and attachment with the subcontinent. They have tried to express their own experiences of India through their works, which speak for itself. Dalrymple and Aitken discuss the attitude of Indian society on different sexual orientations and identities.

The authors share multitude of similarities apart from their nationalities, love for India and the spirit of travelling and exploring. For instance while Dalrymple tries hard but fails to avoid the discreet line of orientalist stereotyping, Aitken is able to achieve this. He moves easily through the lines of vivid expression without giving in to the seduction of stereotyping. However, his work is also remarkable for his blunt criticism of the hypocrisy and ignorance he finds in India. The author is through and through an authentic traveller who has no qualms about admonishing what he feels is not right. For instance he says:

> "While I could not deny the genuine atmosphere of devotion for the river goddess Ganga Mai I was irritated by all the talk of spiritual purity by people who excreted into the very river whose water they drank claiming it held magical properties, the queued up at the ashram dispensary for pills to cure their dysentery. Whatever else popular faith in the Himalaya was known for it certainly wasn't amenable to the cold logic of the mind."

The author breaks the double-faced religious pretentiousness of the people by clearly stating what he saw. The author is clear in the intent when he says that there was indeed some genuine faith while the rest was pure superstition and ignorant faith. Dalrymple discusses the plight of trans genders or the Hijras of the Indian community while he also manages to snatch an interview with a super secretive group of hijaras in Delhi. While he tries to present the unusual sexual life of Delhi he ends up ebbing more of a voyeur than a neutral author as he masculines himself as the powerful narrator. There is a sense of mystique that is maintained throughout the course of the book which presents the transgender community in a rather poor light further "othering" them. Bill Aitken doesn't much ponder over the sexual life of the Himalaya other than few instances of boyish sexual encounters in a monastery, which is subtly referred to in chapter 24. The author systematically criticizes the orthodox Hindu philosophy for not accepting the "love's wayward possibilities". While a look at Dalrymple's work suggests a willful attempt at a mélange of humor and information but falls flat. He states:

> "Razia was the most unlikely of the three. A Kashmiri Muslim, she claimed to have been to the Doon School (the Indian Eton) and to have completed a Mater's Degree in English at Bombay University. I was never able to establish whether she was telling the truth – virtually all the hijras I talked to shrouded the facts of their lives in a thick wrap of fantasies –but she was certainly from a middle-class background and spoke fluent English."

Another instance when he says:

> "Panna, Razia's friend, was a very different creature. She was a very large hijra: nearly six feet tall. Her face was covered with scars of smallpox and she had a huge protruding belly; a shadow of light stubble freckled her chin. She would never have won a beauty contest. But she was one of the shyest of all the hijras I met, and one of the most gentle; her life revolved entirely around the baby she had just adopted. Her story emerged only after I had got to know her very well."

Rebecca Dorgelo remarks in her article about the narrator's own attempts to segregate himself from the lot of the hijras of the Indian community. There is an evident spur of sympathy but an inconspicuous lack of empathy in the author. The outsider in the Indian Community is further marginalized by the author's writing.

> "The section of *City of Djinns* in which William spends time with some of Delhi's eunuchs, or "hijras," still works to define the protagonist's masculinity, although in a different manner to that of *In Xanadu*. An important qualifier to this is the fact that *City of Djinns* is the story of William's time in Delhi with his wife, Olivia, as opposed to his unattached characterisation in his earlier narrative. This aspect of William's identity is explicitly mentioned when he first meets Chaman, the head of a hijra "household" (176), in an exchange with William's Indian companion, Zakir, who introduces him to Chaman. The text uses recorded speech to

> convey the conversation: "'This is my friend, Mr William.' I smiled. Chaman frowned. 'Is he your boyfriend?' 'No,' said Zakir. 'He's married. To a girl.' Chaman wrinkled up her nose in disgust" (176). The protagonist's exchange with Chaman is always polite, but is represented in such a way as to convey to the reader the extent to which William is holding back from agreement with or admiration of Chaman."

In an effort to identify with William, Chaman uses the figure of Sean Connery (a fellow Scot) as common ground, stating, "In the old times we hijras used to be like your zero zero seven. ...Our job was to listen and tell things to the king. We were just like your Sean Connery" (176). Dalrymple conveys his thoughts to the reader: "Somehow I couldn't imagine Chaman and her household taking on Goldfinger or seducing Ursula Andress, but I let this pass" (176). He consistently refuses to be drawn. Chaman shows William a glamour picture of herself at twenty-five and asks: "'I was beautiful, no?' 'Unique,' I said" (177). The effect of William's contact with the hijras is to characterise the protagonist as an ethnographer in the field, penetrating hidden areas of Delhi society in order to bring (slightly titillating) information to his readers." (Rebbeca Dorgelo, 69)

There are besides instances where the lingual superiority of the narrator is unconsciously established while inciting humor at the cost of the unsuspecting audience of his story. The Indian becomes the very stereotype in his work, which has probably attempted to discard. There is the presence of Indian authenticity in his imitation but somehow it fails to separate itself from the web of superficiality, unreal exaggeration and archetypal clichés.

Works Cited

Dorgelo, Rebecca. *Travelling into History: the Travel Writing and Narrative history of William Dalrymple.*

Mariyam, Sheikh Sana. *Treatment of History in William Dalrymple's Works*

Jain, Monika. Imperialist Nostalgia and Orientalist Vision in William Dalrymple's City of Djinns

Shodhganga

Morris, Jan: Review? *Sawshbuckle and Decay in an Ancient City*: City of Djinns

Ahluwalia,, Dr. Gunmeet Kaur. *Change and the Importance of Sustainable Development as Reflected in Works of some Famous Writers*

Dalrymple, William. *City of Djinns*

Aitken, Bill. *Footloose in the Himalayas.*

CHAPTER 17

Cryopathy and The Roots of Imagination in Margaret Atwood's *The Blind Assassin*

Victor Vinoth V. and Dr. Vijayakumar M

Abstract

The novel *The Blind Assassin*, projecting the idea of a story within a story, exhibits the literary concept of embedded narrative, where layers of meaning can be extracted in terms of characterisation. It is only through the novel's plot line that the trajectory of complex personalities like Laura can be explored. The psychologisation of Laura's worldview can be extracted through the process of plot construction, which ultimately projects the impossibility of objective truth. This article ventures to depict how women are being immured in the self-incarcerated world of their trauma, fear, and anxiety in the male-dominated societal world.

Keywords: Sacrifice, separation, search for identity, suffering, sacrifice.

Introduction

An unnamed pair of lovers meet in the shabby backstreet rooms in *The Blind Assassin* by Atwood. *Iris* is perplexed by *Laura's* death. The author features a strong female principal in a novel-within-a-novel. *Iris* discovers her husband's body on a sailboat while mourning her sister. Atwood's brilliant blending of two tales creates a breath-taking vision and lasting impact. The research paper will focus on Atwood's depiction of Canadian culture and high-class individuals' deep, miserable imaginations of the protagonist's life.

Adultery and a secret love affair between a rich maiden and a fugitive Marxist are woven throughout the paper. Using science fiction themes and Arabian adventure stories, the inner layer of the original contextualizes the astonishing journeys of Atwood's *Blind Assassin* and the silent sacrifice girl. Parallels are drawn between *the blind assassin* and the *silent sacrifice* maiden, and the aristocratic lady and her illegal companion, who are allegories for Laura and her boyfriend, Alex. The repetition of the idea of predators and prey throughout the triple tales, as well as the numerous folds of the work, suggests that Atwood may have purposefully tripled the identities of the characters. Iris Chase's desire to create a family history for her distant granddaughter, Sabrina, sparked the beginning of the *Blind Assassin* conspiracy. Iris Chase, who is now in her eighties, knows how important it is to tell her granddaughter the story of her family so that her life will also have meaning.

After years of not seeing her granddaughter Sabrina, Iris Chase Griffen, who is bedridden with heart difficulties, decides to write a memoir for the little girl she loves. Iris wants her granddaughter to know the truth, so she writes in flashbacks that confuse her current life and cause her narration to seem disjointed to the audience as a result. Laura, a disturbed adolescent who drove off a bridge in her sister's family drama, is mentioned. A posthumous publication of her book "*The Blind Assassin*" led to an outpouring of admiration for Laura from the young ladies she knew. Every year, Iris made it a point to visit the family cemetery. She discovered that there were many unknown Laura enthusiasts still visiting her memorial. It hurt when I kneeled and crammed the wilted flowers Laura's nameless admirers had placed there into the vase. "My shopping bag is made of plastic," (39 BA) the woman says. As if Laura were being conjured, I discovered incense and candles now and then. *Laura, the author of The Blind Assassin, has a cult following that has lasted decades after her death.* Because she has had a significant impact on the family, Iris wants the world to know about it. At the beginning of her book, she tells the story of her upbringing with her sister, Laura.

Iris and Laura had a wonderful life in Port Ticonderoga, Canada. Avilion, the family estate, was where they resided with their parents. Capt. Chase was the owner of a button factory. Avilion, the family residence, is nearing the end of its useful life. Due to World War II and an ever-deepening economic downturn, the splendour they had seen was dwindling. Laura is six years old when her mother Iris dies during delivery. The girls are looked after by Reenie Hincks, a housekeeper. Because of the Great Depression, their father's firm is in a precarious financial position. Iris had no idea what she would be facing if she did not have any money. She had no idea what was causing her father's anxiety.

> How many things can you get for a penny? He was curious. This question took me by surprise and left me unable to respond. Nobody told me. Because Reenie felt we needed to understand the worth of a dollar, neither Laura nor I were given any of our own money. (125)

Because money is a human creation, Aristotle deems it to be a kind of "nonsense" because it is not founded in nature. Political philosophy by Aristotle (Politics 1.3.10, p. 39) Brebis also accuses money of upending established social orders. Because of the depression, the Chase industry was set to close, giving the book industry an advantage.

Objectives of the Study

The objectives of the study are as follows:

- to explore the depiction of melancholy feminist psychology in the novel.
- to figure out what kind of connection there is between Laura's imagined adult life and her real life.
- to elaborate on the nuances existing in the social and political system presented in the blind Assassin.

Methodology

The study has followed a qualitative approach to fulfil its objectives. A review of secondary materials gathered from university libraries, as well as a targeted search of online databases, were carried out. The qualitative approach has helped the study methodically analyse various elements of feminism and feministic concepts present in the novel. The inclusion-exclusion criteria for a systematic sampling method have also been adopted to maintain the reliability and validity of the study.

Phenomenological Representation of Laura's Life

Everyone in the country has been affected by the conflict. All parts of the nation have experienced setbacks, and Chase Industries today faces a scale-down in its operations owing to decreasing demand. He would do everything in his power to keep the plants operating, but layoffs or part-time work may be required. Reenie, the governess, is the only person who can teach the girls how to live as young ladies without the help or direction of a mother. When she was 13 years old, her father took great care of her appearance, posture, and speech. My posture, my words, and the department became more and more interesting to him. My shoulders should be upright, with no slouching. I am not supposed to slouch, chew gum, fidget, or babble when I am in front of a computer screen. Although it was never explicitly stated, sexuality was to be suppressed. Is there a minimum age requirement? Now that I have reached puberty, it is all evident to me. However, I was only perplexed. How did I get into this predicament? (193) As a tribute to his two brothers who perished in World War II, Captain Chase longed to have boys of his own. He sagged as if he did not care about the children. Children have always been seen as a burden by society.

In this context, Simone de Beauvoir's devastating observations on the position of women are particularly relevant. That which is accidental or non-essential about her is what defines and differentiates her from everything else, as she asserts, "While he represents the topic, she represents the other" (Beauvoir 16). He had daughters, and he wanted them to be the finest in the world when it came to their careers and personal lives. Iris and Laura, unlike other youngsters, were not required to attend school. A teacher was hired. To begin, a woman was assigned to the position who deferred to the children's wishes. At 43, Mr. Chase hired a tutor who was around 35 years old to help with his kids' education. It was not uncommon for him to physically punish the girls for their misbehaviour. Both were sick and tired of him. When Laura reported that he placed his hands beneath her top and attempted to touch her underwear, it was the worst of all times. Reenie was informed, and she arranged for Captain Chase to be evicted from the home. Traditional concepts of dominance, such as patriarchal order and male status, underlie torture.

An old fear of and suppression of sexuality – shame, sin, weakness – is used to highlight the tormentor's dominance and the victim's fragility. After being purposely injured, the person subjected to sexual torture is subjected to the most humiliating of humiliations. When the girls are adolescents, their father's girlfriend introduces them to Alex Thomas, a young union organizer and socialist activist, during one of the parties they attend. Alex is popular with females. Workers at the plant get into a riot and try to burn it down. Alex is accused of provoking the commotion since he was renowned for his speeches advocating for the benefit of the employees. Iris and Laura sheltered him in their attic from the police when he went into hiding. Since the dawn of time, "males have valued and seen women as attractive and desirable. Men have a strong desire to dominate women's bodies. He establishes his superiority over her by being able to impose his will on her solely based on the physical attributes of her body" (Millet 34–35). Alexander Golden Weiser writes in Sex and Primitive Society that "women are sex." Using sexuality as an instrument of oppression is a certain way to marginalize and denigrate women throughout the world. It is imperative that she be chased, wooed, conquered, and kept, says the author.

Alex and Hieroglyphs have Captured Laura's attention

Laura is fascinated by Alex's tales about the planet Zycron and Egyptian hieroglyphs, and she often asks him questions. Laura was spellbound by Alex's ability to conjure up vivid images in the minds of everyone who heard him tell tales. Laura was brave enough to conceal Alex in the basement when the police came looking for him. Later, when Iris learns that Alex is hiding in their home, she helps Laura put him in the attic. After Alex's departure, Iris discovers that Laura has fallen in love with Alex. During the celebration, she arranged for a photo with Alex, Laura, and Iris. Without Iris, she had snipped it and stated, "You are not." Except for your hand, none of you had ever come this close to confessing your feelings for Alex Thomas. There's one exception: the day before her death." (169)

Mr. Richard Griffen, a Toronto financier, and vocal president of Royal Classic Knitwear, aspired to topple the Chase industry after it suffered a massive loss. To avoid being sued, he coerced Captain Chase into merging his business with Chase Industries. Richard made Captain Chase's life a living hell to get him to sign over control of his business to him. Captain Chase encourages his daughter, Iris, to marry 35-year-old Richard Griffen to preserve his social standing. Concerned, he enlists the help of his older daughter to watch for their younger sister if anything happens to him. To preserve the family's reputation, he urged that she do so. When I asked my father about Richard, he said he had something to tell me. In his voice, he seemed sincere and contrite, "I believe he's trying to get you to marry him," he added, perplexed. Now that I have said yes, it's up to you whether or not to proceed. "That was followed by a certain amount of it,' he said. He was implying that "we wouldn't have any money' until I married Richard" (276).

The connection between a father and a daughter turns out to be one of commerce. A sacrifice of her aspirations was necessary for

Iris' family business and the honour of her clan. By getting married, Iris' father claims, Iris and Laura's future would be assured, as would the family businesses. The idea of sacrifice has long been associated with women since it is a hallmark of a traditional lady; "The cycle of women's lives has lasted too lengthy in both despair and fantasy, while our active energies have been trained and absorbed into caring for others" (Rich. 247). After all, she had no option but to accept Richard's proposal, so she did just that. In the eyes of males in authority, it did not matter what she liked or disliked. The last thing Iris wanted to do with her life was be used as bait or as a sacrificial victim. To ensure the safety of both herself and her sister, however, she had to offer her blessing for their upcoming marriage.

It did not have a problem with him. He did not do anything for me. Because I had never paid much attention to him, I had little to say about him, even though I had noticed his clothes from time to time; "A man's presence implies what he is capable of doing to you or for you," (278). John Berger said in his book, '*Way of Seeing," that as* a result, a woman's presence establishes the boundaries for what can and cannot be done to her." (44) and (45) of Berger Richard and Iris honeymooned across Europe for many months after their nuptials. Just one week after Iris returned from her wedding, Laura told Iris that their father died from severe drinking and sadness. By the time Laura got the word that he had died, she'd sent telegrams and seen it in the newspaper. That Iris was unable to attend her father's funeral is a huge disappointment to her. But Richard convinces her that he did not tell Iris about her father's death because he didn't want to ruin her vacation to the United States and because he didn't want to ruin the trip for her.

Iris is amazed at the simplicity with which he manages to postpone the problem without causing Iris to get enraged. In Iris' opinion, she has been abandoned and taken advantage of. In the words of her mentor, Reenie, "lose your anger and you lose the battle," she did not want to get into a rage (BA376). Iris, on the other hand, was unable to win anything, even after remaining calm at the loss of her father. Highlights are Anitha Desai's specialty: Highly sensitive and emotional women are "tortured by a humiliating feeling of neglect, loneliness, and despair," according to the author. In the twenty-first chapter of Pathak, When Iris returns to Avilion the next day, she discovers that her father had passed the day before the button factory was shut down. Having agreed that the marriage would preserve the factory, Richard misled Iris and her father. Iris is angry because she believes Richard is to blame for her father's death. Her land and the factory have been included in Richard's empire. It breaks Iris' heart to find out that she got married to Richard for nothing.

No agreement was reached: "Because of my marriage, I had been married to Richard for nothing; I had not rescued the factories or Father. Laura, on the other hand, was there. "Still, she was not out and about in the community" (384–385). When it comes to being a wonderful woman, it is not about dwelling on things that can never be regained but about moving forward in life to make a brighter future for everyone they care about. Despite being deceived and duped, Iris tries to maintain her composure to help Laura have a bright future. Mary Wollstonecraft argues that women are not weak. She claims that a woman's natural strength is weakened during her caring era. She is shaped not by her biological gender but by societal and familial expectations. Iris's reaction to the betrayal she suffered might have been different if she had been financially independent. Attempting to retaliate for the murder of her father at the age of 47 would be futile, and would only generate more issues for her and Laura.

For the first time, a woman advocated for "economic freedom for women" (Gilman 22). The fact that Iris married Richard had never crossed Laura's mind, and she had no interest in finding out more about him. Also, she was enraged because he had tramped on their family's history. However, although her sister, Iris, was married to him, she did not want to retaliate against him. Avilion belonged to Richard, but he could not possess it if Laura remained there. It was decided that Laura should live with him and Iris, despite her objections. Laura declines Richard's invitation since she is a confident young lady. She does not show up by train as Richard had anticipated, so he calls the police.

According to the press, Laura Chase had gone missing, with sensational headlines. Anonymously, a phone call was made on the ninth day, indicating that Laura was working at Sunnyside Amusement Park's waffle stand. They went to the amusement park with Iris and Richard to bring her back from there. Angry with Laura for running away, Richard informed her that, as a juvenile, he had all the legal and moral authority to take care of her since he was her father. He asserts that Laura must comprehend all he asks of her. a young woman, according to him. Iris shudders at his words. "I was frightened about the young woman." It seemed like a slap in the face, as if there were something wrong with being young and a woman. If that's the case, it's a slap in the face. (401) To a young woman, Richard was sending the message that she must constantly follow the norms and regulations set out by the male-dominated society in which she lives. There is no way she is supposed to be moving about with a guy helping her.

Though oppressed, the new women feel confined and restricted in their freedom of expression. "I now throw down my gauntlet and reject the existence of sexual virtues, save for modesty," writes feminist Mary Wollstonecraft in her impassioned treatise A Vindication of the Rights of Women. If my understanding is correct, the truth must be the same for both men and women. I accept that women have different responsibilities, but I argue that the principles that govern their performance must be the same. It is mentioned in Margaret *Tims's book, on page* 43. In addition to being compelled to attend a school that she despises, Laura must live with Richard, the man who killed her father under duress.

Laura's Outlandish Behaviour

Due to her strange behaviour, Laura was dismissed from school. Meanwhile, on the streets of Toronto, Iris spots Alex. A secret romance between Iris and Alex results in Iris being pregnant. She sees this as a kind of retribution for Richard's betrayal of her and her family. Laura was taken to a mental institution one day by Richard and Winifred, who said that she had gone mad. Laura had finally lost her cool, according to Winifred. When she spoke, she exclaimed, "Snapped," like Laura was a bean. We should have obtained aid for the poor kid sooner, but we thought things were looking well for her (523) Because Laura was seven months pregnant, Iris was prohibited from meeting her. As Laura's paranoia escalated, Iris was informed that not only was she accusing Richard of intending to murder her, but she was also expecting a child. Iris gives birth to a daughter, Aimee, after a few months.

This established that Alex was Aimee's father since the infant had dark characteristics like Alex's, with black hair and a dark complexion. Iris was delighted to learn that Alex was the father of her daughter, and it fuelled her desire for retribution against Richard. Iris was the only one who knew that Richard was not Aimee's 49-year-old father, and he was overjoyed about becoming a parent. Surprisingly, society is shaped by the idea that a mother is a fact and a father is a conviction. Having children is the only weapon women have against men's egos. Several months later, Iris gets a telegram announcing Alex's death while serving in World War II. She gets the telegram since Alex has included her in the next-of-kin list and she has her phone number. However, Iris does not want Richard to know that she has been following her sister's path. According to Richard, Laura's lawyer withdrew her from the institution after a few months.

Using the ruse that Reenie was on her deathbed, she asked Richard for permission to see her, claiming that she wanted to view Aimee's photo as a last desire for the deceased. As she searched for her sister, Iris had to use falsehoods as a method of getting there. Reenie was the only one who could help her discover more about Laura, and she knew it. With the help of the lawyer hired by the Chase family, Reenie, who was dismissed by Richard, is trying to get Laura out of the facility. Reenie admits that Richard and his sister subjected Laura to a great deal of pain. To aid her sister, Iris is unwilling to go against her husband, who is very wealthy and powerful. Furthermore, she did not want her child to grow up in a miserable situation without her father's support. When it comes to subordination, Mary Astell points out in Some Reflections on Marriage that it is "custom-oriented." She goes on to say that the institution of marriage has long been a tool used by society to oppress women. Women are oppressed in patriarchal societies. For Lis Stanley and Sue Wise, feminism's essence lies in its emphasis on the personal, its insistence on the validity of women's experience, and the argument that understanding and analyzing everyday life, where oppression, as well as everything else, is rooted, is the only way to gain an understanding of 50 women's expression. (p. 135, Stanley and Wise) Iris and Reenie would be aware of Laura's problems if they had read her notes. Moreover, she said that Iris would be able to locate her notes with relative ease. After a few months of being married, Iris realizes that her relationship with Richard is on the verge of breaking apart because she seems to be sick all the time.

Conclusion

Her health has suffered as a result of her two miscarriages. But he is always on the go, having sex with other women. As Winifred said, back then, men had a plethora of desires, which they tended to bury in the depths of their psyches, only to erupt like a plague now and again. A genuine man could not hope to win against them; they were crafty and powerful. (584) Wives suffer a certain amount of shame when their husbands take great satisfaction in having several mistresses, and this kind of behaviour is also recognized. "The wretched condition of very sensitive and emotional women, tormented by a humiliating sense of neglect, loneliness, and desperation," Anita Desai writes on the 45th page of Pathak in her book. But he is always on the go, having sex with other women. As Winifred said, back then, men had a plethora of desires, which they tended to bury in the depths of their psyches, only to erupt like a plague now and again. A genuine man could not hope to win against them; they were crafty and powerful. (584) Wives suffer a certain amount of shame when their husbands take great satisfaction in having several mistresses, and this kind of behaviour is also recognized. "The wretched condition of very sensitive and emotional women, tormented by a humiliating sense of neglect, loneliness, and desperation," (Anita Desai writes on the 45th page of Pathak in her book)She refuses to divorce him since he is her sole source of income and housing.

Divorce would harm Richard's political career since no one wants a leader who comes from a dysfunctional family, and even Richard understands that this is true. He had no intention of divorcing me since I was his legal wife. In those days, national leadership positions were not open to divorced males. I could only use the power I had in this position if I used it. Only if I pretended I did not know anything did it become useful. (584) In society, married women are held in high esteem. If she wants to hold a position of authority or participate in the cultural norms of her community, she must marry and lead the life of a wife.

Only if she is living with her spouse does a woman deserve respect, regardless of what sort of person he may be. Even if he has every right to indulge his fantasies, in society, a woman who has an extramarital affair is seen with suspicion. According to J.S. Mill, "No slave is a slave to the same lengths and in such a complete sense as a wife is" (Mill. 121). Laura calls Iris a few months later to set up a meeting and expresses her desire to meet with her. When Iris sees her sister, she is overjoyed. Inquiring minds wanted to know where she had been and what she'd been up to over the last several days. As Laura says, she was aborted in the mental hospital by the physicians there. To avoid Richard, she advises Iris to get away from him. In response to Iris's question regarding who fathered her unborn child, she said that if she did not already know, she would not tell her. She admits that to keep Alex safe, she had to make a pact with the individual.

This was an excellent deal. Because he threatened to turn Alex in to the authorities if she did not agree to sleep with the guy, he coerced her into feeling that she had no choice but to comply. As a result, she became a silent maiden and offered herself as a sacrifice. Laura's story baffles Iris, who assumes that Laura must be Alex's mother; if she did not agree to sleep with the guy, he coerced her into feeling that she had no choice but to comply. As a result, she became a silent maiden and offered herself as a sacrifice. Laura's story baffles Iris, who assumes that Laura must be Alex's mother. Laura learns about Alex's death through Iris. He died, and she received a telegram because she had an affair with him. Iris wanted Laura to realize at some point that she was so naive that she made the decision that led to her death. Laura believed that God had protected Alex because of her sacrifice and that he would return once the war was over. "I kept my half of the agreement, and it worked," Laura added. God is not a liar. Afterwards, Alex enlisted in the military. After returning from his trip to Spain, Laura drove away in her vehicle (594). She grabbed Iris' handbag, which was still on the table. Iris is startled by Laura's out-of-the-blue behaviour. If Richard or Winifred found out, she would be in danger. While waiting for Laura to call, she becomes irritated and drives off a bridge the following day. Eyewitnesses have told us that Laura committed suicide by driving off the bridge and plunging into a deep valley. A few school journals left behind by Laura are examined by Iris after her death. In Laura's notes, she learns that Richard fathered Laura's child. That was all there was to it. Nothing remained a mystery. It had been there in front of my eyes the whole time. Was I so naive that I missed this? So it's not Alex Thomas. Alex, never in a million years. "For Laura, Alex was a pawn in another realm." (611) Iris felt uneasy when the truth was given without evidence.

To avoid Richard's grasp, she waited until after the funeral rituals and ceremony had concluded before making plans to leave. To salvage the relationship, she did not want to go too low. Richard's avarice had cost her everything: her father, her house, and now her beloved sister. She takes a risk by separating herself from Richard and his family and living a life free of guilt. Instead of endangering Richard's political future, she decided against pressing for a divorce. Iris, on the other hand, recognized his pity and was labelled a saint for spreading the rumour that Iris was insane, so they had to live apart. Iris wanted to honour Laura's memory by exacting revenge on Richard and Winifred for the pain and suffering they had inflicted on her and Laura. *The Blind Assassin* is a book written and published by Iris under Laura's identity. Only at the very end of the book does it become clear that Iris is the author. Laura was my left hand, and I was hers, too. As a team, we wrote the book. It's a book for lefties. "Regardless of how you look at it, one of us is always out of sight." (627).

Works Cited

Appacha, Kavi.(2012). Haradasa Nalnataka, Registrar, *Kodava Sahitya Academy.*

Appaiah, P.S., *A History of Kodagu* (From the Earliest Times to the 16th Century)

Astell's Mary, "Reflections Upon Marriage," *https://www.bl.uk/collection-items/mary-astells-reflections-upon-marriage*

Bartlett, Sarah. (2009). Great Britain, Press.

Beauvoir, de Simone. (1997). *The Second Sex*, Vintage Publication.

Dasan, M. (2003). Beyond Resistance: *Critical Essays on Canadian First Nations* Writing, editor: Calicut University Press.

Liz Stanley, and Sue Wise, (1983). Breaking Out: *Feminist Consciousness and Feminist Research,* by Routledge and Degan Paul.

Burger, J. (1990). "Way of seeing," paperback, 176 pages, Penguin Publication, p. 44, 45.

David and Mary The Hindu, (1999) *2nd Ganapathy, is the herald of women's liberation.* Kodavas (Coorgs): Their Culture and Customs, Literary Review, Weekly Edition XIII.

Desai, Anita. (1987). *"Stairs to the Attic: Anita Desai's Novels"* was published by Print Well Publishers in according to an interview with Jasbir Jain.

James, Strachey. (1964), *Femininity in New Introductory Lectures on Psychoanalysis*, Vol. 2, translated and edited by, Penguin Books Ltd.

Sarah, Gamble. (2001). *Feminism and postfeminism* The Routledge Companion, edited by Routledge, Freud, Sigmund.

Freud, Sigmund. (1973). *New Introductory Lectures on Psychoanalysis, trans and* edited by James Strachey, Penguin Books Ltd, p.173

Gilman Charlotte Perkin, (2021). *The yellow wallpaper of realism in literature.* https://www.bard.edu/library/arendt/pdfs/Aristotle-Politics.pdf.

Levi, Strauss, and Claude. (1978). *Myth and significance Routledge* and Kyan Paul.

Millet, Kate. (1998). *Sexual Politics.* Indiana Publication, Rome, Print.

Girish Karnad. (2018). *Mythologizing History and Historicizing Myth*: Girish Karnad's Plays, Girish Sanbun Publishers.

Benjamin Jowett, (1999). *Aristotle's Politics*, translated by, botched books, page 39; 1, 3, 10. Aristotle (Politics 1.3.10), page 39.

Rich, A. (2005). "A Study of Adrienne Cecile Rich's Works from *a Feminist Perspective.*" p. 247.

Stanley and Wise. (1983). Putting It into Practice: Using Feminist Fractured Foundationalism in *Researching Children in the Concentration Camps of the South African War, p. 135.*

Atwood, M. (2000) *The Blind Assassin*, Bloomsbury Publication.

David Lodge, and Pearson. (2007). The Death of the Author, *in Modern Criticism and Theory*: A Reader and Editor.

William Toye. (1963). The Oxford Companion to Canadian Literature, Oxford University Press, General editor.

P.S. Appaiah, (2006). *The Secrets of Kodava* (Coorg) Language Unveiled.

Wollstonecraft, Mary A. (1972). "*Vindication of the Rights of Women.*"

Woolf, Virginia. (1942). Professions for Women, *The Death of the Moth, and Other Essays* Harcourt Brace, p. 202.

Vinoth V.V. & Vijayakumar M. (2022). The Dystopian Scourge of Women in Gilead Society as Portrayed in Margaret Atwood's The Handmaid's Tale. In the Journal of Theory and Practice in Language Studies, Vol. 12, No. 12, P. 2704–2711.

CHAPTER 18

How Far is too Far? – An Elaborate Interpretation of the Transhumanistic Movies and their Depiction of Characters as Transmogrified Humans

Harry B. and Dr. Vijaykumar M'

Abstract

Transhumanism is the belief that people should learn to compassionately improve other people's lives. It belongs to a group of ideologies that aspire to lead us to a posthuman state. This chapter discusses how movies depict the idea of transhumanism in societal greediness and the lust for power, and how when a human evolves into a higher being, he loses his idea of lust and intrusive behaviour. The problem that most people have with transhumanism is the concept of inequality, which would create a situation where those who have had their bodies modified to surpass the normal human abilities could then use this advantage to overpower others Transhumans share many aspects of humanism, including a respect for reason and science, a commitment to progress, and a value of human or transhuman existence in this life.

Introduction

Transhumanism is a stoical and philosophical moment devoted to promoting the research and development of robust human enhancement technologies. Such technologies would augment or increase human sensory reception, and emotional or cognitive capacity, as well as radically improve human health and extend human life spans. Such modifications resulting from the addition of biological or physical technologies would be more or less permanent and integrated into the human body.

The intellectual and cultural movement promotes the idea that it is both possible and desirable to fundamentally improve the state of humanity through the application of reasoning, particularly by creating and disseminating technologies that will stop ageing and greatly increase human intelligence, physical prowess, and psychological capability. Such technologies would augment or increase human sensory reception, and emotional or cognitive capacity, as well as radically improve human health and extend human life spans. (Magnuson and marks, 2022)

The associated investigation of the moral dilemmas raised by the creation and application of such technologies. Transhumanism is the intellectual and cultural movement that promotes the idea that it is both possible and desirable to fundamentally improve the state of humanity through the application of reasoning, particularly by creating and disseminating technologies that will stop ageing and greatly increase human intelligence, physical prowess, and psychological capability.

The over Humans and the Hope of Future

The movement of transhumanism problematizes the current understanding of humanity, not necessarily through its past and present legacies, but through the possibilities inscribed within its possible biological and technological evolution.

A transhuman is a creature that resembles a human in most ways yet possesses superhuman strength and agility. Improved intelligence, alertness, strength, or durability are a few examples of these skills.It is improbable that there will be a definite point at which humans become transhuman. In contrast, technology will ingratiate itself more deeply with the human body. Technology has long been viewed as a self-extension. (bostrom, 2014)

Science and technology are the main assets of interest for each of these positions, but with different emphases. Transhumanism roots itself in the Enlightenment and does not expropriate rational humanism. In the West, humans have historically been positioned on a hierarchical scale with the non-human realm. Not every human being has been considered as such: women, African-American descendents, gays and lesbians, differently-abled people, among others. And still, transhumanist reflections do not fully engage with a critical and historical account of humanity, which is often presented in a generic and "fit-for-all" way.

Science fiction movies recreate precise transhumanism features, which portray a modified and evolved human capacity to a higher degree and are able to incorporate neurobiological operations into machines. Although this type of movie may be attractive due to its unconventional science, the movies do show the lack of ontological continuity between humans and machines. Some examples of transhumanism include anti-aging and artificial intelligence. (Brown, 2019) Trans humans are often represented in films as a negative aspect of humanity and shown as mad science, where there is a negative plot twist causing damage, robotic evolution, and the integration of humans.

The core of transhumanism is to encourage the use of biotransformative technologies in order to create human organisms with the ultimate human organism so as to overcome this fundamental limitation. The movies are like Lucy, limitless, selfless, and ever-updating. These movies are about the enhancement of human brain structure and performance to become a super human.Mormon teachings about humans becoming gods connect with transhumanist ideas about using technology to enhance the human condition. Mormon Transhumanism embraces science and religion to work toward these corresponding aims.(Lincoln cannon,2015)

It shouldn't come as a surprise that the transhumanism movement has many bold ideas that would create excellent plotlines for movies. Through science fiction films, we have long had the opportunity to observe what a world populated by nanobots or AI would look like. We get to witness these concepts come to life on screen in one way or another, usually as a part of a cautionary tale.

Moral Enhancement necessary for a Way out

Transhumanism has been addressed in a wide range of ways in the film industry, from blockbusters like The Matrix and Avatar to lesser-known jewels like Splice and Ghost In The Shell. It shouldn't come as a surprise that the transhumanism movement has many bold ideas that would create excellent plotlines for movies. Through science fiction films, we have long had the opportunity to observe what a world populated by nanobots or AI would look like. We get to witness these concepts come to life on screen in one way or another, usually as a part of a cautionary tale. Transhumanism has been addressed in a wide range of ways in the film industry, from blockbusters like The Matrix and Avatar to lesser-known jewels like Splice and Ghost In The Shell. Limitless, one of the more realistic transhumanist films, is about a struggling writer who meets a drug dealer acquaintance and accepts his offer to try some NZT-48, a top-secret substance that promises to fix all of his problems. The medicine does all of that and more while boosting his mental power, enabling him to write a book, choose stocks, master foreign languages, and control those around him with relative ease. The plot then involves a pharmaceutical firm and a race to obtain more of the medicine, but to be completely honest, I was distracted by Bradley Cooper's eyes and wasn't paying attention. The main character in Limitless remains entirely human while evolving into something we can only now imagine, but within contexts where we can still understand his experiences, unlike lesser films that might rely on their protagonist becoming less human to depict their transcendence. He's merely supercharging his synapses, which makes his brain fire so quickly that he can practically access every piece of knowledge he's ever acquired or encountered at once. He isn't developing a superpower or having his brain enhanced with technology. Perhaps fantastical, yet something that fits with many neuroscientists' hypotheses about our brains' capacity for memory. The fact that nootropics, also known as cognitive stimulants, are real is another fantastic aspect of this film. Although none are quite as potent as NZT-48, many are still used for therapeutic purposes and even in everyday life for academics. Chemical "doping" of our intelligence will soon become commonplace; otherwise, you run the risk of being... restricted.

In an another film, Gattaca speaks about the enhancement of the future generation. The story of a typical man born into a culture where genetically modifying kids to be better is standard is told in Gattaca, a transhumanist film considered to be one of the all-time greats. The man must assume the identity of a genetically superior person at tremendous risk to himself if he is ever discovered in order to realize his ambition of traveling to space. This movie is fantastic because of how unbelievable and plausible everything feels. It demonstrates many reproductive technologies that are already commonplace. And with the development of genetic technologies like CRISPR, the prospect of a society in which being a completely normal human implies falling short of expectations becomes uncomfortably plausible. However, Gattaca has a more important point to communicate that differs greatly from the rest of its cautions. It is a statement on the degree to which genetics truly determines a person's fate or not. Among the more overt terror of what it would be like to live in a genetic caste system, this message is sometimes overlooked. However "utopic" or "dystopic" the future of humanity may turn out to be, Gattaca's main message is that if we can hold onto even a small portion of the human qualities that cannot be screened into or out of our DNA, like courage, will, and dedication, then each of us will still have a chance to leave our mark. (MSc)

One kind of enhanced human is modified genetically. There is another set of transhuman ideas which is technological enhancement, like in the movie Robo Cop. In the film, a police officer who was on the verge of death is granted another shot at life and a cybernetic body that, in theory, will enable him to be the ideal combination of an unstoppable robot and a thinking, emotional human. He must struggle to hold onto the final vestiges of his humanity after being betrayed by the company that sponsored his regenesis and was only concerned with creating the ideal, order-following soldier. Some observers are concerned that transhumanism would result in the presence of two separate sorts of beings, the human and the post-human, and that they would be seen as having a considerably lower moral status.

What Exactly does it Mean to be Human? Human Moral Psychology in a World of advanced Technology

This is the key transhumanist question here. And to be honest, the film does a good job of addressing the question. It appears to argue, among other things, that the biological human body itself is irrelevant.According to RoboCop, having our own memories or a fully autonomous will may not even constitute being a human. It seems that emotion is what is needed. And not just the illusion of it that any Alexa can imitate, but the convoluted, irrational web of ideas and emotions that threatens what we could refer to as – for lack of a better term – our soul. is the core of who we are. Because the moment the movie's hero is free of his emotions, he stops, to use the movie's own words, "hesitating." And all people must hesitate when making tough choices, or else humanity will truly perish and we will all be reduced to robots. Regardless of which version you like, RoboCop is an excellent illustration of the risks.

Superheroes fall into a category of their own because they are by definition more than humans, so some would argue that this isn't strictly a legitimate entry. However, a lot of superheroes begin as regular people before discovering abilities that allow them to break beyond such boundaries. And more specifically, some heroes don't possess any special abilities at all; instead, they use their intellect and technological know-how to separate themselves from the crowd of ordinary people and become extraordinary. This can be seen in movies such as X-Men, Spiderman, Iron Man, and many others If you understand the concept of a fantastic transhumanist film, Iron Man is for you.

In it, Tony Stark creates a piece of technology that renders him the most unbeatable soldier after being compelled to do so by dire circumstances and fatal injuries.Iron Man is an interesting representation of the transhumanist movement's rising belief that impairments can not only be treated but also present opportunities for people to achieve meaningful enhancements in place of their limitations. Iron Man is a hero who advanced human enhancement to its logical conclusion while also making it seem pretty dang cool, similar to amputees competing on carbon fibre blades.

Conclusion

This essays on transhumanism allow us to appreciate the power of transhumanism as a secularized religion through the narration of movies, inviting us to engage transhumanism on intellectual, social, political, ethical, and philosophical grounds. We may not like where the transhumanist imagination is taking us, but if we want to understand the world we live in, we cannot ignore transhumanism. (Tirosh-Samuelson – 2012) Rather, we should comprehend its complexities, including tensions, contradictions, and paradoxes, as well as its deep desire to transcend human biological existence. One of the most perplexing paradoxes of transhumanism is the possibility of freedom. On the one hand, transhumanism urges humans to take control of evolution in the name of an idealized secular eschaton in order to liberate humans from biological evolution's constraints; on the other hand, the imagined future is actually dictated by human-made technology. Another paradox concerns the dialectic of enchantment: as a child of Enlightenment rationalism, transhumanism appears to prioritise secular rationalism over religious belief, disenchanting the world. However, by imbuing man-made technology with salvific meaning, transhumanism "re-enchants" the secular. Most poignantly, transhumanist eschatology reimagines the place and role of technology in historical change because technology is seen as the driving force of cultural change, but because technology operates on an exponential trajectory, it contradicts the "intuitively linear" view of history. In short, if we are to comprehend the complexities of the current postsecular era, we must investigate transhumanism. (Brown, 2019)

Works Cited

Magnuson, Markus Amalthea. *What Is Transhumanism?* whatistranshumanism.org, https://whatistranshumanism.org/. Accessed 7 Aug. 2022.

Encyclopedia Britannica. www.britannica.com, https://www.britannica.com/topic/transhumanism. Accessed 7 Aug. 2022.

CNN, Karina Tsui. *CNN.* www.cnn.com, https://www.cnn.com/style/article/david-vintiner-transhumanism/index.html. Accessed 8 Aug. 2022.

Brown, Erin Clare. *Medium.* gen.medium.com, 27 Sept. 2019, https://gen.medium.com/meet-the-mormon-transhumanists-seeking-salvation-in-the-singularity-a7e3784d6c04.

MSc, Peter Joosten. *Peter Joosten MSc.* www.peterjoosten.org, 12 June 2020, https://www.peterjoosten.org/transhumanism-movies/.

Tirosh-Samuelson, Hava. "Transhumanism As A Secularist Faith." *Transhumanism As A Secularist Faith*, swab.zlibcdn.com, https://swab.zlibcdn.com/dtoken/0b81e1871bdd7f62323121140a477545. 9 Dec. 2012.

Nick bostrom, "Thesimulation argument", november2014, http://www.simulation-argument.com/simulation.html, accessed Aug. 2022

Dolidon, Annabelle. "Transhumanism and Its Ethical Dilemmas." *Jstor*, https://www.jstor.org/stable/10.5621/sciefictstud.43.2.0390. Accessed 9 Aug. 2022.

CHAPTER 19

Tushar Gandhi's *The Lost Diary of Kastur, My Ba* – An Appreciation Beyond Memoirs

Dr. Rajshree Roselean Kapoor

Overview

Gandhi Research Foundation employees in Jalgaon came across a damaged and decaying diary in the Kasturba Ashram in Indore a few years ago. Kasturba Gandhi's diary, which ran from January to September of 1933 and consisted of 135 pages, was discovered. In a way, her diary mirrored Kasturba's fate: it was ignored and forgotten. This volume is a reproduction of her diary, with the original Gujarati text transcribed and an English translation provided by her great-grandson, Tushar Gandhi.

Kasturba was labelled as uneducated and illiterate her entire life. When Tushar Gandhi first told his relatives about the diary, they laughed at the idea, saying, "She was illiterate." She was unable to put her thoughts on paper. The more of Kasturba's diary Tushar read, the more he realised he had been wrong. It showed that she was her own person, someone you could hang out with and who was also a satyagrahi in her own right despite her lack of formal education.

For the first time, readers will hear directly from Kasturba in *The Lost Diary of Kastur, My Ba*. This book gives a glimpse into what it was like to be married to the "Mahatma" through a look at their daily lives together. This woman was present as history was being made, not only able to observe and comprehend the event but also actively take part in it. It also details her two arrests that year for participating in satyagraha, rather than as Bapu's wife. This book, published 150 years after Kasturba's birth, portrays her for the first time as a unique individual and a strong female leader.

Bapu greeted Ba by saying, "*Oh, so they have brought you to be with me." Ba turned to her husband and said, "No, I have been arrested because I disobeyed their prohibitory order and spoke at the meeting in your place." For myself, I am a prisoner. Noting with a grin that she wasn't there to be his wife, Bapu said, "So, you are here as a satyagrahi."*

Because her husband, the charismatic Mohandas Karamchand Gandhi, was the centre of India's collective consciousness at the time, Kasturba Gandhi's creative agency is often overlooked. Their great-grandson, Tushar Gandhi, decided to look at things from Kasturba's point of view, reading about her life with Mohandas and the political and cultural journey they took together.

Kasturba's diary, written in "colloquial and grammatically deficient" Gujarati between January and September of 1933 and discovered by chance a couple of years ago by the staff of the Gandhi Research Foundation in Jalgaon, is translated into English here. Furthermore, it paints a detailed picture of Kasturba's existence. The reader is given the opportunity to rediscover this remarkable woman for who she really is, a person who is not wholly separate from Mohandas but who is nonetheless on the lookout for a way to express herself creatively and fully.

To begin, here is a passage from her diary entry dated September 4, 1933:

At four o'clock, we pray.

Some of the Gita's verses. Preparations for the day. Served Bapuji dinner at 5:30. After that, I got into the tub and scrubbed myself down. Consumed a cup of coffee. Went for a stroll with Bapuji. I returned to the Gita and read it. I left the house at 8:30 to prepare some vegetables for Bapuji. At 10, he sat down to eat. We had lunch at eleven. We eventually crashed for the night. Then she wove two hundred strands. A young woman with a college education might get frustrated reading the diary of a 'uneducated and unlettered' woman. A religiously devoted wife may be revealed in her habits of praying, spinning, and feeding Bapu milk and fruit. The relationship between Kasturba and Mohandas is a dialectic one, with love and trust present amidst pain and struggle; however, if she goes beyond the textbook knowledge of feminism, develops the courage to become empathic, and feels the vibrations of Kasturba's inner world, she may find that it is symmetrical. It wasn't simple being Gandhi's lifelong companion. Kasturba went through the ups and downs of life, including his constant "experiments with truth," his journey as a political and spiritual nomad from South Africa to India, his moral stubbornness, and, above all, his tense relationship with their eldest son Harilal. Contrary to popular belief, Gandhi was not an insensitive patriarch. With the birth of Ramdas, their third child, in 1897, Kasturba experienced significant blood loss. Tushar Gandhi does an excellent job of capturing the charm of their relationship:

Kastur and the children were nursed by Mohan (Gandhi). Kastur was embarrassed, but Mohan ignored her protests. He sponged her down, emptied her bedpan, and fed her in bed. Very quickly, Kastur began feeling better, and life returned to normal. The songs shared in this bond served as an inspiration. Instead of being the "passive" wife of a great man, Kasturba found her voice and joined her husband in the fight for India's independence. Despite her religiosity and simplicity, Kasturba radiated the spirit of love, courage, and endurance in her extraordinary work with women and children in Champaran; the way in which she began to address meetings in villages and lead marches; or, for that matter, in her death in the prison in 1944.

Introduction

Ba was not a disciplined writer. We always believed she could not write, was unlettered. This diary dispels that false belief. While translating diary from Gujrati, I faced a dilemma. Ba's written language, even Gujrati, was colloquial and grammatically very deficient. The dilemma I faced was should I refine what she had written and write it correctly while translating or should I retain the disjointed, disconnected, unruly, Haphazard manner in which she wrote so that readers would get the flavour Ba's writing in the translation, the way she had managed to write it in her diary? I decided I would not impose my language on Ba allow readers to savour Ba's diary and presenting it to the readers.

Those who feel I should have corrected Ba's writing, please accept my apologies. I believe my job is to present Ba's in her own words as she wrote them.

Kastur: Her Life

On April 1869 A baby girl was born to vrajkunvar and Gokuldas Mukanji Kapadia nagar sheth or honorary mayor of Porbandar. She was named Kastur. Kastur's exact birth date isn't available. She was a sister of two brothers, Khushaldas, older than her, and Madhavdas, younger. 1876 Kastur was betrothed to Mohandas, son of putli and Karamchand Gandhi of Porbandar, now serving as divan of Rajkot, when she and mohan were seven. May 1881 married Mohandas in a lavish ceremony both were thirteen years old. Kastur moved to Rajkot to begin life as Mohan's bride, and daughter-in-law of the Gandhis, at 'Ka Ba Gandhi no Delo' the Gandhi family home at Rajkot, built by Karamchand Gandhi, who served the prince of Thakore of Rajkot as divan, prime minister. Karamchand Gandhi was colloquially called 'KaBa' shortened of Karamchand KaBA', shortened from Karamchand Bappa. 16november 1885 Karamchand Gandhi, her father-in-law, died after a prolonged illness. 25November 1885 Kastur gave birth prematurely to a son, who died in a couple of days. A double tragedy for young Kastur, who was left to grieve and death of her first-born all by herself, while the rest of the household and her husband grieved the death of the patriarch of the Gandhi family, Karamchand Bappa. 1887 Mohan passed his matriculation exam and enrolled at samaldas College in Bhavnagar. As he left, kastur told him that she was once again expecting their child. Six months later, unable to cope with English education and the separation from kastur, Mohan dropped out of college and returned home, a failure. A great disappointment from young Kastur and the Gandhi family. August 1888 Kastur gave birth to her second son, their first to survive. They named him Harilal. After dropped out college, the family was distressed the future look bleak. At this time, putli Ba was counselled by a friend of Karamchand Bappa, Mavji Dave, to send Mohandas to England, vilayet, to study law there and become a British-qualified barrister, which would make him most qualified to be appointed as divan of any principality in Kathiyavad, since now all the administrative decisions were taken by British Resident in the Principalities. After a lot pof discussion, the elders in the family consented. Kastur accepted the family decision when funds were required to finance Mohan's education abroad, Kastur offered the jewellery gifted to her by her father. Mohan swore a solemn promise to his mother and I am certain also to Kastur to stay away from meat, wine and women while abroad, in the presence of a jain monk. He left Rajkot for Bombay on 10 august 1998. For Kastur, it would be a three-year-long separation. On 4 september 1988, Mohan left for England on board the SS clyde. 1888-91 A lonely period of Kastur, separated from her husband, expelled and ostracized by their community, living as a dependant on the meagre income of her two elder Brothers-in-law. Her only consolation was her closeness to her mother-in-law, Putli Ba and the apple of her eye, her son, little Hari. The highlight of the separation was when mohan sent back a close-up portrait photograph of his from London. When Kastur saw it she could not recognize the person for a moment, the stranger in the photograph was some Western saheb, not her Mohan. On closer scrutiny, she recognized some of his features his big ears, his sensuous mouth and the glint in his eyes but how much he had changed. Kastur would often visit her parents in Porbandar. These were interludes which helped her to survive separation from her husband, the community boycott and the poverty faced by her in-laws. In Porbandar, at her father's home, Kastur relived the carefree, blissful times of her childhood along with her son, Hari. As she had done on many an evening when she was a child, she would climbup to the terrace and sit there alone, lost in there thoughts, enjoying the breathtakingly beautiful sunsets over the Arabian sea. But fate was to deal her a cruel blow. Putli Ba fell ill in the spring of 1891 and died within a few weeks, the family was grief stricken. It was a devastating tragedy for Kastur, her anchor, her main support in those difficult times, her surrogate mother and mother-in-law had so suddenly departed. She had also become closer to her sister-in-law but she was very attached to putli Ba. Since the tragedy struck at a time when Mohandas was preparing for his final exams in London, the family decide not to inform him about his mother's passing. Mohan was extremely attached to his mother and it was feared that he would not be able to bear the news of her demise.(Gandhi, 2022)

In London, Mohan who had appeared for and passed the British Matriculation exam, earlier graduated as a lawyer, along with diplomas in latin and French, enrolled at the Bar, Then, Barrister M.K Gandhi set sail on board the SS Assam for India. In August 1891, he disembarked in Bombay, where his brother Laxmi das had come to receive him. Mohan was eager matriculation exam earlier, graduated as a lawyer, along with diplomas in Latin and French, and enrolled at the Bar. Then, Barrister M.K. Gandhi set sail on board the SS Assam for India. In August 1891, he disembarked in Bombay, where his brother Lakshmidas had come to receive him. Mohan was eager to reach Rajkot, to tell his mother that he had remained true to the oath he had sworn to her, to tell his wife that he had remained faithful to her, and to once again be with her. Mohan was impatient.

When Lakshmidas informed him about their mother's demise, Mohan was distraught; he broke down and was inconsolable. Lakshmidas told Mohan that their mother wanted that Mohan make peace with the community elders and seek their forgiveness. Honouring his mother's wish, Mohan appeased the elders, accepted the fine and punishment imposed, and performed the rituals of atonement; then he and the family were once again accepted into the folds of the community. The brothers travelled to Nasik, where the purification rituals were conducted. The post-death rights were also performed by the brothers for their mother. Finally, the brothers began the journey home. After three years, Kastur set eyes once again on a stranger; he looked different even from the photograph he had sent from London. But then Kastur saw the plint in the eves the sensual curve of his lips looked different even from the photograph he had sent from London. But then Kastur saw the glint in the eyes, the sensual curve of his lips and the unmistakable big ears this stranger was her Mohan, the love of her life, her husband, now a vilayati vakeel. On NOVEMBER 1891 being pushed by Kastur, Mohan decided to shift to Bombay and establish his law practice there. He moved to Bombay, where he rented a home and office space. It was at this time that news from home informed Mohan that Kastur was expecting again. Meanwhile, the law practice turned out to be a miserable failure and he was forced to return to Rajkot. He decided to help his brother, and to draft appeals and petitions to earn some money and supplement the family income so that they could pay back the debts incurred on his foreign education. Mohan was good at this work and did quite well, although his earnings were meagre. 28 OCTOBER 1892 Kastur gave birth again, her third-born, second surviving son my grandfather. They named the boy Manilal. The parents were overjoyed but also anxious; the father wasn't earning enough to support the expanding family, and there was an unpaid debt. Their situation was desperate. MARCH 1893

Out of the blue, a missive arrived from South Africa offering Barrister Mohandas Gandhi a one-year assignment to assist the White lawyers Mohandas Gandhi a one-year assignment to assist the White lawyers of an Indian businessman, Dada Abdulla, in a complex legal dispute. However, I believe this must have happened due to the contacts of Kastur's father, Gokuldas Makanji Kapadia. Gokuldas had businesses all over India and abroad, extending right up to Africa. He owned ships and an international banking and finance operation of promissory notes honoured in all major Indian ports, on the Arabian coast and in ports in East Africa. Dada Abdulla was also in a similar line of business based in Durban. He too was originally from Kathiyavad, and very likely knew Gokuldas. When he required the services of a Gujarati lawyer educated in England, he would have requested Gokuldas for help, and Gokuldas would have naturally recommended his unemployed son-in-law. Dada Abdulla would not have entrusted such an important task that required deft handling to an unknown stranger with no references. Mohan grasped the opportunity, partially out of desperation and partially due to the excitement of travelling abroad and discovering a new land. His attempts at establishing a career had failed so far, and now he was a father of two in a family that had unpaid debt incurred because of him. He had the responsibility of the upkeep of his own Kastur was relieved. She would be once again separated from her husband, left behind alone with her two little sons, but at least this time he would be earning. She and her two sons bid goodbye to Mohan as he boarded a train for Bombay in April 1893. There, he would board a ship and set sail for distant South Africa. The separation was only for a year, she consoled herself, but at the back of her mind there was anxiety about what would happen when this assignment was over and her husband returned home, once again without a job, with no income. He was not going to earn enough to take care of the entire family, and at the end of the year the debt would remain unpaid.

1893-94 on this year passed quickly for Kastur; she learned that her husband was doing reasonably well in South Africa, his employers were pleased with his services and that he was also doing work for the community. This was a new aspect of her husband's life, gleaned from the sketchy information she got from her sister-in-law, who in turn heard bits and pieces from her husband, Lakshmidas. The brother regularly received letters from Mohan, along with remittances. As the year drew to an end, Kastur started preparing for the return of her husband. She longed for him, missed him and felt lonely; her longing was physical too. Mohan completed his assignment for Dada Abdulla and was all set to return to India. But fate had other plans. On the eve of his departure, Dada Abdulla and others from the Indian community had gathered to honour Barrister Gandhi for the services he had rendered and the battles he had fought for the rights and dignity of the community. A farewell party had been organized. As the community got together, Mohan caught a glimpse of a news item in the Natal Mercury newspaper, with the heading 'Indian Franchise'. It stated that a bill had been introduced in the Natal Legislative Assembly to deprive Indians of their right to vote. Barrister Gandhi immediately saw the threat it posed to the existence of the Indian community in South Africa and its well-being, and warned the assembled community elders about it. They prevailed on him to cancel his plans to return to India and lead the fight for their rights. They offered to pay him a salary, but Mohan refused to accept any remuneration for such community service. The Indians then promised to provide him enough legal work so he could earn a handsome living. Mohan agreed to stay back and fight for the rights of Indians in Natal, especially the Girmitya, Indian indentured labourers. When Kastur learnt that her husband was staying back in South Africa and would be helping out the Indian community there, she became aware that he was being talked about as a leader. She was proud of him as well as apprehensive of what this meant. What would this change in him be like? What would its consequences be for the family? She did not like these long separations. Even though when they were together, he would soon become irritating and annoying. His insistence on educating her, forcing her to learn Western manners was irritating. This caused a lot of friction between the two, but Mohan was persistent, and this annoyed Kastur a lot. Kastur liked his presence, she craved for his love and affection. She loved his passion too, and missed their love-making. Another worry was that both her sons were losing out on their father's presence in their formative years. Although Hari remembered the fun he had with his father, he was naturally closer to Lakshmidas, with whom he lived all the time, rather than the stranger who visited occasionally. Little Mani, meanwhile, had no recollection of his father. This troubled Kastur Soon, though, things started looking up. Mohan was regularly sending money from South Africa and the debt was rapidly being paid off. The family was also living much more comfortably and Mohan was becoming an ample provider. But he was still so far away, and Kastur was lonely.

One year stretched to three. The Gandhi family was now well off, and it felt like the days of poverty were over. Mohan was doing very well in South Africa. Kastur learnt that he had got a large house, Beach Grove Villa, in Durban, in a prestigious area of town close to the ocean. Kastur was full of pride for her husband's achievement. She had grown up in a seaside town, and her best childhood memory was sitting on the terrace of her father's home watching the sun set on the Arabian Sea. Growing up, she had spent many an hour sitting there, deep in thought. Now her husband had rented a house, which would be her own home by the sea. She could not wait to join him there and live with her husband and their family. To be mistress of her own home! When would it happen? She did not know. But the thought was thrilling. (Tushar Gandhi, 2022)

Finally, Kastur got to know that her husband was coming back for a short visit and intended to take his wife and sons back to South Africa. But the man who landed in Bombay in June 1896 and reached Rajkot on 7 July was once again a stranger to Kastur. Gone was the reticent, hesitant young man full of self-doubt, the one who had repeatedly failed at all he attempted. The man who returned from South Africa was different-confident, assured, determined and extremely focused. Even after his return, Mohan continued to be busy and preoccupied with affairs in South Africa There was a constant stream of with affairs in South Africa. There was a constant stream of a couple of years ago, the damaged diary at Kastur Gandhi, from January to correspondence from there, and he was always busy replying to it. Writing letters and articles and sending them off. Kastur realized that in the three years that had gone by, her husband had once again changed, and had become a big man'-someone important! He would correspond with people in India, England and South Africa, and what surprised Kastur was that they all seemed to be replying to her husband. It was from Rajkot that Mohan wrote about the plight of Asians in Natal and the discrimination they faced there. He wrote a series of articles on the subject, the most famous among them titled 'Grievances of the British Indians in South Africa'. He dispassionately wrote about the plight of Indians in the British colony of Natal, the fact that they were being discriminated against due to the colour of their skin. He held forth on the immorality of such practices without sensationalizing them. He was determined to send out his words to as many people of importance as possible and to newspapers, periodicals and journals in India. He was creating awareness, garnering sympathy and support for his South African cause amongst Indians and Britishers in India. Kastur watched, fascinated. At night, in bed, he would explain everything, in the intervals between their love-making. Kastur was thankful that her husband had not changed too much; she enjoyed and reciprocated his passion. During the day, he would be busy getting copies of his pamphlet printed in Rajkot and despatching them. Kastur saw that her husband was working too hard, so she suggested that he take the help of their sons and nephews to do the work of addressing the mail and posting it. Hari had very neat handwriting and Mani was old enough to seal envelopes and affix stamps. Soon, Mohan enlisted the services of all the children in the family as well as all the school going children in the neighbourhood. He started paying them for their labours by giving them the stamps which were on all the letters he received. He awakened an interest in philately in many of them and get them started as stamp collectors. Kastur was overjoyed. Her status in the family had risen; she was the wife of the provider. Her husband had somehow become an important person, and, best of all, he still loved her passionately. A couple of years ago, the damaged diary at Kastur Gandhi, from January to The shop printing copies of Mohan's pamphlet ran out of paper, and so its cover page was printed on green paper-thus, it came to be known as the 'Green Pamphlet. Just then, there was an outbreak of the plague would spread to their city, and so decided to survey the sanitation facilities and hygiene of the living quarters in the town. Mohan immediately volunteered and began inspecting the latrines in the homes of the affluent. But when it came to the homes and localities of those considered to be lower caste and 'Untouchables', shunned by Hindus, caste taboos kicked in and no one wanted to enter them. Mohan had never subscribed to these caste hierarchies and prejudices and so immediately volunteered to interact with the 'Untouchables' and inspect their bastis. To his surprise, he discovered that they practiced much more healthy and hygienic sanitary habits. But in his own home, he still had to accept the strict caste-based practices and bathe and change clothes before entering. Kastur too would not allow any relaxations in the cleansing ritual, and poured eleven buckets of water over her fully clothed husband's head before allowing him inside the home!

While Kastur basked in her husband's love and took pride in his achievements, the anxiety of travelling across the sea to a distant and strange land, and for the first time being so far away from her family and her parents, was always at the back of her mind. For the first time in her life she would not be able to visit her parents and her birth home when she wished, as she had gotten used to doing after her marriage. But the realization that her husband was a man of respect in that land was something she was eager to witness herself, apart from wanting to take charge of her own home. And so the preparations began. Mohan insisted she learn to wear clothes in the Western manner, like the attire of Parsi women: long-sleeved blouses, manner, like the attire of Parsi women: long-sleeved blouses, sometimes with collars and lacy frills, longer, embroidered saris, long socks and shoes. Mohan insisted Kastur take to this attire and made her and the children wear shoes and practise walking in them all the time before they left for South Africa. 30 NOVEMBER 1896 Tragedy struck the family with the death of Mohan's older sister Raliyat's husband, Vrandavandas, who left behind a son, Gokaldas, and a widow. Now Mohan was responsible for them too. It was decided that Gokaldas would go with the Gandhi family to South Africa and Raliyat would shift to Rajkot. The 'Green Pamphlet' was widely read in India, making the people aware for the first time of the plight of Indians in South Africa. Mohan became known as the voice of oppressed Indians there. A correspondent of the news agency Reuters wired a brief account of the 'Green Pamphlet and the stir it had caused in India to his London office, which in turn cabled an even briefer and more sensational account to their office in Durban. The Natal Mercury headlined the report and gave it further publicity, alleging that Barrister Gandhi had maligned the White citizens of the colony of Notel and defamed them but making baseless allocations alleging that Barrister Gandhi had maligned the White citizens of the colony of Natal and defamed them by making baseless allegations. This caused a lot of anger and resentment amongst the colonials in Natal, an anger which was fanned by opportunist politicians and community leaders. Then the news came that Gandhi was arriving with two shiploads of 'coolies' to swamp the colony. The Whites swore they would not let the 'coolie barrister' and his Black hordes set foot on the soil of Natal. They would dump them in the sea as soon as they arrived.

Mohan was unaware of these developments. Preparations for the departure were gathering pace, and Kastur was busy packing and preparing for the journey. She was happy that her nephew Gokaldas was going to accompany them. He was just a few months younger than her first-born would have been had he survived. In one part of her heart, Kastur still felt a hollowness for the child she had so tragically lost.

The Gandhis-Mohandas, Kastur, Harilal, Manilal and Gokaldas – departed from Bombay for Durban on board the SS Courland. The journey, Kastur's first on a ship, was scary, and to compound it her husband insisted on using the time to train his family to learn Western etiquette. How to walk, how to carry themselves, how to eat-not with hands but with fork, knife and spoon-and how to chew with the mouth closed. They must not speak with a mouthful of food. It was all unbearable for Kastur and the children, but Mohan was a hard taskmaster-there was no escape from the daily exercises. But there was more terror to come.(Avijit Pathak, 2023)

Fourteen days into the voyage, both ships, the Courland and the Nadir, both owned by Dada Abdullah, were caught in a severe monsoon storm at sea. The waters were wild and full of huge waves. The passengers were confined to their cabins, all hatches were battened down and all luggage tied up to prevent accidents. Most of the passengers were seasick, and the remaining were terrified. Kastur clung on to the children and prayed to God to save them. Since her husband seemed to be immune to the fears other were experiencing, the captain enlisted him to help keep the passengers calm. Kastur was left alone as the ship rolled and listed and they were tossed around in the cabins. Finally, after two days of torture and terror, the storm abated, the seas became calm and the ships once again began to sail smoothly. The ships reached the port of Durban but the pilot instructed the captains that they would not be allowed to dock; they were to be quarantined outside the Durban harbour and remain anchored until further orders were issued. The quarantine lasted twenty-five days. Finally, on 13 January 1897, both the ships were allowed to dock and everyone was allowed to disembark, except the Gandhi family. Finally the Captain informed the Gandhis that Mrs Gandhi and the children were to alight and would be taken to Parsi Rustomji's home but Mr Gandhi was to remain on board. Kastur's introduction to South Africa was terrificing and traumatic. When they all evited the dock Africa was terrifying and traumatic. When they all exited the dock, there was an angry mob at the gate to the port; it seemed to be baying for blood. She and the children were whisked away to a stranger's home. Late that evening, when her husband came there, his clothes were torn, he was wounded and bleeding he seemed to have been beaten up mercilessly. Then, the home of their host came under attack by a mob which was baying for her husband's blood. 'What has he done?!' The thought recurred in Kastur's panic-stricken mind over and over again. They heard stones crashing against the walls and windows of the house shatter and angry outbursts from outside. They cowered in fear inside. Later, her husband was secretly whisked away by the police, disguised as a sepoy, just before louts from the mob invaded the home, searching for Mohan. Finally at 2 a.m., peace and order were restored, and Kastur was informed that her husband was safe and secure. Only then she was able to doze off. 'What has he done now?!' she thought as she finally fell asleep.

Mohan joined them two days later, and finally took Kastur and the children to Beach Grove Villa, their home. She asked him about the disturbances that had occurred as soon as they reached Durban. 'What have you done now?!' she asked. 'Don't worry, my darling; they were have you done now?!' she asked. 'Don't worry, my darling; they were misguided souls,' Mohan brushed off her concerns. But I thought they would kill you! What have you done to anger them so much?" 'Nothing my darling, it's just a misunderstanding, they will soon realize their mistake and repent. Do not fret.' She would learn about her husband's exploits slowly, occasionally from him, and mostly from others. Soon, Kastur settled into life in Durban. It was a completely new experience for her a busy here were so different from those she had grown up with and lived in the midst of all her life. But she was the queen of her home and the Regina of her husband's heart and she had conceived again. This time Mohan convinced Kastur to let her child be delivered by a professional doctor. She was horrified, a strange man being involved in such an intimate manner? It was difficult for her to accept, but it was difficult to refuse her husband once he had decided something. Kastur went into labour. The doctor and a nurse were sent for, but the nurse could not reach in time, and so Mohan volunteered to assist the doctor. Kastur's labour pains lasted for a long time, and she was exhausted. But after a stressful and difficult birth, their third son, Ramdas, was born. However, Kastur had lost a lot of blood. This weakened her and led the doctor to advise bed rest, which meant Kapadia and Vrajkunvar simply vanished from her life and ceased to exist. Kastur and her sons settled into the Gandhi home in Rajkot.

Mohan travelled to Bombay and onwards to Calcutta accompanying some Congress men. There he met Gopalkrishna Gokhale in the later half of December. He tried to enlist the support of the Indian National Congress for the cause of Indians in South Africa but failed to get a resolution of support tabled at the convention. He then travelled to Burma, then back to Calcutta and on his way back he travelled across India to Benares, Allahabad, Agra, Delhi, Jaipur and then back to Rajkot. At Rajkot, Mavji Dave, the old friend of Karamchand Bappa, once again mentored Mohan and passed on three cases to him, to start him off. Mohan won all three, and soon established his reputation as a clever lawyer. But Kastur felt that her husband was not at ease; there was a restlessness in him, a growing disturbance within him. Once again, he seemed to be the wavering and uncertain boy of old, not the focused and determined person he had been in South Africa. With the coaxing of Gokhale and the urging of Mavji Dave, Mohan decided to move to Bombay and set up his practice there. Before leaving, in July 1902, he enrolled his son Harilal and his nephew Gokaldas in boarding schools one in Benares and one in Gondal, Kathiyavad; each had only one vacancy. Who would go where was decided by the drawing of coins, the one picking the higher-value coin would go to Benares, and the other to Gondal. As it turned out, Gokaldas went to Benares and Harilal to Gondal. Insulting the community. She tried her best to convince him to accept them, but failed; once Mohan made up his mind, no one and nothing could change it. Finally, Kastur said that she would keep the gifts personally given to her; she too had dutifully served the community and the gifts were given in appreciation of the services she had rendered. But Mohan would not allow that either. She begged, wept, cajoled and cited her responsibility towards her sons, her need to have something to give her future daughters-in-law, but Mohan had shrewdly enlisted both elder sons to his side. They solemnly told Kastur that when required they would earn and buy jewellery for their wives. Kastur admitted defeat and reluctantly gave up the jewellery and gifts given to her. After many grand farewells, the family left South Africa.

The Gandhis arrived in India and went directly to Rajkot and settled into the family home. There is no record of this, but during her absence, both Kastur's parents had passed away. Strangely, after Kastur's departure for South Africa in 1896, there is no recorded history about her parents; it feels as if both Gokuldas Makanji Kastur suffering terribly and Mohan witnessing her agony silently. Eventually, their fourth son was born; they named him Devadas. Once again, Mohan took care of the exhausted Kastur and the newborn infant, cleaning and bathing both mother and baby. He was so efficient that when the doctor came and examined Kastur and the baby, he complimented Mohan on a job well done. But the birth had taken a toll on Kastur's health, and she was bedridden for almost a month. Once again, Mohan took care of her, the household and the children almost single-handedly till Kastur recovered and was strong enough to take over the management of the household. In October, Mohan decided that his work in South Africa was over. The community was now capable of fighting its own battles, and he could return to India. He informed Kastur and requested her to begin winding up the household and pack for the move. Mohan informed the community and promised to remain aware and informed about the situation in South Africa, and said that if ever it was required he would be back. The Indian community in Durban gave a rousing farewell to Mohan and the Gandhi family, showering on them many gifts, including a purse containing a handsome amount of money which they had collected. Much precious jewellery was gifted to Kastur too. Mohan was not willing to accept the purse or the gifts. He decided to form a trust and deposit all the gifts and the money as a corpus for the trust, to be used for the welfare of the community. When he informed Kastur, she refused to accept Mohan's decision. She felt that by not accepting the gifts and the purse, Mohan would be Kastur was very anxious, and it led to many arguments between the two of them. However, while they argued and fought, both played their part as parents with responsibility and efficiency to ensure that life went on smoothly. Mohan was busy with legal work and looking after the welfare and well-being of the community, and Kastur efficiently and lovingly managed the affairs of a busy household and a growing family. In August 1899, she conceived again.

October 1899

The Anglo-Boer War broke out in South Africa, and Mohan decided that in order to prove the loyalty of the Indian subjects to the Crown, they needed to set an example. He raised the Indian Stretcher Bearer Corps and volunteered to serve the British forces in the war. During Mohan's absence, Kastur looked after the home, family and boarders, unaware that he and his fellow stretcher bearers were operating on the battlefront, putting themselves at risk from bullets and cannonballs, carrying off the wounded to the safety of the field hospitals often more than 20 miles away from the battlefront. It was only after Mohan returned that she heard the entire story of the war, and of the heroic deeds of her husband and the men he led. Kastur went into labour, with neither a doctor nor a midwife available. Mohan would have to deliver the baby all by himself. He bundled up the elder children, and told Hari to take care of his brothers. He prepared the birth room, readied Ba and waited for the birth of their child. Like the previous delivery, this one too was difficult, with Kastur went into labour, with neither a doctor nor a midwife available. Mohan would have to deliver the baby all by himself. He bundled up the elder children, and told Hari to take care of his brothers. He prepared the birth room, readied Ba and waited for the birth of their child. Like the previous delivery, this one too was difficult, with Kastur suffering terribly and Mohan witnessing her agony silently. Eventually, their fourth son was born; they named him Devadas. Once again, Mohan took care of the exhausted Kastur and the newborn infant, cleaning and bathing both mother and baby. He was so efficient that when the doctor came and examined Kastur and the baby, he complimented Mohan on a job well done. But the birth had taken a toll on Kastur's health, and she was bedridden for almost a month. Once again, Mohan took care of her, the household and the children almost single-handedly till Kastur recovered and was strong enough to take over the management of the household. Kastur that when required they would earn and buy jewellery for their wives. Kastur admitted defeat and reluctantly gave up the jewellery and gifts given to her. After many grand farewells, the family left South Africa. There is no record of this, but during her absence, both Kastur's parents had passed away. Strangely, after Kastur's departure for South Africa in 1896, there is no recorded history about her parents; it feels as if both Gokuldas Makanji Kapadia and Vrajkunvar simply vanished from her life and ceased to exist. Kastur and her sons settled into the Gandhi home in Rajkot.

Mohan travelled to Bombay and onwards to Calcutta accompanying some Congress men. There he met Gopalkrishna Gokhale in the later half of December. He tried to enlist the support of the Indian National Congress for the cause of Indians in South Africa but failed to get a resolution of support tabled at the convention. He then travelled to Burma, then back to Calcutta and on his way back he travelled across India to Benares, Allahabad, Agra, Delhi, Jaipur and then back to Rajkot.

At Rajkot, Mavji Dave, the old friend of Karamchand Bappa, once again mentored Mohan and passed on three cases to him, to start him off. Mohan won all three, and soon established his reputation as a clever lawyer. But Kastur felt that her husband was not at ease; there was a restlessness in him, a growing disturbance within him. Once again, he seemed to be the wavering and uncertain boy of old, not the focused and determined person he had been in South Africa. With the coaxing of Gokhale and the urging of Mavji Dave, Mohan decided to move to Bombay and set up his practice there. Before leaving, in July 1902, he enrolled his son Harilal and his nephew Gokaldas in boarding schools-one in Benares and one in Gondal, Kathiyavad; each had only one vacancy. Who would go where was decided by the drawing of coins, the one picking the higher-value coin would go to Benares, and the other to Gondal. As it turned out, Gokaldas went to Benares and Harilal to Gondal. (Tushar Gandhi, 2008)

Conclusion

Some years ago, workers from the Gandhi Research Foundation in Jalgaon discovered a decaying and damaged diary in the Kasturba Ashram in Indore. The diary of Kasturba Gandhi, written between January and September of 1933, was found to span 135 pages. Kasturba's diary ended up being ignored and forgotten, much like her. This book is a transcription of her diary written in Gujarati, with an English translation provided by her great-grandson Tushar Gandhi. Kasturba spent her entire life having her intelligence and literacy discounted. After Tushar Gandhi mentioned the diary to his family, they laughed and said, "She was illiterate." When she tried to write down her ideas, nothing came out right. Tushar realised he was wrong the more he read Kasturba's diary. It demonstrated that, despite her lack of formal education, she was her own person, someone you could hang out with and who was also a satyagrahi. Within the pages of The Lost Diary of Kastur, My Ba, readers will hear directly from Kasturba. This paper provides a window into what it was like to be the Mahatma's wife by detailing the couple's routine activities. This woman was there as history was made, and she did more than just watch; she helped make history. In addition, it describes her two arrests that year, both of which were unrelated to her role as Bapu's wife and both of which occurred during satyagraha. Even though she was born 150 years before the publication of this book, it is the first time that Kasturba has been presented as a complex person and a formidable female leader. Tushar Gandhi is the son of Sunanda and Arun Gandhi and the great-grandson of Kasturba and Mohandas Gandhi through their second son Manilal and daughter-in-law Sushila. Aside from leading the Gandhi Research Foundation and the Lok Seva Trust in Jalgaon, where he was born, he is also the president of the Mahatma Gandhi Foundation. In 2005, to celebrate the Dandi Kooch's 75th anniversary, he led a group of people on a re-enactment of the entire 241-mile journey. His walk along the entire route from Sabarmati Ashram to Dandi bolstered his case for including it on India's list of historical heritage routes. Currently, Tushar, his wife Sonal, and their two children, Vivan and Kasturi, call Mumbai home.

Works Cited

Avijit Pathak. (2023). *The Lost Diary of Kastur, My Ba' by Tushar Gandhi: Living with the Mahatma.* https://www.tribuneindia.com/news/reviews/story/the-lost-diary-of-kastur-my-ba-by-tushar-gandhi-living-with-the-mahatma-407011

Gandhi, T. A. (2022). *The Lost Diary of Kastur, My Ba Kindle Edition.* https://www.amazon.com/Lost-Diary-Kastur-My-Ba-ebook/dp/B09YVTLZJT

Tushar Gandhi. (2008). The lost diary of Kastur, My Ba. *Harper Collinsindia.* https://www.google.co.in/books/edition/The_Lost_Diary_of_Kastur_My_Ba/lPlsEAAAQBAJ?hl=en&gbpv=1

Tushar Gandhi. (2022). "Kasturba Gandhi's sole diary to be published as a new book by her great-grandson Tushar Gandhi." *Times of India.* https://timesofindia.indiatimes.com/life-style/books/features/kasturba-gandhis-sole-diary-to-be-p

CHAPTER 20

Journey of Life and its Connected Themes in Dylan Thomas' *Altarwise by Owl-light*

Dr. N. Sumathi

Abstract

Journey of life is analysed as a voyage taken by a sailor through different stages of voyage in parallel with different stages of life with an undertone of religion and sex. Thomas attempts a conventional Christian interpretation of life. Life from conception to the doomsday has been the subject matter of the ten sonnets of *Altarwise by Owl-light*. The sonnets derive different interpretations of several layers of meanings in astrological, Christianity, common man's journey of life and the poet's stages of life in the creation of poetry. The themes connected to life are death, love, sex which the boy undergoes through his boyhood, adolescence, youth, manhood and old age and death. Karl Saphiro on Thomas' poetic method commented that "Thomas poetry was a holocaust, sowing of the wind." Saphiro comments that "the metaphorical riddles are characteristic of Thomas and are particularly salient in *Altarwise by Owl-light*". Elder Olson believes that "the cycle marks a turning point not only in the technique but also in content." Moynihan notes that "Thomas' language implies so much than the mere words". The themes of sacrifice, revelation, spiritual certainty, fearful struggle of the poet, incarnation, voyage of life etc. The themes are coloured by religious and sexual overtones.

Keywords: Life – Journey of life – Religion – Spirituality – Sensuousness – Incarnation – Revelation – Stages of life

Introduction

The first seven sonnets are published in December, 1937 in "Life and Letters Today" (XIII, pg. 73-75). The other three sonnets are published in May 1936 in "Contemporary Poetry and Prose" VIII, IX and X sonnets in July. The ten sonnets are later collected in *Twenty Five Poems.* According to Elder Olson, sonnet cycle is considered to be astrological. The sun's annual passage through the signs of the zodiac which also represents the twelve labours of Hercules, the Sun Hero is represented in the ten sonnets. The Sun is placed in parallel to man and the span of human life is drawn in comparison to Hercules through the phenomenon of seasons.

Moynihan notes that "the sonnets are Thomas' depiction of fallen world, the world of exodus or wilderness, the world of wanderer, the outcast voyager." He has identified the sonnets to be the journey of life with different periods of man's life from birth to maturity and to death. He further points out that "Thomas is describing Christ and himself in the sonnets". Christ in human form is partly God and human being and man can be elevated into the level of God through his lofty virtues.

First sonnet describes the Christ birth at the cradle of the poet, who is described as "dog among the fairies" and "old cock from nowhere". Sonnet II describes the early childhood as "the child that sucketh long is shooting up" and "soon sets alight a long stick form the cradle". Man is partly God and partly devil comes under the lineage of Adam who is created in the image of God, the rungs of Abaddon and the angel of the bottomless pit. Sonnet III describes the stages of youth and adolescence marked by the loss of innocence in terms of the murder of Abel ("the lamb") by Cain ("Adam's wether" and "black ram"). Sonnet IV gives experiences of first awareness of death and passing time and the age of enquiry. The questions of adolescent about the meaning of life are God, death and sex drive etc... Sonnet V explores the discovery of hypocrisies of conventional religion. The poet rebels against the "fake gentleman", a preacher who is "tipsy from salvation's bottle", and as the Byzantine Adam, rebels against his teaching to become an outcast like Jonah and a wanderer like Ishmael. Sonnet VI describes man enters into life through sexual experience. The man wanders and travels over the sea, an image of "primordial chaos". Sonnet VII knocks the voyager (the poet) with the nature of reality of death, mortality and passing of time. "Time's tune" "sucks the bell-voiced Adam out of magic", stealing man's faith. Sonnet VIII denotes the crucifixion of Christ as well as poet. Christ image of crucifixion denotes the man's redemption of sins and attainment of salvation through the sacrifice. Sonnet IX brings out the poet's dilemma of belief and disbelief in orthodox Christianity and it may be described as rejection of the religion and its beliefs as "death from a bandage" as the religion creates in mind, the fear of death and sin. Sonnet X brings out resurrection of Christ as well as human being form an organic cycle and new life springs. The ten sonnets in the poem signifies the stages in the life of any man as well as the stages in the life of Jesus Christ and poet.

According to Olson's theory, Sonnet I describes nature is mortal as the stars reflect changing seasons. Death affirms the conception as the mortal being undergoes changes in time. Sonnet II describes the annual passage of the sun as vain because sun descends when it reaches the top of the spiral. Sonnet III describes the persona imagining the sun describing a span of time from the winter to succeeding autumnal equinox. The significance of winter that man is born out to death and must die to make other things born out of his death. Sonnet IV describes that the persona asks many meaningless questions due to lack of faith. He sees that the motion of the stars is sinister because they indicate the passage of time. Sonnet V describes the stars appearing as cowboys, cards, Biblical characters and nightmare figures. Life is like a nightmare dream of death. Sonnet VI shows that man and the sun are both burning candles. Man is wounded by birth and eventually bleeds to death. Sonnet VII places the persona to reject time and places his faith in the cross of Christ, seen in the heavens as a constellation. Sonnet VIII suggests that the cross signifies the sacrifice and like Christ, man has to sacrifice and there is no immortality or redemption. Sonnet IX justifies the Egyptian effort to withstand death and writing is the only resurrection which preserves the spirit. Sonnet X affirms the resurrection with the reappearance of the cross in the sky. Daniel Jones has remarked as "The heavens now spell out the message of God. Let time go on, bringing us closer to the Judgement day".

According to Tindall, the theme of the sonnet sequence is Thomas himself. The sonnet begins with the birth of the poet, his childhood and ends with his writing and publication of his poems. Sonnet I deals with the gentleman either his father or himself waiting to be born. Thomas brings the conflict between the father and son which Freud talks about. The father and the son can refer to Thomas' father and himself or the God and Christ (referring to Christ and the father). Sonnet II describes the growing up of child to die. Nature reaffirms life after death and death after life and through death, there is a hope of resurrection. Sonnet III brings in the metaphor of sheep referring to the lamb old days of childhood and seasons change parallel to the change in man. Thomas is described as a young lamb "to be a black ram, the boss of the fold". Sonnet IV describes the young Thomas troubling his mother embarrassing questions about sex and obstetrics. Sonnet V refers to the boy a little older and plays at beginning a voyage. The mother's protection and the "climbing sea" threaten the child's freedom. Sonnet VI describes the reflection of the wounded parents with Thomas' face as "a cartoon of slashes". Sonnet VII said that the young poet's words are a "book of trees". The poems are the Lord's Prayer and stamping it on a grain of rice shows modesty. His poems are like the sufferings of cross. Sonnet VIII describes suffering as the creator as the poet is crucified and his muse weeps. He leans on his father as well as mother as both have shaped him. Sonnet IX describes mummies as the images of printing in books. When the mummies set in the books, they occupy the poems too. They come alive and resurrected through the printing of poems in books. The poems reflect the shift in time. Sonnet X describes the poet to balance his poetry. He refuses the "dummy bay" of orthodox Christianity. His poetry is "the blown word" which confuses "December's thorn" and "a brow of holly" in an unorthodox arrangement. The "sea ghost" refers to the building worm of Thomas which may refer to the poet's writing finger and in Biblical sense, Eve's serpent and in sexual connotation, it is phallus. Thus the poem has three levels of meanings – creativity and the poet, Biblical meaning and sexual connotations.

Understanding of life is gained by a voyage through life. The voyage of life is attended by doubts, fears, wonder and uncertainty. The perplexity of life makes the poet crave for a spiritual awakening and guidance in the time-fold and death-ridden world. He seeks to understand the value of sufferings and sacrifice in life and in the scheme of universe. Altarwise denotes the religious connotations of worship particularly sacrifice. The voyage of life described in the sonnets is both Christian and secular. Thomas' imagery strides on two levels – Biblical and Sexual. Sex, birth, death and renewal are expressed through the Christian analogy of birth, crucifixion and resurrection. Christ is the archetypal image of life. The journey of life begins form the womb to tomb and then again to womb. The owl-light symbolises the darkness in the womb. The sonnet cycle of Altarwise By Owl-light uses imagery of two main sources drawn from the Bible and Freud. Sacred and erotic images are merged to reveal the kind of sacramental nature of sex. Basic Christian concepts of original sin, incarnation and atonement are projected through sex. Religion and sex interweave the theme of obscurity and paradox of life and death. The complexity of the poem lies in the handling of imagery in the poem. The origins of images in the poem have greatly influenced the themes. Edith Sitwell has noted on the difficulty of the sonnet cycle as "It is largely the result of the intense concentration of each phrase, packed with meaning, of the fusion of two profound thoughts." This intense concentration of imagery in the sonnet cycle is described by Daniel Jones as "almost claustrophobic". Daniel Jones has observed that "the complexity and concentration of imagery interweaves the difficulty of the sonnet cycle".

Francis Scarfe observes that the themes of the sonnets are "life-death antagonism" bound up with Biblical mythology and sexual symbolism. Sonnet II describes the universal sense of sin. Sex and sin are identified and death is always present. Sonnet III describes Thomas' capacity for montage. Sonnet IV is the passage of sexual symbolism in which love and sex are identified as a prelude to nativity. Sonnet VI conveys the horrors of birth in a brutally effective language. Sonnet VII describes Christ's identification with man, God and the universe. Sonnet VIII symbolizes the birth of love through the death of sex (crucifixion). Sonnet IX ends on a combined note of creation and destruction. The vision of the worm creating is gained only after the sexual immolation of the male. Thomas is trying to reconcile the creative and destructive elements of sex

Sonnet I depicts the conception and birth of life in womb. The womb is signified through owl-light and "half way house" which is a house between mortal and immortal. The idea of womb as a tomb and tomb as a womb is derived from Medieval and Renaissance. The child lies "graveward" in the mother's womb assuring the death before its birth. Man's journey towards tomb starts when he begins to breathe. Man rises to live eternally after death according to Christianity. Thomas identifies the birth of man particularly himself, the birth of Christ

Life sparked off in the "shapeless country" (the womb) shoots up in Sonnet II and "soon sets alight a long stick from the cradle". The child soon becomes sexually strong. He attains manhood, and sets another cradle rooking as he proceeds through life. Life's journey to light ("Jacob to the stars", Sonnet II) is a movement towards death. The menacing "cross-bones" and "the cavern over black stairs" refers to the horrors of life accompanies the voyage of life.

Man grows in the ladder of sin and death, a ladder horrifying symbol of "the horizontal cross-bones of Abaddon" and "verticals of Adam". Death is the ultimate reality. "Death is all metaphors, shape in one history". The "short spark" is an electrical image of life force that "set alight a long stick" which consumes itself and at the same time sets alight new life. The hope of renewal and continuity is offered in the last few lines of Sonnet II even though the course of life is the token of death.

> Hairs of your head, then said the hollow agent,
> Are but the roots of nettles and of feathers
> Over these groundworks thrusting through a pavement
> And hemlock – headed in the wood of weathers.

There is a constant transformation of life into different forms through the agents of death – "hollow agent". This "hollow agent" may refer to the holy spirit as suggested by Clark Emery. "And what he says breathes more of hope than of despair". The crumbling flesh nourishes "the roots of nettles and feathers" which raise their heads out of the earth into "the wood of weathers", of seasons, of reality. There is an ever renewal of green life which is death-ridden, "hemlock-headed". "Over these groundworks thrusting through a pavement" is the life force. The three ways to immortality which defeats death are orthodox Christian means, sexual intercourse, and immersion into the life-stuff are the three ways of attaining immortality.

Sonnet III welcomes the child into adolescence of the sheep from spring lamb to spring ram is expressed through ovine imagery: "Adam's wether in the flock of horns... Horned down with skullfoot...The black ram.... Alone alive among his mutton fold". "Climbing grave" refers to the womb where life grows towards death. The image of copulation is to be found in the following lines:

> That Adam's wether in the flock of horns,
> Butt of the tree-tailed worm that mounted Eve,
> Horned down with skullfoot and the skull of toes
> On thunderous pavements in the garden time" (Sonnet III)

"Adam's wether" who "horned down with skullfoot" "on thunderous pavements in the garden of time" is father. The father in his creative but self-consuming thrust conveys vital stuff to the son. "I took my marrow-ladle / Out of the wrinkled undertaker's van" and put on "the descended bone" of son and death. He is now the "black ram" "alone alive among the mutton fold", alive among the eves. The vital continuity through propagation is maintained, "We rise from the vaults of death and put on the descended bones of death and in turn, die to provide the marrow of another's life". (Elder Olson)

> The black ram, shuffling of the year, old winter,
> Alone alive among his mutton fold,
> We rung our weathering changes on the ladder,
> Said the antipodes and twice spring chimed.

The above lines depict the generation and regeneration in nature and man. The earth regenerates itself in the spring. Life and death are described as ladders and antipodes ring the cyclic changes in life and death ladders.

The age of questions preoccupy the Sonnet IV. The boy puts forth the questions about sex embarrass the mother (referred to as "wounded whisper"). The boy questions the Christian faith with equally nagging questions. The questions show the greater awareness in boy as well as the poet. Through scepticism the poet moves to light, undergoes the process of spiritual re-birth.

> What is the metre of the dictionary?
> The size of genesis? The short spark's gender?
> Shade without shape? The shape of Pharaoh's echo?

The mysterious questions that life puzzles the man with made the boy ask too many questions about the mysteries of life. It is beyond the comprehension of the intellect. "What is the size of being before it takes into shape? Can there be a soul divorced from the body, shadow from shape? What is the sex of "the short spark" which is the generative force? "What of a bamboo man among your acres?" "Can the scarecrow of the bamboo poles be the father of the child in the mother's or Hary's womb?" (Kleinman). The growing boy in his voyage through life becomes aware of death. "A bamboo man may also refer to marrowless skeleton." "What of a bamboo man?" "Questions are hunchbacks to the poker marrow". These questions "about the meaning of life are deformities, hindrances, to the natural inclinations of the "poker marrow the life forces, the newly discovered sexual drive." (Moynihan). Sceptics are ""hunchbacks" to the man of faith. The "boneyards" is a metaphor of mother's body. "A crooked boy" is a cynic.

The image of photography sets at rest all the questions of the cynic. The answer to all questions is in one word love. The embryo in the mother's womb, the "bread-sided field", bears the stamp of love, since it is conceived in love.

> Love's reflection of the mushroom features,
> Stills snapped by night in the bread-sided field

Sonnet V shows the religious experience of the boy and his discovery of the hypocrisy of the conventional religion. Thomas makes a reference to the Gabriel's apocalyptic trump and of preaching in the chapel

> And from the windy west came two-gunned Gabriel,
> From Jesu's sleeve trumped up the king of spots,
> The sheath-decked jacks, queen with a shuffled heart;
> Said the fake gentleman in suit of spades
> Black-tongued and tipsy from salvation's bottle

Gabriel, an angel of the annunciation and the last trump comes as a cowboy or a western two-gunned marshal. "Trump" introduces the imagery of playing cards, and this also suggests trickery. The tricky "two-gunned Gabriel" "trumped up" from "Jesu's sleeve" "the king of spots" "the angel of death", the hosts of the sinners, and Babylon. The trickery of the chapel consists in the "salvation bottle" which makes one "tipsy". But the boy remains "black-tongued". The preachers of religion are "fake" gentlemen, and hypocritical liars. Thomas, the "Byzantine Adam" revolts against the preacher's idea of salvation and damnation.

Rose my Byzantine Adam in the night

This rising in the night i.e., creation symbolises protest against the life-denying abstinence preached by the religious preachers. In "Jonah's Moby", two images are telescoped, the images from the Bible and "Moby Dick". "Medusa" represents the sensuality. Thomas always an inner inhibition accompanying sexual drive. The lustful songs of the sirens come from the waste sea alluring and tormenting the hero; the psychological fear is never absent. Evil and death are associated with sexuality, but not in any theological sense.

The initiation into life through sexual experience occurs in Sonnet VI. The voyager blows tallow from the "tower" of father's creative candle. Sexual experience is essential for the development of personality. The voyager unites father and mother principles in his own creative efforts. The image "tide-traced crater" combines fire and water to express this cooperation. Creation involves, as it were, a cosmic energy. The cataclysmic upheaval is expressed through seismic imagery, "tide-traced crater", "lava's light split through the oyster vowels", "burned sea silence", "pluck", "lop", introduces surgical imagery.

> Adam, time's joker on a witch of cardboard
> Spelt out the seven seas, an evil index
> The bagpipe-breasted ladies in the deadweed
> Blew out the blood gauze through the wound of manwax

"Adam, time's joker", the father principle, writes on a page, "on a witch of cardboard", the mother principle, Adam begets poems. These poems spell out "the seven seas" which indicate the prolong journey that awaits the voyager. It is on "evil index" since all voyage ends in death. In all creation, women are necessary through dangerous. Women are always associated with death and sensuality in Thomas, "the bagpipe-breasted ladies" blow out the gauze (bandage) that precents wounded men from bleeding to death and thus extinguish the candle of man. (Kleinman)

Sonnet VII states that the way to defeat time is to have faith, faith in the Lord. The Lord's prayer is the staff of life. The "book of trees" which is "Bible-leaved" should be studies instead of "book of water" which tells of time and death. In Thomas' poems, words are always associated with trees. All religion should be stripped "to this tree". Religion stripped to its essence is the word (John 1:1).

Doom on Deniers at the Wind-turned Statement

"The denier at a wind-turned statement is a denier of the word's embodiment – that is, of spirit breathed into body (incarnation); of the body's transformation... on the road tree of death. Such a denier denies the full natural cycle. Doom on such..." (Emery)

But time seems omnipotent. "Ladies with the tests of music" sets the "time's tune". Time, like a sponge, sucks the faith of "the ball-voiced Adam" and that "from the world beginning".

Time is the Tune my Ladies Lend their Heartbreak

Ladies give their heartbeat to their children. But the children are in time, they in turn will break the hearts of their mothers. "Time's tune" grows out of their heartbreak. From the bare pavilion of the sky to the earth ("the house of bread") below, time "tracks the sound of shape on man and cloud". Time leaves it a point on all the objects of all seasons. Time pursues the rose and icicle, man and cloud through their changes. So time is not so powerful as it appears.

Individual life may come to any end but the cyclical continuity of life defies time. Clouds change but do not die. Life asserts itself through death defeating continuity. Time stalks on everything that comes into existence, but it can never wipe it out. Life ever renews itself and this Thomas has already said in Sonnet II.

> Time's relentless pursuit of life brings the inevitable end to the voyager.
> This was the crucifixion on the mountain
> Time's nerve in vinegar, the gallow grave
> As tarred with blood on the bright thorns I wept;
> The rold's my wound, God's Mary in her grief,
> Bent like three trees and bird-papped through her shift,
> With pins for teardrops is the long wound's woman
>
> (Sonnet VIII)\

In "The world is my wound", the "world" is an image of body of God or Christ and the "wound" is an image of suffering and death. The suffering of the world is the suffering of the God. In "God's Mary in her grief", the crucifixion of her son is her wound. Mary epitomises all mothers. Mothers suffer heartbreak through the idea of their children on who time stalks. Mary is the "long wound's woman", the spouse of "the long world's gentleman" (Sonnet I). She suffers the agony of childbirth. This is her crucifixion which all mothers suffer to maintain the continuity of life. She is bird-papped through her shift", meaning she is bird-breasted. This recalls the image of the mother as "the planet-ductd pelican of circle" (Sonnet II) who sacrifices herself suckling her offspring on her heart's blood. Mary bent down in grief "like three trees in a striking image of agony. The crucifixion of Christ is the sacrifice made for the welfare of the world. His sacrifice involves the whole world which is slow to realise its significance. The death of Christ was predestined ("heaven – driven"). The crucifixion is implicit in the nativity. It is in the scheme of the universe. Christ dies to nourish the life of others, "from pole to pole".

> This was the sky, Jack Christ, each minstrel angel
> Drove in the heaven-driven of the nails
> Till the three-coloured rainbow form my nipples
> From pole to pole leapt sound the snail-waked world

Child is the heavenly surgeon, "all glory's surgeon", who sees death. Christ is the death of death. In this historic accent, sex is exalted to love,

> In the light of legend and pelican image is may be said that "the child-hero raises the symbol of potency, his father's phallus which enables him to "suffer the heaven's children through my heartbeat." The signal act of

> reaching majority, thus is the apotheosis of the child, the crucifixion and castration of the father (D.F .Mackay). "Blowclock witness of the sun" may refer to the darkness of the world during the crucifixion and the extinction of time. Thomas combines closely physical life and spiritual life. Christ is "time's nerve". His bitter sacrifice has made time weak. The continuity of life has made death impotent. "This mountain minute" is an image which combines time and space, great and smell. The crucifixion on the mountain has a great cosmic significance. Genesis, birth, growth, love led to this moment. (Kleinman). "All glory's cowbones" offers his body for the life of others.

After the crucifixion in Sonner VIII comes the theme of burial and resurrection in Sonnet IX. We are in a pagan world, attempts have been made to gain release from the captivity of time and attain immortality. The corpse is preserved in Egyptian embalmment.

> ...the queen in splints
> Buckle to lint and lcoth their natron footsteps
> Draw on the glove of prints, dead Cairo's henna
> Pour like a halo on the caps and serpents

The spirit of the writer is embalmed in writing, in "oil and letter". The "leaped calligrapher" and embalmer offer a defiance of death and provide resurrection. But the inscribed mummy cloth is the glove of the hand of time which contains death and not life. "This was the resurrection in the desert". The scholars with their mask of scholarship find death in the gold mask on the mummy's face, infer "death from a bandage". The "linen spirit" "entombment in mummy cloth." consigns the phallic "long gentleman to busts and furies in the pyramided "world in the end". (Olson)

All the glories and fancies collected in the odyssey oflife are deed weights of stones in the pyramid. The triangle landscape is an image of the pyramids and the female principle. "The deed around my neck" is an image of albatross round the neck of the Ancient Mariner and symbolically suggests the crime committed and punishment that the wanderer in his nightmarish journey through life.

There is no escape from death and time but the hint of life is given in "linen spirit" that unites the long gentleman's phallic tool with "dusts and furies". "Furious are the deadly women, sirens medusa of the earlier sonnets where they represent feminine principle and sexuality which occurs the continuity of life.

The meaning life has offered to the voyager to whom Christian teachings offer no consolation and answer, Sonnet X attempts to answer. The "tale's sailor" will anchor "half-way" off the "dummy bay" (harbour) of Christian faith and cease from the search for the meaning of life in conventional Christianity and hold, like Atlas, "Time is ship-recked gospel" on the "globe" of his poetry. The sea farer has realised "December's thorn surround in a brow of holly". The polar opposites meet in life; pain is found in the midst of joy, birth in death. The single miracle of the world is the persistence of ever-recurring life through death and this has kept alive the Christian virtues of faith, hope and love. "Let the first Peter" (Sonnet X about father, pealing like a stick in mother's blue channel" to sow the flesh of child Thomas and the holy child around a ghost) (Tindall).

The child will rise and fall "with its two bark towers" and the ever proceed life will be "green as beginning". The two forces of life and death will become one at the end on the day of Judgement, the "nest of mercies" will be built by "the rude, rod" phallus which is creative and destructive at the same time. The "worm" builds with "venom" and venom contains new life. Golden "straw" are those of mothers'. Mercy is to be seen in the natural cyclical process of life and death in which nothing is lost.

> ...to that day
> When the worm builds with the gold straws of venom
> My nest of mercies in the rude, rod tree.

> "It is the power of love which remains as the vindication of life and survival; the fact that the processes of life go on, that the process of generation in man and nature never falls, and that the seasons change, is itself witness of some beneficent will at the heart of the universe." (John Ackerman)

Conclusion

The journey of life starts with the birth and a voyage towards the death. Death is not the ultimate end but the process of regeneration and new life as every poem of Dylan Thomas states. The voyager is the wanderer in the sonnets and he undergoes the various stages of revelation at different levels – from birth, boyhood, adolescence, youth, manhood, old age and death. The voyager expresses fearful struggle at times and at times reveals the wonder and awe and sometimes doubt and questioning the faith of the religion but rooted in the forefathers. Kleinman believes that "the sonnets are deeply moving statements of religious perplexity concluding in spiritual certainty. They reflect the wonder, awe, doubt and faith of a young poet who could not reconcile the capacity of divine pity with the necessity of human sacrifice. The paradox of the incarnation and passion affected Thomas early in his career. There is revelation in the sonnets of a fearful struggle of the poet with his God. Concentric to the theme of struggle is the theme of sacrifice; the agonizing story of Abraham and Isaac is implicit in the sonnets." Thomas has used the Biblical reference to Adam and Eve and other characters and astrological reference to the Sun and Hercules, stars and influence of stars, Capricorn and Cancer. The sonnets in detail exemplify the journey of life which is often mysterious voyage as the sailor's.

Works Cited

Ackerman, John, *The Welsh Background. Dylan Thomas: A Collection of Critical Essays.* Edited by C. B. Cox. Englewood Cliffs, N.J.: Prentice-Hall, Inc., 1966, 75-78

Jones, Daniel, ed. *The Poetry of Dylan Thomas.* New York: James Laughlin, 1971, pp.83.

Kleinman, Hyman. *The Religious Sonnets of Dylan Thomas: A Study in Imagery and Meaning,* University of California Press, 1963, pp.46.

Mackay. D.F., *Aspects of Energy in the Poetry of Dylan Thomas and Sylvia Plath Critical Quarterly* (ed. C.B. Cox and A.E. Dyson), Vol. 18. No.1, Spring 1974, p.22.

Moynihan, William T. *The Craft and Art of Dylan Thomas.* New York: Cornell University Press, 1966, pp. 37.

Olson, Elder. *The Poetry of Dylan Thomas.* Chicago: University of Chicago Press, 1954, pp. 72.

Scarfe, Francis. *Dylan Thomas: A Pioneer. Auden and After: The Liberation of Poetry,* 1930-1941. London, pp. 102.

Shapiro, Karl. *Adam and Eve. This Is My Best.* Edited by Whit Burnett. New York: Doubleday & Company, 1970, pp. 180-185.

Stearns, Marshall. *Unsex the Skeleton: Notes on the Poetry of Dylan Thomas, Transformation Three,* 1946, pp. 145-158.

Tindall, William York. *A Reader's Guide to Dylan Thomas.* New York: The Noonday Press, 1962, pp. 103-104.

CHAPTER 21

Fiction v/s Nonfiction: A Critical Comparative Evaluation in English Literature

Anubhav

Life is a mixture of experiences. These experiences may be either good or bad. Good experiences remain in our mind throughout life, and bad experiences we tend to forget. I've never seen a normal human being telling about a non-significant bad event. It is a human tendency to remember and repeat the good things and forget the bad ones, in the name of a bad day. These good and bad experiences teach something to all of us. Good experiences give us sweet memories to cherish and bad experiences give us learning, about what to erase and what not to repeat. These entire experiences combine together to form life. These experiences remain in a passive state and come out when we are asked to narrate our experience to somebody or when we think about any critical situation in our free time, these earlier experiences form the basis of our current decision, Yes these decisions might differ according to the circumstances but a human being takes the help of these experiences to arrive at it, and all these present decisions carry from within, the soul of experiences of the past, which help us to frame the path for the future. When a human being writes something it comes out in the form of a book. These books may be fiction, nonfiction or a mix of both. Books are nothing but written human experiences in a crisp manner with a title or label over it. Fictional books are purely imaginative and Co incidental. For example: Harry Potter. Nobody has ever seen the school of Hogwarts in real. Nobody has seen a small ball and brooms flying and turning in mid-air. When JK Rowling was asked about whether she was sure about the success of the Harry Potter Series she said: "*I don't know what struck me when I started writing about Harry Potter. For me it was a way to give something new to children which they read with zeal and interest apart and different from the fiction which seemed more comic and non life like, thank god it succeeded(laughs)"* as she said in an interview with BBC World in 2004.

Non Fiction writings comprise of the basic genres like autobiographies, memoirs, travelogues, science, self-help etc.These books are nothing but real life experiences of the authors.

All these fictional and non fictional writings are placed in a vast system which is placed under another vast system. Let us understand it with the help of a Venn diagram

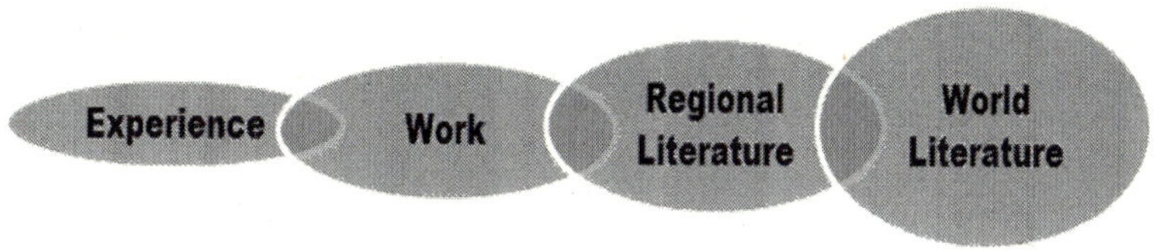

The same Venn diagram shown above works for nonfiction as well. There is something in common which is the basic experience. According to the theory of tragedy by Aristotle as he writes in his *Poetics*, plot plays a major role. In any novel or text there is a proper beginning, middle and end. In nonfiction as well, there is a proper description of everything. For example if we write an autobiography, we start from the beginning, describing about the childhood and then moving to the present age. If we write a diary, it is also chronological. There is a proper sequencing of things datewise. It is never like we mention a future date on previous page and the present date later on.

There is a proper order of ideas when we write something. First of all we experience something in life, than we think of narrating our experience to others. This is where a work forms in our mind. The work when completed is compared to other works of the same language and genre and this comparison evaluates our work as significant or non significant. When the work attains the staid level of significance in regional literature, its readership increases up to the next stage and it becomes significant on the world stage as well. As we can see, that the text transforms itself. There are multiple interpretations of it. And these interpretations vary differently i.e. according to mood, region and situation. For example if a person sitting in India, reads a text, for instance *The Last Girl, by Nadia Murad and Jenna Krajeski,* the interpretation drawn would lack reality as the text is centered around the Gulf region of Iran and Iraq, where the

Islamic State is active as a terrorist organization. Let's take another example of the book of Malala Yousafzai, *I am Malala* along with Christina Lamb. In this book the Nobel Peace Prize winner narrates her experience of how she was shot by the Taliban in the head and how she survived. Now we, sitting in the comfort of our homes would interpret it differently, as compared to the school students, in front of whom the incident happened. They would tell us the real experience, which is not narrated in any book, the real terror in the eyes, the deafening silence of the guns firing shot by shot, and killing people in the name of moral policing against education. So the nonfiction books are more realistic and interesting to read. It is not a judgment or prejudice, but the efforts that are put in writing any book be it fiction or nonfiction is a thing which cannot be ignored. The fiction books bring in the importance of imagination, when the author thinks of the real life characters and places them according to the situation one by one, where the situations are also hyper real in a sense that the readers know the genre is fiction, but they still read it and relate its characters to the real life happenings. For example, the books of the well-known popular choice author Chetan Bhagat, are all fiction, but we still connect to them. Why? It is because of their writing style and power of narration. The book *The Girl in Room 105* is a good piece to read where Chetan Bhagat narrates the story of Keshav and Zara, the girl from Kashmir, about how they fell in love during the hostel days and broke up four years ago. As Chetan Bhagat itself calls it "*It is not a love story it is an unlove story, about how a girl calls her ex boyfriend on the eve of her birthday and the boy found the girl dead and cold in Room 105 in her hostel.*

We can compare two authors of same style, but comparing two random authors of any age would be a big mistake. This is what we have to consider. For example comparing Munshi Premchand with Charles Dickens, of course we can try that if we are in research field, but for a layman to try and read both of them side by side would be an arduous task to do and almost close to impossible.

As far as sports autobiographies are concerned the challenges are different. To create the same atmosphere as experienced in the stadium, just by narration itself shows the efforts put in behind writing a sports autobiography. It gives you the feeling that you are thinking from the mind of the cricketer or athlete and it gives you a thrilling experience which is worth reading. For example the famous

South African Cricketer wrote his autobiography and we get a glimpse of how religious he is when he says in Chapter 1 of his book

> "I am all because of Jesus Christ. I am just a medium, it's all his will. When the first ball crunched off the bat to the boundary I looked up and Christ said to me, there is something special waiting for you today child, just blast off."

He narrates the readers that the coach told Davey (David Miller) to wait and instructed me to put my pads on during the match where he broke the world record of the fastest century in one day internationals against West Indies during the Pink ODI, a hundred off just 31 balls faced, the fastest of all time.

The books written also take into account the time invested by the readers to read. In earlier times the books were quite bulky and heavy, narrating every setting and situation first and then getting on to the story part. The story moved slowly page by page and when it came to the end the readers have read 600 pages already. For example Tom Jones by Henry Fielding in Fingerprint Publishing has 816 pages in all, and David Copperfield of the same publishing has 1416 pages in total. In the busy world of today nobody has that much time. Books and newspapers were the only mediums of entertainment in earlier times. The books also were not like today as we get them. The chapters of the novels were published as episodes five days a week and the readers read it with keen interest, just like we watch TV Serials in modern times. Whereas today a novel if bulky tends to get ignored if the reader is a layman, because they read the book for entertainment only and not for critical evaluation of the book. Some people by mistake buy bestsellers thinking if they are best sellers they ought to be the best but it is a myth.

First of all they must be aware of their genre of interest and after knowing their genre of interest, they must research the said book about their content, rather than blindly trusting the best seller tag on it because this tag takes into consideration many critical factors, of which a reader is unawares. And then they regret of wasting out their precious hard earned bucks.

Thriller Series authors are getting popular now a days like James Dashner and Dan Brown. Dan Brown who is famous for his three major works *The Da Vinci Code, the Lost Symbol, and Angels and Demons.* The Da Vinci Code is about a cold brutal murder at *The Louvre* in France when an elderly curator of the above mentioned museum is put to death. It is a murder mystery and second of the five books of

The Robert Langdon Series. After the Da Vinci Code came out the Lost Symbol which is just a mere extension of the events of the earlier novel. Angels and Demons is the earliest published book where the character of Robert Langdon is introduced and he is given the task of investigating the murder of Leonardo Vetra, a scientist and to detect his connections with the *Illuminati*, a secret society which Langdon thinks, is responsible for the murder of the said scientist.

People tend to like and usually incline towards thrillers because of their fast paced action. Young generation have a scientific mindset as we move towards science stream, and people of the arts stream bend towards romantic fiction and Classics in a general sense. The fast pace of the thrillers create an adrenaline rush and we are not able to put it down. Once read completely we move towards another part of the same series thinking about the same age old question, What happened next? And that is where we develop interest towards reading books. Once we begin reading books, there is nothing more peaceful and pleasurable experience. For those who don't like to read books, there are movie adaptations of the same, but movies are movies. Like a chapatti made on a village chulah has that smoked flavor within, which is unmatched as compared to one which is made on a gas burner, the same is the case. The directors and producers tend to add their own creativity and spice, rightly so because they cannot show everything which is written, but it distorts the original flavor. The novel (or the Chapatti) is the same having the same ingredients, but the tastes are different. The text loses its original essence when the mixture is so much as Bacon said "*A mixture of a little lie to the truth tends to add pleasure but the more is added the more distasteful the truth becomes.*"

Just like Maggie masala is added to the raw Maggie to create a taste which is edible, the same is the case with genres. The author adds the masala of his or her choice to the raw idea which is created in the mind. The masala can be regular, hot and spicy or a simple raw classic one, more suitable to adults as they like the classics and could feel the old melody much better. They usually tend to go page by page like a slow horse cart moving on a rainy day enjoying every bit of the pleasant weather. They are not fast paced like the young generation. The factor of age plays a big role. As we move towards the old age the choices we make, as we read and our tree of imagination matures fully, the choices become more sombre, delightful and ripe. Young people in their twenties or thirties are quite impatient and immature to understand the complex mindset which is required to write a classic novel. For them a novel is a piece to read once only. The more short and romantic the chapters are, the more they like it. That is why some young authors of the contemporary age are more popular. Those who like myths can read Devdutt Pattnaik and Amish Tripathi to understand the characters of their choice in a better way.

In the final say and on a final note it can be said that there is no comparison between fiction and nonfiction. Both have a concrete base on which a superstructure is built. People usually compare but the mindset, concentration and creativity which is required to write a masterpiece, be it fiction or nonfiction is not found in every human being. It is not an innate or inherited trait but an acquired one. People critically evaluate the majestic masterpieces written, but tend to forget the efforts put in by the author to bring a piece out. It's all about the mindset, whether to create or to distort. Both are two faces of the same coin. People toss it and it would fall, one way or the other. The coin is the work, minted by the author in the mint of his brain first and then put on paper. The onus is on the reader itself to interpret the way he or she likes and then pass on the work into the hands of other readers to interpret. As Roland Bartes writes

> "The author is dead as soon as the work is presented before the readers. The onus is on them now to interpret the work, the way they want and according to the tastes they like"

Works Cited

Brown, Dan. *Angels and Demons*, RUHK, 2009.

.... *The Da Vinci Code*, RUHK, 2009.

.... *The Lost Symbol*, RUHK, 2010.

Yousafzai, Malala. *I am Malala*, W & N, 2014.

De Villiers, Abraham Benjamin. *AB The Autobiography*, Pan, 2016.

Murad, Nadia. *The Last Girl*, Virago, 2018.

Bhagat, Chetan. *The Girl in Room 105*, Westland, 2018.

Fielding, Henry. Tom Jones, Fingerprint Publishing, 2020.

Dickens, Charles. *David Copperfield,* Fingerprint Publishing, 2020.

CHAPTER 22

The Voice behind Persona; A Critical Evaluation of Non-Fictional Writings of Salman Rushdie

Dr Rajesh Trivedi

The fame of Salman Rushdie as a novelist can be attributed to two main factors; first the technical innovativeness that unifies a number of influences not just from literature and novel writing but also from the allied species of literature and secondly the bold thematic framework that entail his treatment of religion and religious figures and his political views that owe their origin to the idealism of a Cambridge educated intellectual and the discomfiture caused by deviations from the ideal eventually leads to the birth and burgeoning of controversies. It is pre-eminently the reason why almost all his novels have fallen prey to controversies on political or religious grounds. It is truly unfortunate that the elements constituting the point of view of the author have rarely been discussed in completeness. The crisis of identity is one of the major factors defining the point of view of the author and much of the controversial delineation of characters and situations in the narratives of Salman Rushdie are attributed to the crisis of identity. Rushdie is the novelist with acute social and political consciousness that contribute incessantly to the point of view of his narrators-whether he is a first person narrator or third person narrator. The authorial intrusions in the narratives also contribute to compliment the point of view of the narrator that makes the crux of his technique of narration and ratification of the essential nature of the point of view. Rushdie has published a number of non-fictional works. He published a book on reportage titled *The Jaguar Smile; A Nicaraguan Journey* (1987), a collection of essay of various topics titled *Imaginary Homelands* (1991) that arrest his interest and consequently contribute to the form and nature of his point of view, and a book on film criticism *The Wizard of Oz* (1993). His major works for television are *The Painter and the Pest* (1985) and *The Riddles of Midnight* (1987). The present paper aims at exploring various constituent elements of the point of view of the narrators of the novels of Salman Rushdie and to rationalize the contents leading to the complexities of the themes and techniques of his novels. The research paper mainly focuses on the Rushdie's collection of essays – *Imaginary Homelands* and the travelogue – *The Jaguar Smile; A Nicaraguan Journey.* The interviews of Rushdie from different journals and magazines have also been referred to.

The crisis of identity has been one of the recurring features of the thematic framework of the works of Salman Rushdie. All the protagonists of his major novels are subjected to this agony of fragmentation and rupturing of identity which is nothing but the reflection of the personal agony of the loss of origin. Salman Rushdie was born in Bombay in the year 1947, which is unambiguously the most eventful year in the history of modern India. He spent his first thirteen years in Bombay and during this period he was sent to Cathedral High School in Bombay. At the age of thirteen, Rushdie was sent to Rugby which marks the earliest realization of the fragmentation of identity. He recollects his days at Rugby with great pains and recollects;

> I was miserable at Rugby. Here at Rugby I was suddenly an Indian. There are no Indians in India. There are classes of course and regional identifications. Here in England, it is largely understood as race-and at the school – boy level, back then that was no fun. (Rushdie, Interview, *Parade*, June1989, 50)

The loneliness and isolate which Rushdie was subjected to as a small school going child, exercised a lasting influence on his creativity. The most decisive blow on the creativity of Rushdie is manifest in multiple identities. Rushdie, after completing the schooling at Rugby was reluctant to proceed with higher education but to respect the wish of his Cambridge educated father, he joined the under graduate courses at Kings College Cambridge. After completing his graduation in 1968, he returned to his homeland, but now it was not India but Pakistan as his family had left Bombay for Karachi. Rushdie's agony of the loss of origin seeks best expression in the title essay of *Imaginary Homelands.* He, during his visit to Bombay, recollects that he opened the telephone directory and saw his father's name. He further recollects;

> And amazingly, there it was; his name; our old address; the unchanged telephone number as if we had never gone away to the unmentionable country across the border. It was an eerie discovery. I felt as if we were being claimed, or informed that the facts of faraway life were illusions, and that this continuity was a reality. (Rushdie, *Imaginary Homelands*, 09)

The above quoted passage gives us the erupting nostalgia of the author for the roots and in the same essay, he makes clear the agony of cultural transplant 'for those of us who have migrated.' He writes;

> We are Hindus who have crossed the black water; we are Muslims who eat pork. And as a result – as my use of the Christian notion of the Fall indicates – we are now partly of the West. Our identity is at once plural and partial. Sometimes we feel that we straddle two cultures; at other time, that we fall between two stools. But however shifting and ambiguous this ground may be, it is not an infertile territory to occupy. (Rushdie, *Imaginary Homelands*, 15)

Rushdie endured the loss of homeland and went to Pakistan to receive more question marks on his identity not just as an individual but also as a writer and man of creative predilections. Pervading fanaticism in Pakistan disqualified the secular and progressive mind of Rushdie for the stay and citizenship in that country and the result was another escape and now it was back to London. Rushdie, in his essay titled "Censorship," recollects his 'first direct encounter with censorship', when he was 'commissioned' to write a piece' about his impressions on returning home.' He writes;

> I remember very little about this piece (mercifully memory is a censor too), except that it was not all too political. It tended, I think, to linger melodramatically on images of dyeing horses with flies settling on their eyeballs. You can imagine the sort of thing. Anyway, I submitted my piece and a couple of weeks later, was told by the magazine's editor that the Press Council, the national censors have banned it completely. (Rushdie, *Imaginary Homelands*, 37-38)

He also recollects his second painful encounter with censorship when he produced Edward Albee's *The Zoo Story* for Pakistan TV and the play was banned just because 'the word pork cannot be spoken on Pakistan Television' (Imaginary Homelands, 38).

Rushdie's experiences in his new homeland – Pakistan – obliged an inevitable escape to England where he found the milieu more conducive to creative pursuits. The escape to England marks the culmination of the fragmentation of identity after successive attacks and the need to redefine it. Dr R S Pathak in his famous article titled "Salman Rushdie's Treatment of Alienation" refers to Taviss's analysis and interpretation of the term alienation and opines that

'Taviss subsumes them under two kinds i.e. social alienation and self-alienation.' He further observes that 'in Rushdie's novel we come across both the forms of alienation.' (Pathak, *Indian English Fiction; Problems and Promises*, 157). It is noticeable that both the forms of alienation in the works of Rushdie are manifest in mutual complementation and separating one from the other is an uphill task as they owe their origin to a common cause; the rootlessness and angst and a perpetual quest for the origin and identity. If the loss of roots accounts for the pervasion of self-alienation in the thematic framework of the novels of Rushdie then the rupturing of ideals of the Cambridge educated intellectual locatable along social and political dimensions of the countries that make his origin ie, India and Pakistan eventually lead to the genesis and pervasion of social alienation. For Rushdie, novel is nothing but a tool to express the lack of comfort caused by the uncertainty or origin. He says;

> What is being expressed is discomfort with plural identity. And what I am saying to you – and saying in the novels – is that we have got to come to terms with this. We are increasingly becoming a world of migrants made up of tits and bits; and fragments from here, there. And we are here and we have never left anywhere we have been.(*Parade*, June 1989,51)

The excerpt taken from the interview quoted above makes clear the factors responsible for self-alienation in the novels of Rushdie. The views of M K Naik capture attention who 'the theme of identity and its fate' to be at the center of the thematic network of *Midnight's Children* which unifies all its aspects. He says;

> Both action and character repeatedly emphasize this theme and show the numerous ways in which identity is made to suffer. Identity is taken as a sham, as mistaken and confused, fractured and fragmented, merged and super imposed, subjected to oblivion as dwarfed and reduced to animal level, totally lost and barren and as sterile. (Naik, 46)

Naik writes the above arguments in relation with *Midnight's Children* but the same hold perfectly relevant in relation with all the novels of Salman Rushdie. All his protagonist suffer a loss of identity and eventually endure the crisis along various dimensions. Flapping Eagle is a roaming spirit in search of something that has no specific origin or identity. Saleem Sinai of *Midnight's Children* and Omar Khayyam of *Shame* represent the painful loss of identity along multiple dimensions. The subjective aspect of the loss of identity is fused with crisis of identity of the protagonists along social and political dimensions on the respective countries.

The crisis of identity attributed to self-alienation is manifest in a diverse manner traceable along every aspect of human existence. In *Grimus*, the protagonist Flapping Eagle is an 'orphan' with 'uncertain sex' in time of his birth. The crisis of identity of the protagonist becomes more poignant with he says that he was 'inexplicably to be fair skinned and tallish' as against the expected appearance of his race. Similarly Flapping Eagle's search for his sister Birth Dog – if judged in the broader context – draws a close metaphorical parallel with an expatriate's search for identity which eventually proves to be 'a voyage through the waste land that had destroyed his appetite for the greatest treasure; life.' (Rushdie, *Grimus*, 90) In Midnight's Children and Shame there is more profound and poignant realization of the sense of alienation manifest along either dimension. In *Midnight's Children*, the narrator creates a perfect equilibrium between his physical appearance and the mindset bearing the crises. The protagonist narrator admits that he is 'tearing' himself 'apart' as he "can't even agree with himself (Rushdie, *Midnight's Children*, 503). He also confesses that he has begun to 'crack all over like an old jug.' (Rushdie, *Midnight's Children,* 37). He is born precisely at the midnight of 15 August, 1947 marking the great divide between colonial and independent India. M K Naik takes this synchronicity as metaphorical to the crisis of identity According to him, the birth of Saleem Sinai at the precise moment of India's Independence 'is itself symptomatic of identity crisis.' (Naik, 46) The birth image in the *Midnight's Children* also brings forth the idea of the crisis of the political identity of an individual in the complex matrix of socio-political processes. The incongruities in the physical appearance of Saleem Sinai continue to be more piercing and consequently alienating with the surroundings. The protagonist 'lacks something in the region of chin' and there is a 'dark patch' that has 'colored his eastern ear' (Rushdie, *Midnight's Children* 144). The lack of harmony in the appearance of Saleem Sinai is further intensified by a series of events that account for the humiliation of the protagonist. The most painful of all such events takes place in the geography class when his geography teacher pulls a 'a clump of hair out.' Saleem recollects;

> Mr Zagallo stood like a statue with a clump of my hair in his fist. While I –too shocked to feel any pain – felt the patch on my head where Mr Zagallo had created a monkish tonsure, a circle where hair would never grow again and realized that the curse of my birth which connected me tp my country had managed to find yet another more unexpected expression of itself. (Rushdie, *Midnight's Children* 278)

There are a number of events that further intensifies the identity crisis associated with the character. One of the most painful humiliations takes place during the Emergency when Saleem is made impotent by a group of good doctors. He recalls;

> They were good doctors; they left nothing to chance, not for us the simple vas-tubectomies performed on the teeming masses; because there was a chance; just a chance that such operations could be reversed....ectomies could be performed, but irreversibly; testicles were removed from the sacs; and wombs vanished forever. (Rushdie, *Midnight's Children* 523)

Saleem's marriage with Parvati is another major attack on his identity as an individual delineated through the masterstroke of irony. He is rendered impotent in a sterilization campaign launched by Sanjay Gandhi, and marries Parvati and begets Adam Sinai who is the son of Shiva, the character representing destruction and devastation. The series of humiliations eventually make of soliloquize;

> Why alone of more than five thousand million should I have to bear the burden of destiny? (Rushdie, *Midnight's Children* 457)

The protagonist of *Shame*, Omar Khayyam Shakil is another very strong representation of the crisis of identity in socio-political matrix. It is noticeable that *Shame* is much more political than *Midnight's Children*. Rushdie admits;

> *Shame* is much more overtly political novel. It starts much closer to a political idea than *Midnight's Children*, because in that novel I wanted to write about growing up in Bombay before I wanted to write about anything else. With *Shame*, in the beginning, there is germ of this peculiar relationship between Zia and Bhutto. (Rushdie, *Gentleman*; April1984;66)

In *Shame*, the protagonist Omar Khayyam Shakil is delineated with more poignant irony than the Saleem Sinai in *Midnight's Children*. Fantasy is again a prominent device that serves to design the birth image. Omar Khayyam Shakil is born of three mothers who demonstrate simultaneous growth of the symptoms of pregnancy as 'identically their wombs ballooned to the pregnancy's full terms and the three wombs eventually burst and give birth to a single child. The childhood of the protagonist is another prominent revelation of the crisis of identity associated with the protagonist of the novel. The use of archetypal image captures our attention as Omar Khayyam Shakil is 'afflicted from his earliest days from a sense of inversion, of a world turned upside down.' There is something even worse and that is the fear of living at the edge of the 'edge of the world so close that he might fall of any moment,' (Rushdie, *Shame*, 21) Omar Khayyam's nuptial conjugation with Sufiya Zinobia is another masterstroke that serves to represent the crisis of identity at its most painful manifestation. If Omar Khayyam represents lethargy and inertia, Sufiya is simmering violence in the mind of heart of the people inhabiting a place like Pakistan. Together Omar Khayyam and Sufiya Zinobia represent the axis of shame and shamelessness. When Sufiya marries Shakil she didn't even know what did 'it mean to have an husband and what they are meant for.' The crisis of identity, knit around Omar Khayyam becomes more poignant, when Sufiya realizes that 'there is a thing which women do with their husband at night.' She further realizes that 'she doesn't do it,' but, 'Shahbano does it for her.' (Rushdie, *Shame*, 214-215)

The Satanic Verses is Knit around the idea of the crisis of identity locatable along religious dimensions. Both the major characters of the novel; Gibreel Farishta and Saladeen Chamacha, are divided characters and have their own pains and pangs. In the famous essay "In Good Faith" Rushdie makes the point clear that '*The Satanic Verses*" is the story of two divided selves.' He further sums up the contents of one of the most controversial novels of the century and says;

> In case of Saladin Chamcha, the division is secular and secular and societal; he is torn to put plainly between Bombay and London, between East and West. For the other Gibreeel Farishta, the division is spiritual, a rift in the soul. He has lost his faith and is strung out between his immense need to believe and his new inability to do so. The novel is about their quest for wholeness.

He further clarifies the same idea by saying that the name Gibreel is 'not to insult or abuse real Archangel Gabriel,' and further elaborates;

> Gibreel is a movie star and movie stars hang above us in the darkness larger than life, half way to divine. To give Gibreel an angel's name was to give him a secular equivalent of angelic half divinity. When he loses his faith, however his name becomes the source of all his torments. (Rushdie, *Imaginary Homelands*, 397)

Rushdie in the essay makes the motif clear which owes it identity to the immigration and expatriation eventually leading to the loss of religious identity as the migrants of the sorts of Rushdie risk their faith and nation and race and origin and suffer the torments for no fault of their own.

Rushdie's novel; *Haroun and the Sea of Stories*, known more as children's classic, is knit around the crisis of identity of a creator that looms about here in case of Rushdie as result of the long period spent in exile after the religious decree issue by Ayatollah Khomeini resulting into unending threat to his life. 'One can hardly read the novel,' says Gerald Marzorati, 'as anything other than an allegory of Rudhie's own predicament.' (Marzorati, *Parade*; January, 1991, 17) The novel is centered around two major characters; Rashid Khalifa and his son Haroun Khalifa. The personal despair becomes evident as the action of the novels is centered in a city 'so ruinously sad that it had forgotten even its name. (Rushdie, *Haroun and the Sea of Stories*, 15) The phlegm and despair becomes more painful when Rashid Khalifa loses his gift of gab.

> 'Ark,' that was all that came out. The Shah of Blah sounded like a stupid crow. Ark ark ark.' . (Rushdie, *Haroun and the Sea of Stories,* 15)

What follows the loss of the gift of gab is an endless journey into the wonderland and the consequent retrieval of the lost gift of gab of the Shah of Blah. It is an interesting note that the novel, unlike the preceding masterpieces of Rushdie ends with the ray of hope as the City remembers it name;

> 'Kahani' said the policeman brightly as he floated down the flooded streets. 'Isn't it a beautiful name for a city? It means story you know. (Rushdie, *Haroun and the Sea of Stories*, 15).

The crisis of identity continues to rule over the thematic domain of the novels of Salman Rushdie. The Moor's Last Sigh is a relatively more intensified representation of the crisis of identity of protagonist of Midnight's Children and Shalimar the Clown locates the same in a more intensely political backdrop. However in all these novels the identity of the protagonist as that of the Rushdie himself in found fractured and fragmented, craving for definition and determination.

Rushdie's non fictional works, especially *Imaginary Homelands* and *The Jaguar Smiles* serve much to throw light on the political predilections of the author and bring into focus the political ideals nurtured by the author. It is noticeable that the political idealism of Rushdie is as much the cause of controversy as his views on religion. Both the non-fictional works make it clear that he nurtures the dream of a secular socialist and progressive India. He develops the concept of a socialist India where the liberalism and humanism play a prominent role in defining his ideals. The most important aspect that looms up in the non-fictional writings of Rushdie is that it rests on the ideals of freedom of expression, liberty and human rights prevailing in every section of the society. The absence of religious fanaticism and sectarianism is ever prevailing ideals of Rushdie's political ideology. Rushdie's fond and passionate inclination towards the Nehru is an apt testimony of his political predilections. Rushdie, in his essay titled "Dynasty" says that 'Jawaharlal Nehru represents the dream's noblest part, its most idealistic phase.' Indira Gandhi for him is a 'figure of decline' and he takes Sanjay Gandhi to be a further debasement of the currency' (Rushduie, *Imaginary Homelands*, 48). Elaborating his view on the political method of Nehru, he says;

> It was therefore of great value and importance that the Congress Party under Nehru based its electoral appeal on safeguarding the rights of the minorities. It forged a unique electoral coalition between India's Muslims, Harijans and Brahmin Hindus-the only large nationwide groupings – and for a long time seemed invincible as result.
>
> (Rushduie, *Imaginary Homelands*, 72)

It is clear that Nehru is an embodiment of Rushdie's political ideals as he is the only political figure whom he admires wholeheartedly. Orest Martyshin supports Rushdie's view when he says that Nehru 'didn't succumb to the sentiments of the mob or that of some of his colleagues in the government who demanded revenge and massacre of Muslims' and he 'tried to convince the Muslims that they were not foreigners in India.' (Martyshin41-42) Martyshin further elaborates Nehru was never 'tired of repeating that while he was the Prime Minister, India would never become a Hindu state' (Martyshin176). Martyshin's views draw an exact parallel with the ideals of Rushdie which he locates in the most influential political figure he always idolized as ideal.

The controversial delineations in the novels of Salman Rushdie owe their genesis and vitality to the idealism of the Cambridge educated intellect. The characters of the Widow and Shiva zoom up as a result of the disruption of the political ideals of Rushdie. The character of the Widow often identified with Mrs Indira Gandhi created the ripples of controversy in India. The character is structured on the surrealistic images of the paintings of Picasso and Salvador Dali is painted verbally with camouflaging images with Mrs Gandhi. The character of the Widow is delineated with black and green foreground and background and is introduced with nightmare and breathless fear. The narrator points out;

> Now one by one the children mmff are stifled quite the Widow's hand is lifting one by one the children green their blood is black unloosed by cutting – fingernails it splashes black on the walls (of green) as one by one

> the curling hands lifts children high as sky the sky is black there are no stars the Widow laughs her tongue is green but see her teeth are black (Rushdie, *Midnight's Children*, 249)

It is important to note that the Widow does not replicate Mrs Indira Gandhi but she through some gentle camouflaging constructs a surrealist image embodying the political vices of contemporary India. The character of Shiva who represents the debasement of the Nehru-Gandhi Dynasty Shiva with his ruthlessness and cruelty represents the cruelest phase of the Dynasty. He, with his ruthlessness and cruelty, offers a sharp and scintillating contrast to Saleem Sinai the timid and vulnerable protagonist of the novel. He offers a threat to him as when Saleem first confronts Shiva he 'saw in his mind a terrifying image of a short rat faced youth which filled down teeth and two of the biggest knees the world has ever seen' (Rushdie, *Midnight's Children*, 262). Shiva is a representation of vicious political ideal that were in practice during the Emergency, the worst phase in the history of the nation. The idea is more explicitly ratified through synchronicity between the nuclear explosion taking place in Rajasthan and the arrival of Shiva in the protagonist's life. He exclaims;

> Was Shiva's explosion into my life truly synchronous with India's arrival, without prior warning at the nuclear age? (Rushdie, *Midnight's Children*, 486)

The political meanings inherent in the character of Shiva become more clear as he is a 'firm admirer of Mrs Indira Gandhi 'largely because of his hatred for her opponent Morarji Desai who was 'intolerably ancient' and as 'Chief Minister of Bombay' he 'had once been responsible for the banning alcohol and persecution of young goondas' (Rushdie, *Midnight's Children*, 487). The burgeoning pathos of the protagonist and finally delineated with the unique admixture of social, political and sexual strength eventually leading to chaos in every section of the social fabric of India. In the backdrop of his essays on political figures of the Indian sub-continent in the *Imaginary Homelands* it becomes clear that Shiva represents the destructive power that brings forth nothing but devastation.

The political characters of Rushdie's third novel *Shame* can also be understood best in the context structured by his essays in the *Imaginary Homelands.* Omar Khayyam draws a close parallel with Saleem Sinai of *Midnight's Children.* Pakistan, the location where the action of the novel is centered, during the regime of Zia UL Haq 'has become a nightmarish surreal land, in which battlefield armaments meant for Afghan rebels are more of less traded openly on country's black market.' Rushdie cadidly asserts that Zia was 'Islam's enemy' as 'to be a believer is not meant by any means to be a zealot' (Rushdie, *Imaginary Homelands*, 54). The two characters of contextual significance-Iskander Harappa and Raza Hyder are not just the caricatures of Z A Bhutto and Zia ul Haq respectively but they represent two different strains of Pakistani politics and eventually it is Hyder who deposes Harappa and takes over the throne signifying the victory of fanaticism over progressive politics and eventually ratifying the rupturing of dream of Zinnah who firmly declared in the Parliament that 'Pakistan is not a theocracy or anything like it' (Zakaria228). Rushdie creates two more characters of prophetic significance. They are Arjumand Harappa and Sufiya Zinobia. Arjmumand Harappa is the democratic alternative to fanatic politics and Sufiya Zinobia is the possible threat to the future of Pakistan enduring vicious political practices in the country. Rushdie in his Obituary to Zia ul Haq points out the inevitable need to seek alternative to political processes of Pakistan and says;

> I am talking of course about Benazir Bhutto and the coalition of political parties she leads, and which she now works hard to preserve. This obduracy of Pakistani Army, the fissiparous nature of the coalition (now that its great uniting foe has gone, and the contortions of geopolitics conspire to deprive her of it. (Rushdie, *Imaginary Homelands*, 55)

It is noticeable that If Arjumand Harppa is a possible democratic future of Pakistan then Sufiya Zinobia is a possible alternative. The views of Uma Parmeshwaran capture out attention when she says that Sufiya can be 'likened to the spirit of Pakistani blushing at indignities heaped upon her by her own kith and kins.' The views quoted above make us realize Sufiya Zinobia as an apt alternative to political processes in Pakistan. She further opines that 'her lack of mental development and her emotional instability could well be Rushdie's statement on Pakistan' (KIrpal129).

Rushdie's travelogue – *The Jaguar Smile; A Nicaraguan Journey* is another profound revelation of his political predilections that serve to construct the point of view of most of his narrators. The book, which is said to an 'anti-colonial stance' by S S Sharma is an apt representation of Rushdie's adherence to humanistic values and liberalism. Sharma further points out that

> *The Jaguar Smile* is a good example of anti-colonial liberalism and it goes Rushdie's credit that he refuses to be swayed altogether by any system however progressive it may seem to be (Taneja and Dhawan 196).

The views of Sharma make it clear that *The Jaguar Smile* is steeped in political overtones and is a profound revelation of the political ideology of the author. Rushdie identifies himself with the 'successful revolt against the great power' and writes;

> When the Reagan administration waged it war against Nicaragua, I recognized deeper affinity with that small country in a continent (Central America) upon which I had never set foot. I grew daily more interested in its affairs, because after all, I was myself a child of successful revolt against a great power, my consciousness, the product of the triumph of Indian revolution. (Rushdie, *The Jaguar Smile*, 12)

The book, as the narrative grows, makes us clear the author's anti-colonial stance and his hatred for colonial oppression and sympathy for the tyrannical approach of Reagan administration. He points out that Reagan administration was not interested in international law at least not when its custodians were found against the U S (Rushdie, *The Jaguar Smile,* 39-40). Rushdie takes Nicaragua to be a country of 'ghosts' as he always had a feeling that everyone who mattered had already died.' He candidly asserts that to understand living in Nicaragua, it is necessary to begin with the dead.' Rushdie goes on to the extent of saying that Managua, the capital of Nicaragua 'sprawls over its own corpse' (Rushdie, *The Jaguar Smile*, 16). Rushdie shares with readers the poor economic condition of Nicaragua when he says that the Nicaraguan economy 'suffered and estimated $2million worth damage.' Her further informs th to be at the 'the country had lost one entire year's production in last five years' (Rushdie, *The Jaguar Smile*, 39). Poor medical facilities are another major source of concern for the master. The pregnant women of this country are the most pitiable lot of the people of Nicaragua. 'Childbirth in Managua was all natural, he observes, 'there simply weren't any drugs to be had,' and 'women were given no training in breathing and pushing.' The basic thing which he is told is 'how to survive and feed children during the Contra attack' (Rushdie, *The Jaguar Smile*, 141). It is but obvious that Rushdie holds Reagan administration responsible for the violation of human values in Nicaragua. Rushdie also lays stress on the need to reinstitute the humanistic values and democratic processes conservation of human rights. The curbing of freedom of speech is another agonizing factor which tortures his sensibilities. The painfully exclaims that 'the government of writers had turned into the government of censors' (Rushdie, *The Jaguar Smile*, 48).

It is clear from the above discussion that the anger and angst mirrored in the novels of Rushdie can easily be traced in *The Jaguar Smile*. The violation of democratic processes, human values and rupturing of democratic ideals are the main factors contributing to the idealism which gave birth to the controversies that loomed up after the publication of *Midnight's Children* and *Shame*. It is rightly said that the third part of *Midnight's Children* is at marked tonal variation with the preceding parts of the same novel. However the reason can be traced to the fact the time span of the history of modern Indian witnessed the worst kind of violation of noble political values paving way for the violation of human rights.

Rushdie's views on religion are unambiguously one of the most outstanding aspects of his creativity. It is surprising for the readers of Rushdie that despite is secular and somewhat irreverent approach to religion-as seen in *The Satanic Verses*, he approaches religion with gravity and seriousness. A good number of essays collected in *Imaginary Homelands* acquaint us with the same fact. Discussing the role and function of divinity, he firmly says that 'the idea of god is at once repository for our awestruck wonderment at life.' Elaborating the idea, Rushdie takes the concept of divinity to be 'an answer to the great question of existence and a rule book too.' The death of communism in Central Europe obliges him to observe the deep religious spirit with which so many of the makers of these revolutions are imbued.' He further opines tbat 'it is not only a particular ideology that has failed but the idea that man and woman could ever define themselves in terms that exclude their spiritual need. (Rushdie, *Imaginary Homelands*, 421-422). It is clear from the views of Rushdie quoted above that for him spiritual needs play a vital role in defining the existence of man. It is however a scintillating paradox that Rushdie always locates a well-defined relation between religion and politics and hold political processes responsible for the iconic stature of many modern religious figures. In his famous essay- "In God We Trust" Rushdie discusses at length the mutual inter-dependence between religion and politics. He takes religion and politics to be the 'manifestations of our dreaming selves.' In politics, Rushdie locates the sense of superiority naturally associated with man whereas in religion he locates human will to submit himself before some unquestionable authority. He identifies politics with the 'optimistic dreams' and in the politics we seek to express our 'dreams of improvement, or betterment, of progress,' and, on the other hand, he examines religious inclinations of man at a sharp contrast with his political aspirations and opines that religious spirit asks us to accept our inferiority to a non-corporeal omnipresent, omnipotent supreme being who is both our creator and judge' (Rushdie, *Imaginary Homelands*, 378). Rushdie affirms his thesis on inter-dependence between politics and religion by referring to two main political figures. Jesus Christ and Ayatollah Khomeini. He traces the genesis of Christianity to a political cause b y alluding to the findings of famous historian Hyam Maccoby who claims that 'crucifixion in time of Christ was the penalty exclusively for the persons found guilty of the acts of political not theological subversion.' On the basis of Maccoby's findings, Rushdie claims that 'Christ died as political revolutionary but was largely depoliticized and wrapped in mysteries by Paul...' (Rushdie, *Imaginary Homelands*, 381). He also cites the example of Ayatollah Khomeini whom he takes to be an embodiment of 'the idea of Iranian Nation. He analyses the political revolution of Iran and infers that Shah of Iran Raza Palhevi never 'dared to move as ruthlessly against the mosque, against the clergy as he did against his secular enemies' which led to the 'gravitation' of 'opposition' to theologians resulting into a 'power vacuum' and, he further opines, "Khomeini stepped into it with massive authority' (Rushdie, *Imaginary Homelands*, 381).

The two instance of human history cited above make clear Rushdie's views on the inter-dependence of religion and politics. The two examples also make clear his fond passion for rationalizing religion into practical and convincing terms which sows the seeds for flowering of controversies. *Midnight's Children* and *Shame* fell prey to political controversies and *The Satanic Verses* created the ripples of controversy across the world on religious grounds. *The Moor's Last Sigh* published in the year 1997 again fell prey to controversy on political grounds for delineation of political characters.

The study of non-fictional works of Salman Rushdie brings into focus the prominent aspects of his life and mind which brings us close to the realization of the thematic essentials of his novel and the author's 'secret identity' which according to the him is 'the greatest and most subversive gift' of a 'novel form' (Rushdie, *Imaginary Homelands*, 381). The constituent elements of the point of view of his narrator come out with great transparency and enable us to appreciate his fiction with more objectivity and acumen. The crisis of identity which we associate naturally with an expatriate's sensibility seeks reflection in the identity of all his protagonists; however, it is realized along various planes of human existence. The rebellious intellect of a Cambridge educated person with self-conscious approach to every constituent feature of the work at hand is also viewed through the kaleidoscope of his non-fictional writings brings forth the truth clouded by controversies. It is thus clear that non fictional writings of any author acquaint us with the finer aspects of the creativity and various constituent elements of his point of view. In case of Salman Rushdie, it is clear that he takes up complex themes for his novels and proportionally complex point of view and the identity of the narrator. Both the non-non fictional works of Salman Rushdie serve much to unfold the knots of complexities characterizing the points of view of his narrators and their constituent emotions and ideas.

Works Cited

Martyshin Orest, *Jawaharlal Nehru and His Political Views*. Mascow; Progressive Publishers, 1989.

Marzorati, Gerald. "Fiction's embattled Infidel" *Parade*, June1989, 50

Nailk, M K. "A Life of Fragments; the Fate of Identity in Midnight's Children" *Studies in Indian English Literature*. New Delhi; Sterling Publishers, 1989.

Parmeswaran Uma, *The Perforated Sheet*. New Delhi; East West, 1988.

Pathak R S. "Salman Rushdie's Treatment of Alienation" *Indian Fiction in English' Problems and Promises*. New Delhi; Northern Books, 1990.

Rushdie, Salman, *Grimus*, 1975; Granada, London, 1977.

Rushdie, Salman, *Midnight's Children*, 1980; New Delhi; Avon Books, 1982.

Rushdie, Salman, *Shame*, London; Rupa and Co, 1983.

Salman Rushdie, *The Jaguar Smile; A Nicaraguan Journey*. London, Picador; 1987

Rushdie, Salman, *Haroun and the Sea of Stories*, London; Granta Books, 1990.

Rushdie, Salman, *Imaginary Homelands*, London; Granta Books. 1990.

Sharma S S. "An Anti-Colonial Stance; The Jaguar Smile" *The Novels of Salman Rushdie*. Ed G R Taneja and R K Dhawan. New Delhi; Indian Society for Commonwealth Studies. 1992.

Zakariya Rafiq, *The Struggle within Islam; the Conflict between Religion and Politics*, New Delhi, Penguin, 1988.

Contributors

1. **Anubhav**, Research Scholar, Department of English, Om Sterling Global University, Hisar, Haryana, email: kalkalanubhav@gmail.com
2. **Aswin Mohan**, M.A English Literature, email: aswinmohan2016@ gmail.com
3. **Dr. Rajshree Roselean Kapoor** is an Assistant Professor in English Department of Government Science College Model and Autonomous College Jabalpur, Madhya Pradesh. She has attended and presented Research papers in various Conferences and Seminars at the State, National and International level. Her first edited Book title "In Translation: Literature Accross The World" was published in 2021 by Authorspress New Delhi.
4. **Dr. R. Sujatha Rani** Lecturer of English, Rajiv Gandhi University of Knowledge Technologies, YSR Kadapa, Andhra Pradesh, email: sujatharani.r@gmail.com
5. **Dr. Rajesh Trivedi**, Professor-Department of English, Shree Ram Institute of Technology, Jabalpur.
6. **Dr. Tejendra Singh Shiv**, Asst. Professor (English), Govt. J. S. T. P. G. College, Balaghagt.
7. **Dr. Avdhut Atre**, Research Guide, Vishwakarma University.
8. **Dr. N. Sumathi**, Assistant Professor, Department of English and other Foreign Languages, College of Sciences and Humanities, SRM Institute of Science and Technology, Ramapuram, Chennai, Ph: 9445620350, email: sumathinarayan@gmail.com
9. **Dr. Saradashree Choudhury**, Assistant Professor, Department of English, Morigaon College, email: sscmg18@gmail.com
10. **Dr. Susheela. B,** Faculty, Department of English, Jyoti Nivas College Autonomous, Bengaluru, email: susheelab634@gmail.com

11. **Dr. Tanu Gupta**, Professor and Head, Department of English, University Institute of Liberal Arts and Humanities, Chandigarh University, Chandigarh University, Ghauran, Mohali, Punjab, India, email:: tanu.e9349@cumail.in
12. **Dr. V. Rema,** Professor & Head, Department of English and other Foreign Languages, SRM Institute of Science and Technology, Bharathi Salai, Ramapuram, Chennai – 600089.
13. **Dr.Vedprakash Borkar**, Assistant Professor of Hindi, National Sanskrit University, Tirupati, Email: hod.efl.rmp@srmist.edu.in
14. **Dr. Vijayakumar M.** is an Associate Professor in the Department of English, School of Social Sciences and Languages, Vellore Institute of Technology, Vellore. He has presented numerous research papers at national and international conferences. His research interests include Indian writing in English, post-colonial studies, diaspora studies, African American literature, and Canadian literature. He has authored a few books and several book chapters. He can be reached at vijayakumar.muthu@vit.ac.in
15. **Harry. B,** Teaching cum Research Assistant (TRA), School of Social Sciences and language, Vellore institute of technology, Vellore 632014.
16. **Jipsa Maria Joy**, MA English
17. **Meenakshi S.,** Department of English, School of Social Sciences and Languages, Vellore Institute of Technology, Vellore.
18. **Ms. Sarika**, Resource person, Department of English, JNRM, Port Blair, Andaman and Nicobar Island, PH NO.: 9476082520, Email: Sarikasony2520@gmail.com
19. **Nathiya. M,** Assistant Professor in English, Department of English and other Foreign Languages, SRM Institute of Science and Technology, Bharathi Salai, Ramapuram, Chennai – 600089, Email: nathiyam2@srmist.edu.in
20. **Nivedita Thakur**, Research Scholar, Vishwakarma University.
21. **Raja Kumar Tenali,** Freelance Writer, Former Lecturer, Visual Communication, Andhra Loyola College, Vijayawada, Email: rktenali@ yahoo.com

22. **Rajeshwari S.,** Department of English, School of Social Sciences and Languages, Vellore Institute of Technology, Vellore.
23. **Ruth Neyah**, Research Scholar, School of Social Sciences and Languages, Vellore Institute of Technology, Vellore, email: ruthneyah.v2019@vitstudent.ac.in
24. **Shruti Mishra,** Research Scholar, University of Lucknow.
25. **Shweta Chauhan**, Research Scholar, Department of English, University Institute of Liberal Arts and Humanities, Chandigarh University, Chandigarh University, Ghauran, Mohali, Punjab, India, email shweta.chauhan669@gmail.com
26. **Victor Vinoth** is a Research Scholar in the Department of English, School of Social Sciences and Languages, Vellore Institute of Technology, Vellore. He had his bachelor's, master's, and MPhil degrees from Madras University, Chennai, Tamil Nadu. He spent seven years teaching in various arts and sciences colleges in Tamil Nadu. He has published ten of his research articles in reputed international journals.

Index